Y0-EKZ-634

California Government & Politics

ANNUAL

Edited by
Thomas R. Hoeber
Charles M. Price

1997-1998

ISBN: 0-930302-45-1
ISSN: 0084-8271

EXECUTIVE BRANCH & STATE FINANCE

California's governor has, as does the President of the United States, power that is counter-balanced by power of the other branches of government and the electorate. The governor reigns supreme in very few areas. One of them is appointments, but many of these are subject to confirmation by the state Senate. California's governor has remarkably few appointments compared to other states because the civil service system has long been established for all but the top policy posts. The governor also has prime responsibility for the fiscal affairs of state, but his budget is subject to alteration by the Legislature. The governor can reduce or eliminate items in the budget passed by the Legislature. This "line-item" veto is a very powerful tool of California Governors. These vetoes, like any others, are subject to override by two-thirds vote of the Senate and Assembly, through this happens only rarely. Former Republican Presidents Ronald Reagan and George Bush supported a line-item veto federal amendment to strengthen the executive's fiscal power. Democratic President Bill Clinton is also an admirer of the line-item veto.

Governors are elected for four-year terms, with a two-term maximum (established by Proposition 140 in November 1990). Historically, only Earl Warren was elected more than twice. The order of succession is the lieutenant governor, Senate president pro tempore, Assembly speaker, secretary of state, attorney general, treasurer and controller. The governor serves as the ceremonial chief of state, as president of the University of California Board of Regents and the State University and Colleges Board of Trustees, as unofficial leader of his party, and as the head of most administrative agencies through his subordinate appointees. The governor is deeply involved in the legislative process, through presentation of the budget, the office's veto power and the traditional presentation of a package of bills constituting a legislative program (and usually outlined in the annual "state-of-the-state" message). When stymied by the legislature, Governor Pete Wilson has also authored initiatives.

Veto power

The veto is perhaps the governors most potent weapon, but it is essentially a negative power. Governors usually wield considerable influence with members of their own party (because they often control the party structure, weak as it is, and because lawmakers like to stay on the good side of a governor so they can get projects for their districts and appointments for their friends). Consequently, vetoes are rarely overridden. When Governor Ronald Reagan had a veto overridden during the 1973-74 session, it was the first over-ride since 1946. Jerry Brown was overridden during his first term on a death-penalty measure and overrides became almost commonplace in 1979, especially on fiscal issues. Neither George Deukmejian nor Pete Wilson has had a veto overridden.

Governors have the power to organize the administrative agencies of state government as they see fit, although the Legislature can veto major reorganization plans. Reagan organized his administration into four agencies headed by the secretaries of health and welfare, business and transportation, agriculture and services, and resources. The Department of Finance reported directly to the Governor. The cabinet met regularly and established policy for the administration.

The Jerry Brown administration employed the case-study method for solving problems and establishing policies. Cabinet sessions at the start were frequent, lengthy and argumentative — far less business-like than in the Reagan years. However Brown put agency executives on a loose leash once they learned what he expected from them. Jerry Brown created a fifth agency, the Youth and Adult Correctional Agency.

George Deukmejian, it was assumed, would be willing to bargain and compromise with the legislature on issues since, as a former legislator, he was used to a give and take process. His unyielding stance during his first year in office on issues like taxes and community college fees surprised many. Despite the fact that he was the sole Republican among the state's statewide office-holders and both houses of the Legislature were Democratic-controlled, Deukmejian wielded the powers of his office with considerable effect.

Deukmejian's Republican successor, Governor Pete Wilson, selected a more moderate and pragmatic group of Cabinet secretaries. Wilson has also established three new cabinet-level agencies: Environmental Protection, Child Development and Education, and Trade and Commerce.

Sharing executive power with the governor are a number of boards and commissions. The governor appoints most of their members and they in turn exercise independent authority. Among them:

University of California of Regents. Aside from the power of the purse, the Regents control the university system.

State University Trustees. This board has less power and prestige than the UC Regents but has been seeking increased independence.

Public Utilities Commission. The PUC sets rates for public utilities and also exercises allied responsibilities.

Franchise Tax Board. This board administers the state income tax and handles other revenue matters.

State Lands Commission. This commission exercises control over the state's oil-rich tidelands and other public properties.

Fair Political Practices Commission. This powerful agency was created by voters in June 1974 to police the state's Political Reform Act covering lobbyist activities, campaign contributions and conflicts of interest.

Energy Resources, Conservation and Development Commission. This commission also went into operation in 1975. It is charged with establishing overall state power policy and with the selection of sites for new power plants.

Agricultural Labor Relations Board. This agency supervises management-labor activities for the agricultural industry.

Lottery Commission. Created by the 1984 initiative to run what is, in effect, one of the nation's largest businesses.

Citizens Compensation Commission. This governmental unit was established by voters with the adoption of Prop. 112 of June 1990. This commission is charged with setting the salary level of all state elected officials except judges.

In a special category is the *State Board of Equalization*, composed of the state controller and four members elected by district. It collects the sales tax and other levies, and supervises county administration of the property tax. From time to time, governors propose elimination of the Board of Equalization and the Franchise Tax Board in favor of creating a Department of Revenue under the governor's control.

Statewide offices

In addition to the governor, the state Constitution requires the election of seven other statewide officials. All are limited to two four-year terms by Proposition 140. See box for a list of current incumbents, the individuals they defeated and their predecessors.

Here is a brief rundown of the duties of these other statewide officials:

• **Lieutenant Governor:** presides over the Senate, serves as a member of numerous state boards and commissions, and exercises the powers of chief executive when the governor leaves the state or is incapacitated.

• **Secretary of State:** the state's chief election officer; maintains all the state's official files and historical documents, including articles of incorporation; receives lobbyists' registrations and their monthly reports; receives campaign-contribution and conflict-of-interest disclosure forms.

• **Attorney General:** the state's chief law enforcement officer, legal advisor to state agencies.

• **Treasurer:** provides all banking services for the state, including sale of bonds and investment of securities.

• **Controller:** the principal accounting and disbursement officer for the state; administers inheritance and gift taxes and performs a variety of functions assigned by the Legislature, including publication of statistics on local government.

• **Superintendent of Public Instruction:** heads the state Department of Education, but most of the public schools are administered by local boards; state education policy is established by the state Board of Education, composed of gubernatorial appointees.

• **Insurance Commissioner:** This is a relatively new position created by the passage of Proposition 103 in 1988. The commissioner oversees the operations of the state

Constitutional Officers

	Incumbent (year first elected)	Defeated Nov. 1994	Predecessor
Governor	Pete Wilson (R) 1990	Kathleen Brown (D)	George Deukmejian (R)
Lieutenant Governor	Gray Davis (D) 1994	Cathie Wright (R)	Leo McCarthy (D)
Secretary of State	Bill Jones (R) 1994	Tony Miller (D)	March Fong Eu (D)
Attorney General	Dan Lungren (R) 1990	Tom Umberg (D)	John Van de Kamp (D)
Treasurer	Matt Fong (R) 1994	Phil Angelides (D)	Kathleen Brown (D)
Insurance Commissioner	Chuck Quackenbush (R) 1994	Art Torres (D)	John Garamendi (D)
Controller	Kathleen Connell (D) 1994	Tom McClintock (R)	Gray Davis (D)
Superintendent of Public Instruction	Delaine Eastin (nonpartisan)1994	Maureen DiMarco	Dave Dawson*

Note: Minor-party candidates omitted.   *Acting upon conviction of a felony of Louis (Bill) Honig

GOVERNOR

BUSINESS, TRANSPORTATION AND HOUSING AGENCY

Dept. of Alcoholic Beverage Control
Dept. of State Banking
Dept. of Corporations
Highway Patrol
Dept. of Housing and Community Development
Dept. of Motor Vehicles
Dept. of Real Estate
Dept. of Savings and Loan
Dept. of Transportation
California Housing Finance Agency
Stephen P. Teale Data Center
Office of Traffic Safety

RESOURCES AGENCY

Dept. of Conservation
Dept. of Fish and Game
Dept. of Forestry & Fire Protection
Dept. of Boating and Waterways
Dept. of Parks and Recreation
Reclamation Board
S.F. Bay Conservation and Development Commission
Dept. of Water Resources
California Conservation Corps
Colorado River Board
Coastal Commission

HEALTH AND WELFARE AGENCY

Dept. of Alcohol and Drug Programs
Employment Development Dept.
Dept. of Developmental Services
Dept. of Health Services
Dept. of Mental Health
Dept. of Rehabilitation
Dept. of Social Services
Dept. of Aging
Office of Statewide Health Planning & Development
Emergency Medical Services Authority
Health & Welfare Data Center
Dept. of Economic Opportunity

STATE AND CONSUMER SERVICES AGENCY

Fire Marshall
Franchise Tax Board
Dept. of General Services
Personnel Board
Dept. of Consumer Affairs
Public Employees Retirement System
Teachers' Retirement System
Dept. of Veterans Affairs
Dept. of Fair Employment and Housing
Building Standards Commission
Museum of Science and Industry

TRADE AND COMMERCE AGENCY

World Trade Commission
California Film Commission
Office of Tourism
Office of Small Business Development

YOUTH AND ADULT CORRECTIONAL AGENCY

Board of Prison Terms
Dept. of Corrections
Board of Corrections
Prison Industries Authority
Youthful Offender Parole Board
Dept. of Youth Authority

ENVIRONMENTAL PROTECTION AGENCY

Air Resources Board
Integrated Waste Management Board
Water Resources Control Board
Dept. of Toxic Substance Control
Dept. of Pesticide Regulation
Office of Environmental Health Hazard Assessment

INDEPENDENT COMMISSIONS

Agricultural Labor Relations Board
Arts Council
Lottery Commission
State Lands Commission
Coastal Commission
Energy Resources, Conservation & Development Commission
Fair Political Practices Commission
"Little Hoover" Commission
Public Employment Relations Board
Public Utilities Commission
Transportation Commission

SECRETARY OF FOOD AND AGRICULTURE

DEPARTMENT OF FINANCE

DEPARTMENT OF INDUSTRIAL RELATIONS

SECRETARY OF CHILD DEVELOPMENT AND EDUCATION

Office of Administrative Law
Office of Planning and Research
Office of Emergency Services
Office of Personnel Administration
Military Department
Office of Criminal Justice Planning
State Public Defender

CALIFORNIA EXECUTIVE BRANCH ORGANIZATION

Department of Insurance and has wide authority to approve or disapprove many types of insurance rates.

State Finance

The governor is required by the state Constitution to present a budget each January — an estimate of the state's expenditures and revenues for the fiscal year starting the following July 1st. In a state growing as fast as California, the budget increases dramatically no matter who is governor.

During the eight years Ronald Reagan was governor, the total budget doubled from $5 billion to $10 billion. Jerry Brown's first budget (1975-76) totaled $11.4 billion, and his final budget (1982-83) totaled $25.3 billion. George Deukmejian's first budget (1983-84) totaled $26.8 billion and his last budget (1990-91) was $51.4 billion. Governor Pete Wilson's 1997-98 budget totaled $66.6 billion.

These figures can be misleading because they do not show how much the cost of state government has risen. Many of the increases were for the exclusive purpose of relieving-pressure on the property tax or on local government, especially after the passage of Proposition 13 in 1978. In fact, about two-thirds of each year's budget consists of allocations to schools and other elements of local government, and about half the state budget is for public education.

Budget process

The budget process in the Legislature involves detailed study of items that are questioned by the Legislature's fiscal specialist, the legislative analyst. For months, subcommittees of the Senate Budget and Fiscal Review Committee and the Assembly Budget Committee pore over the budget and decide which items should be increased, reduced, added or eliminated. Eventually, the budget is packaged by the fiscal committees and sent to the floor of each house. As a practical matter, either the Senate or the Assembly bill becomes the vehicle for enactment of a budget. The first house to act sends its version of the bill to the other, which then puts its own figures into the legislation and sends it back to the house of origin. The changes are routinely rejected, and the budget is placed in the hands of a conference committee composed of members of both chambers. Even though the constitution requires that the budget be sent to the governor by June 15th, it is often much later before both houses are able to adopt a compromise because passage by a two-thirds majority is required.

Revenue

One major portion of the budget — estimated revenues — is not considered at all by the Legislature, except to verify that funds will be sufficient to meet anticipated expenditures.

The difference between revenues and expenditures (with any carry over from the previous year taken into account) produces the projected surplus for the fiscal year.

About 78 percent of the revenue goes into the state general fund. The remaining 22 percent is collected from specific sources and placed in special funds (notably the motor vehicle fund) to be spent for specific purposes. Estimates in the governor's proposed budget for the 1997-98 fiscal year show anticipated revenue from all funds of $64.7 billion ($50.7 billion general fund; $14.0 billion special funds). Specific fund sources and their percent of total revenue are as follows:

Personal income tax, $24.2 billion (37.4%);
Sales tax, $19.3 billion (29.8%);
Bank & corporation taxes, $5.9 billion (9.1%);
Insurance, $1.2 billion (1.8%);
Motor vehicle (inc. gas tax), $8.4 billion (13.0%);
Tobacco, $656 million (1.0%);
Liquor, $262 million (0.4%);
Estate taxes, $655 million (1.0%);
Horse racing fees, $74 million (0.1%);
Other, $4.1 billion (6.6%).

Expenditures

Total proposed 1997-98 expenditures are $66.6 billion, not counting bond funds. Here are the major items of expenditure as proposed by the governor in January 1997:

K-12 Education, $21.1 billion (35.5%);
Health and welfare, $17.9 billion (27.6%);
Higher education, $7.6 billion (11.1%);
Business, transportation and housing, $5.5 billion (7.0%);
Youth and adult corrections, $4.3 billion (6.6%);
Other, $10.2 billion (15.2%).

While the Legislature can revise the budget in any way it sees fit, the governor has only two choices when he receives the bill act at the end of June: he can veto it in its entirety and thus force the Legislature to pass a new bill, or he can reduce and eliminate specific items (this is known as blue-penciling the budget through line-item veto). This latter is the practice traditionally used.

Until the budget is enacted, the Legislature cannot pass appropriations measures unless the governor provides a letter saying that the expenditure is needed on an emergency basis. Once the budget is passed, however, the Legislature can — and usually does — send the governor numerous bills containing appropriations. The governor can cut the entire appropriation or reduce the amount. (Each of these bills can contain only a single appropriation.) 🏛

What future Pete?

Termed out of office in 1998, Pete Wilson must create a legacy of achievement. Otherwise, he simply may be remembered as the unluckiest chief executive in state history. And he may never be known as President Wilson.

by Steve Scott

Reprinted from *California Journal*, June 1996

When recounting the travails of his first five years in office, Governor Pete Wilson is fond of recalling a pre-inauguration lunch he had in 1990 with outgoing Governor George Deukmejian. The lunch, remembers Wilson, began with the state facing a $3 billion deficit. By the time the dishes were cleared, the estimate had been revised to $7 billion. It was, as they say, all downhill from there. Economic depression, natural disasters and budget gaps as large as $14 billion kept Wilson hunkered in survival mode throughout his first term. Although fortune smiled on him long enough to send Kathleen Brown as a re-election opponent in 1994, even his harshest critics would have to concede the point:

Pete Wilson is probably the unluckiest governor in the state's history.

This unprecedented succession of bad breaks has contributed mightily to Wilson's persistent lack of popularity, reaffirmed recently by a Field Poll which showed his presence on the GOP national ticket would cost the party 10 points in California. But bad luck alone can't account for approval ratings that have been, at times, the lowest for any governor since the advent of modern opinion polling. Fair or not, many Californians see Wilson as little more than a dour-faced caretaker in a blue disaster jacket. In a state built by individuals who seized destiny by the reins, the governor's fate always seemed to rest in the hands of others — the Legislature, Congress, the federal administration. Even his most significant achievement to date — controlling the growth of state spending — is tainted in the minds of some by his early advocacy of the largest tax increase in state history. Wilson always seemed to be blaming someone else for his travails, and while the excuses were often valid, they still were just excuses.

Recently, though, there have been signs to suggest the tide of Wilson's fortunes is finally starting to come in. The state's economy has begun to regain its characteristic dynamism and luster, briskly creating new jobs in the high-tech and entertainment sectors. Crime is down, and California voters were optimistic enough this year to begin passing bond issues again.

The long-overdue arrival of hopeful times presents the governor with an opportunity to make good on the promise that greeted his arrival in Sacramento in 1991. "He spent four years trying to put the state's fiscal house in order," said longtime Wilson aide Dan Schnur, now a public-relations executive. "Now he's finally gotten to a point where he can make real progress on his agenda." What many both in and out of state politics are asking is whether Wilson will seize that opportunity. What is his agenda for the final two years of his time as governor? Will he be able to take control of his own destiny, or will it continue to be controlled by outside forces? How important are the last two years of his term to California's future ... and to his own?

Answering these questions requires an understanding of the unique context in which this two-plus-year drama will be played out. First, there is the issue of term limits. Thanks to 1990's Proposition 140, Wilson will be the first governor in history to face a constitutionally-mandated endpoint to his time as governor.

Hero or villain, saint or sinner, Wilson is out in 1998.

There are many who see that limit as providing a window of opportunity for the governor — a chance to follow his heart without worrying about the interest-group pressures which often mess with a politician's head. When Deukmejian voluntarily term-limted himself in 1989 by announcing that he would not seek a third term, he concedes it was, in some ways, a liberating experience.

"When you don't have to consider your decisions in the light of how would this play in the next political campaign, there is a certain amount of relief," said Deukmejian. "You're always trying to do the best you can, but you aren't subjected to as much contact and pressure from interest groups as you might be if you were seeking another term."

As Deukmejian and other second-term governors came to realize, however, there is a price to pay for this opportunity. While most politicians bristle at the mention of the words "lame duck," the fact remains that chief executives on their way out tend to find their influence waning the nearer they get to the end of their term. "As it became apparent that Pete Wilson was going to be my successor, [legislative Democrats] began to refuse to work with us," recalled Deukmejian. "They kept believing ... they could get a better deal from Wilson."

Of course, Deukmejian was somewhat unique among recent governors in that his decision not to run for a third term was, in effect, an announcement of his retirement from public life. A quiet life in the private sector appears to hold no appeal for the ambitious Wilson. While there's an outside chance he might try for the U.S. Senate seat currently held by Democrat Barbara Boxer, most observers see him setting his sights higher. Last year, on the heels of his surprisingly successful re-election bid, Wilson was emboldened to try his hand at presidential politics. The results were calamitous thanks to some self-inflicted wounds and a run of his trademark bad luck. Still, the 1995 debacle left Wilson with a taste for national politics, either as a member of a Bob Dole cabinet or as a presidential candidate himself.

"If Bill Clinton is re-elected, I'd bet a pretty good sum of money that Pete Wilson will run in four years," said Schnur.

So there sits Pete Wilson as he approaches his last two years: term-limited, unpopular, ambitious, helming a state emerging from five years of dark times but still beset with a troubling array of structural and societal maladies. For his next presidential campaign to have a chance of faring better than his last one, many believe Wilson needs to leave more of a legacy than simply being the guy who kept the state from falling into the sea. He needs to post some active policy accomplishments.

"Good government is good politics, and good politics is good government," said GOP political consultant Sal Russo, a veteran of state and national campaigns. "It would be easier if he had a record that he could take and say, 'This is what i'm going to do as president.' I don't think it's a requirement [but] it's easier."

What new initiatives can Californians expect from their governor as his tenure heads into the home stretch? Efforts to secure an interview with Wilson to put that question to him directly were unsuccessful; a spokesman said the administration had only begun the process of mapping out the last two years. By most accounts, though, Wilson has already begun charting his political course by virtue of the issues he has chosen to make his priorities in 1996, as well as the tone of his public utterances.

In terms of his public persona, it sometimes seems as if the presidential campaign hasn't ended. Scarcely a week goes by without some new invective levelled at the Clinton administration over some slight real or perceived. If Clinton doesn't act on a California priority, Wilson blasts the inaction. If some action is taken, Wilson complains that it's not enough. Even when the administration does everything he wants, Wilson still complains, usually that the action wasn't swift enough. The governor's main beef has been the federal government's inability to stem the flow of illegal immigrants across the border. Veteran GOP consultant Tony Quinn says Wilson's focus on federal inaction is just what the doctor ordered, but he warns the governor risks diminishing his credibility by making it a partisan issue.

"He cannot make the case that it's only the Democrats' fault that California has all these problems," said Quinn. "The problems were there with the Bush administration."

Wilson's other main political cause has been his crusade against affirma-

tive action. In addition to engineering the University of California Regents' vote to ban affirmative action in admissions and hiring, the governor is the most visible advocate of the anti-affirmative-action California Civil Rights Initiative. Here again, Quinn questions the value of the effort, even though he agrees with the objective. "These initiatives tend to come and go," said Quinn. "Whatever happens to the civil rights initiative won't affect him one way or another."

In terms of specific policy initiatives, Wilson this year has focused on four areas:

• **Tax cuts.** As he has for each of the previous two years, Wilson is again pushing an across-the-board, 15 percent reduction in personal and corporate income taxes. The gover-nor's budget also calls for a range of specific tax and fee breaks for business and industry. The policy justification for this anti-tax fervor is job creation, but Wilson's critics see his proposal as little more than a bid for absolution from conservative Republicans angered by his advocacy of the largest tax increase in the state's history. "He's introduced this tax cut solely to say that the governor who raised taxes is also the governor who cut taxes," said Democratic political consultant David Townsend.

• **Welfare reform.** In the past, Wilson's version of welfare reform was simple — cut benefits. This year, however, the governor has crafted a more complicated approach, aimed, he says, at "eliminating cash benefits." The governor's plan proposes a series of vouchers — for food, housing, job training, and so forth. These benefits would be time-limited, with incentives which he believes will discourage unwed pregnancies and encourage two-parent families. Here again, there is a political prophylaxis at work. Two of his prospective 2000 presidential rivals — Massachusetts Governor William Weld and Wisconsin Governor Tommy Thompson — have substantial welfare reforms to point to in their own states.

• **Education Reform.** Years of trying to chart a center course on education policy have earned Wilson little good will, so he's decided to veer right. Wilson's state of the state message this year included a call for a system of "opportunity scholarships" for students in low-performing schools. Translation: vouchers, only two years after he publicly opposed a school-voucher initiative. Wilson has also joined the conservative attack on the whole-language approach to reading instruction and has called for scrapping the entire state education code.

• **Privatization.** Earlier this year, Wilson unveiled a broad proposal for reshaping and streamlining government services. Large sections of government would be contracted out to the private sector, such as the Department of Motor Vehicles and the State Compensation Insurance Fund. Departments would be consolidated, regulations would be eliminated, and vast quantities of unused state property would be sold off. Much of this is still in the planning stages; so far, the only state department specifically targeted for elimination is the Department of Boating and Waterways. But administration officials insist the effort is serious.

In reviewing what appear to be the governor's priorities, veteran Wilson watchers will notice something conspicuously absent. It seems that, for now, the pragmatic, pro-government, preventive Pete who bounced into office in 1991 is gone. Sadder and wiser, Wilson's focus on privatization can be seen as evidence that Wilson has joined

other conservatives in believing that government is more a part of the problem than a part of the solution. Some of his preventive programs did make it into law, but they don't get the time or attention he devotes to tax cuts or Clinton bashing.

Democrats have complained about the newer, nastier Wilson for some time. "We thought he represented a return to the sort of progressive type of Republicans we've had in the past," said Senate President pro Tempore Bill Lockyer (D-Hayward). "It didn't work out that way."

But even Wilson's staunchest defenders now concede he is not necessarily the same man he was when he took office. "I don't think it's possible to go through what he's been through and not be changed by it," said Schnur. "People who live through war, or survive some natural calamity, are fundamentally changed by their experiences. In a broader sense, that's what's happened to California, and more specifically, it's what's happened to Pete Wilson."

This tough tone likely will complicate Wilson's relationship with the Legislature as currently constructed; in other words, with Lockyer's Democrats in control of the Senate. Although he has, at times, worked with Democratic leaders to accomplish mutual goals, Wilson is more often confrontational. Even this year, with the state's economy and fiscal situation improving, Wilson is still warning of "a long and unpleasant summer" of budget negotiations. "He's still caught up in the general Republican theme of 'government as the enemy,'" said Lockyer. "As long as that's your fundamental philosophy, it's not likely you'll use government to solve problems."

This prickly relationship with Democrats leaves Wilson no choice but to pull out all the stops this year in pursuit of GOP majorities in both houses of the Legislature. Deukmejian believes the November legislative elections "will be critically important to his ability to accomplish anything in his last two years." Already, the governor has suffered a setback in his quest for a Republican Senate, as his hand-picked candidate for a special election in the Silicon Valley was defeated. But Wilson is still holding out hope and is constantly pushing Republican presidential nominee Bob Dole to campaign vigorously in the state this fall.

In the final analysis, though, even a full Republican house in Sacramento is no guarantee that Wilson will be able to pad his presidential resume. The governor's relationship with GOP conservatives has always been prickly, as was evidenced again this past month when GOP lawmakers scotched his teen- pregnancy initiatives in an Assembly fiscal subcommittee. Wilson can expect more such snubs in the future, especially if Attorney General Dan Lungren begins to assert his position as the presumptive GOP gubernatorial nominee in 1998.

"Historically, a governor's last two years have been their worst two years," said Quinn. "No governor in recent times has been able to reverse what begins to be a bad run of luck."

Bad luck ... just what Pete Wilson needs. 🏛

Wounded Watchdog

The California Coastal Commission has been in the center of the ongoing debate over how much coastal development is too much. The commission has also been a playground for the mischief-making political leaders who appoint its members.

by Noel Brinkerhoff

Reprinted from *California Journal*, March 1997

Whether it's *El Nino, La Nina* or some other havoc-wreaking meteorological phenomenon, it never comes as much of a surprise when California finds itself weathering yet another soggy battle with the elements. Thankfully, these natural furies are never more than a temporary problem for those caught up in them. There does exist, however, another kind of disturbance that knows no seasonal boundary, whose duration can outlast anything sweeping in from the Pacific Ocean. It is a man-made concoction of swirling political pressures arising over the California coastline on a seemingly endless basis, and has trapped within its unforgiving center the state agency responsible for preserving the serene and sandy periphery of this Golden State.

Welcome to what might be called the little black rain cloud of the California Coastal Commission.

Since 1972 when voters adopted the landmark coastal protection initiative Proposition 20, the commission has struggled to carry out a large and difficult mission. With limited funding and a staff of 100, it must help to preserve 1,100 miles and 1.5 million acres of land stretching from Oregon to Mexico, while also balancing the financial needs of private and commercial development. As mandated by the Coastal Act of 1976, it assists coastal communities with the formulation of Local Coastal Programs (LCPs) — plans encompassing land-use, zoning, beach access and conser-

vation priorities which allow issuance of local building permits for new construction. But when local jurisdictions fail to adopt LCPs — as is the case with many — the commission becomes a permitting "beast of burden," with building decisions falling upon the shoulders of politically appointed and vulnerable coastal commissioners.

"The [appointment] system as established by the Coastal Act lends itself to politics getting involved in the whole process," said Senator Bruce McPherson (R-Santa Cruz), whose coastal district takes great interest in commission dealings. Whether it's the governor, speaker of the Assembly or Senate Rules Committee — each of whom appoint four members to the commission's ruling board — the commission has been whipped back and forth by the political machinations of this triad of appointing powers, who likewise are pressured by developers, environmentalists and local politicians to affect the voting decisions, support staff and very tenure of commissioners.

The ascension last year of Assemblyman Cruz Bustamante (D-Fresno) to the speakership serves as just one example of the unstable world commissioners must tolerate. Almost immediately after taking power, Bustamante removed those commissioners appointed by former Speaker Curt Pringle (R-Garden Grove), who had replaced those of his predecessor, Asssemblyman Willie Brown Jr. (D-San Francisco), only a

Photos courtesy of Kim Serrett   Carlsbad, July 1993.

Encinitas, Spring 1996.

year earlier. Though Bustamante has yet to make permanent selections to the commission, he temporarily appointed former Assemblyman Bob Campbell (D-Martinez) just prior to an important commission meeting. This maneuver was viewed by many observers as a way for Bustamante to improve his standing among environmentalists who favor Campbell and coastal Democrats who supported the Central Valley lawmaker for speaker.

"Crude political payback, not sound public policy," was how Commissioner Arnold Steinberg characterized Bustamante's action after getting tossed off the commission. Steinberg, a GOP political pollster, is also a textbook example of what frustrates many Republicans about the commisssion. A home construction project of Steinberg's in Calabasas became entangled in regulatory problems at the commission, prompting Steinberg to sue the panel. Republicans say such wrangles are the product of the commission's free-ranging mandate, and its anti-development bent. As for his experience as a commissioner, Steinberg remains unimpressed. "It struck me as a kind of kangaroo court."

But the "push me/pull me" story of coastal commissioners does not begin with the ouster of Pringle's appointees. During Brown's long reign as Assembly speaker, the San Francisco liberal was notorious for the brazenness with which he interfered with commission appointees. For example, a meeting in 1994 saw Brown appoint attorney Carl Williams to the commission, who was then elected chairman after an alliance was forged between the speaker's appointees and those of Governor Pete Wilson. Never before had a new board member ever been elected as chair, causing Commissioner Gary Giacomini to blast the political maneuver as an act that left the commission "horribly tainted."

"He was an interesting player," League for Coastal Protection Chairman Mel Nutter said of Brown's involvement with the commission. As a former commissioner and chairman from 1977-85, Nutter recalled how Brown "kept people happy and unhappy" by consistently splitting his appointments between environmental and business-oriented individuals.

Michael Fischer, the commission's executive director from 1978-85 and current executive officer for the State Coastal Conservancy, described another Brown-initiated incident when a lobbyist walked right up to commissioners while a meeting was in progress, "handed each of the Brown appointees the cell phone and said, 'It's the speaker.'"

"Subtle it was not," Fischer recalled, who insists that such outside interference was not exclusively limited to Brown. "There were a half dozen times when commissioners either got yanked from the commission just before a meeting or called to the phone during one, and then voting differently afterward," he said. One instance involved then-Senate President pro Tempore David Roberti (D-Los Angeles), who pulled Commissioner Fred Farr just before a meeting, leaving the father of Representative Sam Farr (D-Monterey) "utterly devastated" and "in tears" over his removal. The decision, according to Fischer, was entirely "permit driven."

The political scheming to which commissioners have been subjected also has reached down to their support staff. In July, 1996, the Wilson administration tried unsuccessfully to oust Peter Douglas from his staff position after the executive director opposed projects involving the San Onofre nuclear power plant and Bolsa Chica wetlands. Douglas says he was asked last February by a Wilson administration official to resign, and when he refused, a vote was called on whether the executive director should retain his post as head of the commission's staff.

Ironically, many observers assumed at the time that the effort to dump Douglas was orchestrated by Pringle since his appointees had only recently joined the commission just before the vote.

"We did not initiate that effort," insists Steinberg, adding "We were the new kids on the block, trying not to prejudge the situation." A Republican lawmaker who wished not to be identified further confirmed that "it was the governor's staff that wanted to go after Douglas."

The vote ultimately was tabled after hundreds of people showed up in support of Douglas, though the attempt did not mark the first time commissioners had plotted against Douglas or other staff members. In 1991, Brown appointees David Malcolm and Mark Nathanson tried to orchestrate a coup against Douglas after the executive director thwarted a development plan by Walt Disney Company to fill in 250 acres of Long Beach shoreline. The scheme failed miserably, however, after Malcolm and Nathanson failed to garner any support from other commissioners, who voted to retain Douglas.

Then there was the nearly three-year ordeal Fischer went through at the hands of four appointees of Governor

Peter Douglas

George Deukmejian, who tried unsuccessfully to fire him when he served as executive director. Fisher says he was targeted because of his suppport for Deukmejian's 1982 Democratic rival, Tom Bradley.

With a 12-member board, the Deukmejian appointees needed seven commissioners to call a vote, but failed to garner more than six even after two Brown appointees supported the plan to oust Fischer. "Had the commission been a pleasure appointment of the governor, I would have been gone," Fischer said.

In addition to outside political interference, there also have been instances when some commissioners generated their own controversy by trading votes for campaign contributions and bribes. During the late '70s, when local commissions still existed in support of the state body, four members of the South Coast Regional Coastal Commission lost their seats after it was reported by the *Los Angeles Times* that they had accepted $74,000 in contributions from individuals with projects pending before the commission.

None of the four were indicted since it wasn't illegal at the time to take contributions from commission applicants. The scandal, however, led to the adoption of regulations by the Fair Political Practices Commission that made such activities illegal.

"We are pleased that our new regulations have ended these practices and that we will never again be presented with such a situation," Commission Chairman Leonard Grote told the *Los Angeles Times*. Unfortunately, the regulations didn't prevent an even more egregious act ten years later by another Southern California commissioner.

Again it was Nathanson stirring up trouble, this time by soliciting $250,000 in bribes from a veritable Who's Who of the rich and famous, including movie producer Irwin Winkler and agent-producer Sandy Gallin. There were also others, such as actor Sylvester Stallone and songwriter Carol Bayer Sager, who refused to meet Nathanson's demands for money in exchange for votes. In 1993, Nathanson was convicted on racketeering and tax evasion charges and sentenced to nearly five years in prison.

Another money-related trouble that has plagued the commission for the past 15 years and prevented it from performing all of its tasks involves its dwindling budget. Deukmejian — who wanted desperately to eliminate the commission but lacked the legal authority to do so — used instead his budgetary powers to steadily reduce the commission's effectiveness. From 1982-90, its budget shrunk by almost one-third from $11.1 million to $7.8 million, forcing staff to be reduced from 188 to 110 and the closure of its regional office in Eureka. And despite the transition from a Republican governor openly hostile to the commission to one who likes to tout his environmental credentials, the commission's budget woes have continued, with current-year funding down to $6.9 million.

Mark Nathanson (center) outside Sacramento Federal Courthouse

"Deukmejian began the eroding of its funds," said Gary Patton, general counsel for the Planning

Isla Vista, February 1994.

and Conservation League, "and while Wilson has done a better job, he hasn't gotten it back to where it should be." Republicans argue the funding cuts are needed to rein in an out-of-control agency. Recently, Wilson announced as part of his 1997-98 budget proposal an additional $500,000 for the commission to upgrade its computer technology and another $500,000 in grant money to help local governments complete their Local Coastal Programs.

While politicians in Sacramento have been less than forthcoming in funding, local officials have been slow to carry out their responsibilities. Of the 126 LCPs that should have been completed and certified by 1983, 43 remain undone — including Los Angeles, Santa Monica, Malibu, Monterey and Santa Barbara. And while drafting and completing a local program is a long and complicated task, critics contend that the delay is at least partly due to foot-dragging on the part of locals who prefer to let the commission handle permitting responsibilities.

"Some local jurisdictions are fearful to take the heat in the coastal permit process," says McPherson, who is "personally frustrated that they [LCPs] all haven't been done." By not adopting coastal plans, locals can avoid the pressures of developers and businessmen to approve projects and instead let the commission take the blame for killing projects.

"When I was on the commission, I had at least one local official tell me that they loved having the commission to pass the buck to and beat up on," Nutter said, whose sentiments were echoed by Fischer as well. "Thank God there was the commission to deny the permit," one local reportedly told the former executive director, "otherwise I would have had to vote against it and that would have killed me."

Even when the commission approves an LCP, thus turning over permitting decisions to the jurisdiction in question, there is yet another important function the commission must fulfill: a five-year review of the programs mandated by the Coastal Act. Only two have been conducted since the act was enacted and commission staffers say the task has been all but impossible given current staffing levels.

"It's very important to review LCPs because things are missed the first time around, like polluted run-off," says Douglas, "but we can't do it because of a lack of resources."

If the recent appointment shuffling is any indication, the political winds that swirl around the commission won't die away anytime soon. Governor Wilson's proposed "Coastal Initiative" is seen by some as a way of paring back the commission's authority over coastal matters. But like a storm-battered coastline, this agency has found a way to survive. For the foreseeable future, the Coastal Commission will continue to reside in the eye of any future coastal development windstorms. 🏛

Not Your Average Pothole

Fixing damage from earthquakes and retrofitting to make California's bridges and highways safe in the next big temblor is time-consuming and expensive. Very expensive, as Caltrans and lawmakers have discovered while the state tries to recover from the '89 Loma Prieta and '94 Northridge quakes.

By Ray Sotero

Reprinted from *California Journal*, September 1996

Above: Bay Bridge, Loma Prieta Earthquake, 1989. Courtesy of Cal Trans
Left: Retrofitting Vallejo Bridge, Highway 37. Courtesy of the author.

Talk about sticker shock. In the aftermath of the killer Northridge earthquake in early 1994, in which seven southland bridges collapsed, state engineers reviewed the cost of strengthening seven toll bridges statewide. Their estimate, released in June of 1994, said it would take $650 million to retrofit the toll structures with cables and steel-jacketed columns to help ensure their safety. Five of the bridges were in the Bay Area; the remaining two in Southern California.

Nearly 18 months later, the repair estimate mushroomed to more than $2.1 billion, with up to $1.3 billion alone needed to repair the complex San Francisco-Oakland Bay Bridge. The bulk of those repairs is for the eastern portion of the 60-year-old span, between Yerba Buena Island and the Alameda County shore off Oakland. But that revision has raised sticky questions about financing for bridge-repair projects statewide, and has some worrying about the safety and future of the estimated 12,000 bridges statewide overseen by the California Transportation Department.

Chief among the Caltrans critics: state Senator Quentin Kopp (I-San Francisco), chairman of the Legislature's Senate Transportation Committee. "They [Caltrans leaders] have performed dreadfully, and their figures are entitled to no credibility," said Kopp, who conducted summer hearings on proposed toll increases to help pay for bridge-safety improvements. "As for what the final numbers will be, who knows?"

For their part, Caltrans officials point to what they insist is an accomplished record considering the size of

Left: Bay Bridge, Loma Prieta Earthquake, 1989. Courtesy of Cal Trans

their engineering task: Inspect the 12,000 state and 11,500 city and county bridges and judge their structural integrity. For the state bridges, they then must design a retrofit plan, award a contract and oversee construction. Caltrans supporters also note public support for their work because of voter passage last March of a $2 billion bond measure to help pay for seismic retrofit projects for transportation systems throughout most of California, a task Kopp said exceeds earmarked funds.

Consider the record, Caltrans spokesman Jim Drago said.

On January 17, 1994, Southern California was shaken by the biggest quake there in more than 22 years. It caused $18 billion in damages and caused the collapse of seven highway bridges. Of those seven, five had already been scheduled for retrofitting. More significantly, of the 114 Los Angeles County structures that had been retrofitted prior to the quake, all came through in good shape. By early 1994, when the dust from Northridge had begun to settle, the state's retrofit plan was divided into a four-part attack.

It began with what Caltrans called "phase one" after the fall 1989 Loma Prieta earthquake devastated many Bay Area freeways. Engineers identified 1039 bridges throughout California deemed most in need of urgent retrofitting. By the middle of this year, 988 of those bridges had been strengthened, and most of the remaining 51 bridges are expected to be completed by October, with the overall cost pegged at $780 million, records show. In what the highway agency calls phase two, launched after the 6.9 temblor in Northridge, engineers identified 1364

bridges for strengthening. Construction on nearly 200 of those is either completed or underway, with the remainder in various stages of engineering design, review and analysis. Estimated completion date is the end of 1997, at an estimated cost of $1.05 billion.

So far, so good. Reaching critical mass now, however, is perhaps the hottest political potato of the earthquake retrofitting projects: The toll bridges. They perhaps are the most complex part of the repair plan, and it is here where the biggest shock came over estimated repairs. Their estimates pushed the retrofit budget into the red, and repair estimates for each of the bridges have been revised upward. But none of the costs increased more than for the work needed for the four-mile stretch of the San Francisco-Oakland Bay Bridge. Instead of $250 million, as initially predicted in mid-1994, the repairs were pegged early this year at between $1 billion to $1.3 billion. Caltrans Director James Van Loben Sels attributed the upward revision to greater-than-expected repair needs to the supporting columns and abutments on the eastern-most section of the bridge.

Kopp's hearings, part of a joint effort with the Assembly Transportation Committee, have yet to hammer out a way to come up with an estimated $1.4 billion to help retrofit financing. It's likely, however, that nothing much will be accomplished until the next session of the Legislature. The hearings don't include the most famous of his hometown commuter links, the Golden Gate Bridge. That tower is run by a separate, local authority, which is seeking federal help for about $100 million in strengthening work.

Finally, agencies responsible for locally owned bridges in Los Angeles and Santa Clara counties are charged with assessing retrofitting needs for their non-state, publicly owned bridges. About 1000 bridges have been earmarked for repairs, and as of earlier this year, 41 bridges are done, 24 are under construction and design is completed on 59. Costs will be borne locally.

Financing remains a worry. "We know there isn't enough money, but it'll be made available, one way or another," Kopp predicted, with a sigh. "They'll either raid toll money that hasn't been spent or the highway account" or both, he added.

Whether that money can be used until the highway bonds are exhausted is open to debate. Jim Knox, head of transportation issues for the Planning and Conservation League, a conservation lobbying group, said no tolls or tax dollars could be used until the bond measure, known as Proposition 192, has been expended. That interpretation has been open to debate, but opponents seem bothered most by how the bond-funded retrofitting projects are exempt from environmental review, and also how new road and maintenance projects have been put on hold to make way for the retrofitting.

On another front, California's recent earthquakes have highlighted two major problems with overpass designs: A lack of flexibility in concrete bridges because of design problems, and a lack of restraints at interior expansion joints and at the abutments of the bridges. The latter problem allowed large motion of the highway decks and, as a result, Caltrans embarked on a program to redesign new bridges and to retrofit older overpasses with steel metal jackets, joint restraints, and tying bridges together across their expansion joints and to their abutments.

Later, a study showed this approach resulted in joints that weren't as flexible as needed and the result was a crash program at the University of California campuses in San Diego and Berkeley on how best to strengthen both single column and multi-column overpasses. To deal with the previously unrecognized power of upward thrusting quakes, Caltrans officials insert a steel mat into existing highway decks to prevent columns from pushing through.

If nothing else, floating bonds for highway projects breaks the historical system of paying for road projects with user fees, tolls and gas taxes. In addition, interest on the bonds will have to come from an ever-shrinking general fund. In the meantime, safety-conscious commuters may be edgy, Kopp said: "This says to taxpayers, 'Pray for no earthquake.' and it says that Caltrans is not an efficient organization." 🏛

Ray Sotero since January has been managing editor of Ag Alert, *the largest weekly trade paper in the state. He formerly was deputy bureau chief for five years of the Sacramento Bureau of Gannett News Service/USA TODAY, and, before that, worked in* The Sacramento Bee *Capitol Bureau.*

THE JUDICIAL SYSTEM

The California system of government is the same in bold outline as the government of the United States, with three theoretically equal branches of government operating under the supreme law of the land, the Constitution. Nevertheless, there are some significant differences:

• The California Constitution is far more detailed than the United States Constitution and, thus, the Governor and the Legislature have far less power and freedom than the President and Congress. Matters that are left to the statute-writers in Washington are covered in detail in the California Constitution, taking these issues out of the hands of the Governor and Legislature. The judiciary, on the other hand, may be even more powerful because this branch is in charge of interpreting the constitution.

• The people at large have much more control over California government than over national government because they have the powers of initiative, referendum and recall, giving them the ultimate voice in all matters that are not in conflict with the United States Constitution. Most major fiscal decisions, such as the enactment of general-obligation bond issues and the raising of local taxes, also cannot be made without voter approval.

Constitution

Every few years the California Legislature prints a paperback book with up-to-date versions of the United States and California Constitutions. The document that is the basic law of the entire nation takes up 27 pages; but the California Constitution takes up three times as much space (and twice as much just for the index).

The state constitution contains 21 articles describing, in great detail the bill of rights, the powers of various branches of government and basic state law in such fields as education, local government, corporations, taxation, water, harbor frontages, state debt, homesteading, motor vehicles, civil service, open space, public housing, and even the minimum drinking age.

The California Constitution wasn't always such a long-winded document. The first constitution, adopted in 1849 (one year before California was admitted into the Union), was a basic statement of the rights of the people and the responsibility of the three branches of government. Peter H. Burnett was elected California's first governor in November 1849, and the first Legislature convened shortly thereafter to levy taxes, establish cities and counties, put the courts into operation, and borrow enough money to grease the wheels of state government. Over the next 30 years, only three major changes were made to this constitution. This stands in sharp contrast to the current practice of adopting amendments every election year.

Massive unrest produced a greatly expanded new constitution in 1879. There was tremendous distrust of the state government, especially the Legislature, and demands were made for greater public control over taxation. The state's population had increased 17-fold in its first three decades. A drought and unfavorable economic conditions had produced mass unemployment. The railroad bloc practically ran the state and was an obvious target. Farmers were in revolt against the railroads and other businessmen. Unemployed whites joined the Workingman's Party to seek a ban against imported Chinese labor. Constitutional reform was seen as a solution, and a convention was called in 1878. The result was an extremely detailed document, which was adopted the next year by a comfortable but not overwhelming margin. The document remains the basic law of California, although it has been amended hundreds of times.

But despite the goals of those who demanded the convention, the second constitution did not provide major reform. That was to come later with Hiram Johnson and the Progressives, who instituted the initiative, referendum and recall.

Amending the Constitution

There are three ways amendments to the California Constitution may be placed on the ballot for approval by a majority of the voters: by initiative petition now requiring nearly 700,000 signatures of registered voters, by legislative proposal, and by constitutional convention.

• *The initiative.* Almost every election California voters decide the fate of one or more measures placed on the ballot through the initiative process. The initiative was designed as a method of exerting public control over the Legislature, so that bills ignored by the lawmakers could be put into effect. In recent years, elected officials themselves have sponsored initiatives when they are unable to get their way in the Legislature. Beginning in the late 1970's the initiative has been used more and more frequently by special interest groups, the very element the initiative was created to counter. The initiative can also be used to enact statutes.

• *Legislative proposal.* Every year, legislators introduce dozens of proposed constitutional amendments. A small percentage receive the necessary two-thirds vote of each house to qualify for the ballot. A 1983 law requires that ballot measures be numbered consecutively from election to election, starting with November 1982, to avoid confusion. Thus, for example, the November 1994 ballot measures were numbered 181 to 191.

• *Convention.* The constitution provides that the Legislature may call a constitutional convention by a two-thirds vote of both houses. However, it has not done so since 1878. Instead the Legislature has chosen to form a revision commission because it can control the commission and its recommendations. Such a commission existed from 1963 to1970. The commission had some successes during those years and managed to reduce the size of the constitution considerably. A new constitutional commission was established in 1994 to evaluate and recommend structural reforms in California government.

Judicial Branch

The judiciary may be the most powerful of the three branches of state government because the Constitution is so detailed and because the Supreme Court has the power to strike down acts of the Legislature or initiatives that conflict with the state and federal constitutions. The court also uses its power to void acts of the executive branch that violate

CALIFORNIA'S COURT SYSTEM

U.S. SUPREME COURT

CALIFORNIA SUPREME COURT

Original jurisdiction; habeas corpus, mandamus, certiorari, prohibition

DISTRICT COURTS OF APPEAL

First District	Second District	Third District	Fourth District	Fifth District	Sixth District
San Francisco	Los Angeles	Sacramento	San Bernardino San Diego	Fresno	San Jose

Original jurisdiction; writs of mandamus, prohibition, habeas corpus, ceritorari

SUPERIOR COURTS
ONE IN EACH COUNTY

Original jurisdiction; Civil-amount in controversy exceeds $15,000, mandamus, habeas corpus, equitqable relief, probate, family law and juvenile court matters. Criminal-felonies.

MUNICIPAL COURTS

ONE IN EACH DISTRICT OF MORE THAN 40,000

Civil jurisdiction; amount in controversy, $15,000 or less. Criminal: lesser misdemeanors, preliminary hearings for felonies, infractions

MUNICIPAL COURTS

ONE IN EACH DISTRICT OF 40,000 OR LESS

Civil jurisdiction; amount in controversy, $15,000 or less. Criminal: misdemeanors, preliminary hearings for felonies, infractions

JUDICIAL COUNCIL

Makes rules on judicial procedure; surveys and expedites judicial business.

COMPOSITION:
Chief Justice
Fourteen judge appointees of chief justice
Four elected by State Bar
One Assembly
One Senate

COMMISSION ON JUDICIAL NOMINEE EVALUATION

Evaluates the Governor's prospective judge candidates.

COMPOSITION:
Nineteen elected by State Bar
Six appointed by governor

COMMISSION ON JUDICIAL APPOINTMENTS

Confirms or rejects appointees of Governor to Supreme Court and Courts of Appeal

COMPOSITION:
Chief Justice
Attorney General
Senior Justice on Court of Appeals

COMMISSION ON JUDICIAL PERFORMANCE

Recommends to Supreme Court censure, removal or retirement of judges

COMPOSITION:
Three judges appointed by the Supreme Court
Two lawyers elected by State Bar
Six public members—two each appointed by the governor, Assembly speaker and Senate president pro tem.

RECOMMENDATIONS, ADVICE CONFIRMATION

LINES OF APPEAL OR REVIEW

either a statute or the Constitution.

Under a series of forceful chief justices — among them Phil Gibson, Roger Traynor and Donald Wright — the state's highest tribunal often led the way for the United States Supreme Court. The California Supreme Court built a reputation for activism and independence with decisions that struck down the death penalty (People v. Anderson, 1972), outlawed the state's system of financing public education (Serrano v. Priest, 1971) and invalidated an anti-fair housing initiative approved by the electorate (Mulkey v. Reitman, 1966).

An activist Supreme Court has often been viewed as a second Legislature — more powerful than the first. Governor Ronald Reagan sought to reduce the activism of the court through his appointments, but one of the big disappointments of his eight years as governor was that his appointee for chief justice, Donald Wright, turned out to be another activist.

In 1977, Democratic Governor Edmund G. Brown Jr. had an opportunity to recast the court and by 1981 his appointees comprised a majority on the court. He appointed the court's first woman, Chief Justice Rose Elizabeth Bird; first black, the late Wiley W. Manuel; and first Latino, Cruz Reynoso. Bird was a highly controversial figure when she was appointed and throughout her tenure on the court. While there were many criticisms of the Bird court by conservatives, the most critical was the court's failure to allow any executions during her tenure as Chief Justice. (Polls indicate that over 80 percent of California citizens favored the death penalty.)

In November 1986, in an unprecedented election, three of the Brown-appointed liberals, Justices Bird, Reynoso and Joseph Grodin lost their confirmation elections. This enabled Governor George Deukmejian to appoint three new conservatives to the high court. These three combined with two previous appointments gave the court a conservative majority which it has retained to date.

Lower and appellate courts

The Supreme Court sits at the apex of the California judicial system. There are three lower levels — the municipal courts, the superior courts, and the district courts of appeal. Members of the Supreme Court and the district courts of appeal are appointed by the governor subject to confirmation by the Commission on Judicial Appointments (consisting of the chief justice, the attorney general and one appeals-court justice). In recent years, the commission has called for public hearings on controversial appointees. Bird was approved by a 2-1 vote following a heated public debate. Incumbent judges' names appear on the ballot at the first general election following their appointment and again at the end of each 12-year term. If the incumbent receives a majority of "yes" votes for retention, he or she has another 12-year term.

• *Municipal courts.* These local courts hear misde-

meanor cases, preliminary hearings on some felony charges, small-claims actions and civil cases involving relatively small amounts of money (less than $25,000 in both municipal and justice courts).

• *Superior courts.* These countywide courts hear juvenile criminal cases, felonies, appeals from justice and municipal court decisions, and civil cases that cannot be tried in the municipal courts.

• *Courts of appeal.* These are divided into six districts (based in San Francisco, Los Angeles, Sacramento, San Diego, Fresno, and San Jose). Each division within each court contains three or four justices, with three justices normally sitting on each appeal. The court has jurisdiction over appeals from superior-court actions and decisions of quasi-judicial state boards.

• *The Supreme Court.* The state's highest court handles appeals from the district courts of appeal, although some cases can be taken directly from the trial court to the Supreme Court. In death-penalty cases, for example, appeals automatically go from the superior court to the Supreme Court. The high court also reviews orders of the Public Utilities Commission and has some appointive powers.

Judges of the municipal and superior courts are elected by the people for six-year terms. The governor fills vacancies on the municipal and superior courts. On occasion, there is a wide-open race for a judgeship, but usually the post is filled by appointment and the incumbent retains the judgeship at the ensuing election. District courts of appeal and state supreme court judges are confirmed (they face no actual opponent) in a yes or no vote of the people to twelve year terms. They also must stand for confirmation in the first state election after their appointment.

A judge may be removed or otherwise disciplined by the Supreme Court — but only upon recommendation of the Commission on Judicial Performance. Judges are also subject to impeachment and recall, but the more common disciplinary procedure is through an investigation by the commission and action by the high court.

The state Judicial Council is a 21-member board charged with the overall administration of the court system. It is headed by the chief justice, who in turn appoints most of the members. The Administrative Office of the California Courts is the staff agency charged with carrying out the council's policies and conducting research for the council.

California uses the standard jury system. Grand juries (19 citizens in most counties, 23 in Los Angeles) investigate public agencies and have the power to hand down criminal indictments. However, the state Supreme Court ruled in 1978 that preliminary (probable-cause) hearings must be held, whether or not a suspect is indicted. Trial juries usually consist of 12 registered voters, but both sides in a case can agree to a smaller panel or waive a jury and submit the case to a judge. A unanimous vote is needed for acquittal or conviction in a criminal case. 🏛

End of the Lucas era

A decade ago, California voters ousted three Supreme Court judges after a bitter campaign centered on the death penalty. Malcolm Lucas became chief justice after that election. Did voters get what they bargained for?

By Bob Egelko

Reprinted from *California Journal*, July 1996

The state Supreme Court of Chief Justice Malcolm Lucas was unique in modern California history: It was a court installed by the voters.

For the first time since the state instituted non-partisan, yes-or-no retention elections for Supreme Court and appellate justices in 1934, voters said "no" in 1986, ousting Chief Justice Rose Bird and liberal colleagues Cruz Reynoso and Joseph Grodin. In the same election, Governor George Deukmejian was returned to office after pledging to overhaul the court. He then elevated Lucas, his former law partner and the leading dissenter on the Supreme Court since 1984, to chief justice and promoted appeals court Justices John Arguelles, David Eagleson and Marcus Kaufman to the high court, giving conservatives a majority for the first time in 30 years.

Lucas' recent retirement, more than nine years after Bird was ousted, provides an occasion to ask whether voters got what they wanted.

First and foremost, the public wanted the death penalty. The focus of the campaign against Bird was her court's reversal of 64 of the 68 death sentences it had considered. The Lucas court turned the numbers around, upholding 85 percent of its capital cases overall, and nearly 95 percent in the last four years — the nation's highest affirmance rate during that period. But implementing capital punishment has proven to be a more complex problem than the 1986 campaign slogans ("Cast Three Votes for the Death Penalty") suggested. Only three Lucas court defendants have been executed; scores of cases are bottled up in the federal courts, which have set aside at least a half-dozen California death

sentences; meanwhile, the state court struggles with a seemingly intractable backlog and a growing shortage of lawyers willing to take capital cases.

One segment of the public, contributors to the anti-Bird and pro-Deukmejian campaigns, also wanted a court more friendly to business. Liberal courts had expanded consumers' rights, interpreted environmental and civil rights laws broadly, and opened the courthouse doors to a wide array of liability suits on topics ranging from product defects to employee firings and denials of insurance coverage.

The Lucas court was more receptive to business concerns. Early rulings that restricted suits against insurers and employers voiced fears about the harmful effects of litigation on the business climate. But employees have regained some ground in recent years as the membership of the court changed, and the justices, while discouraging liability suits against insurance companies, have upheld regulation of insurers by ballot initiative. The court has left previous environmental rulings largely intact, rejecting property-rights doctrines embraced by the U.S. Supreme Court. The justices anticipated current anti-smoking litigation by allowing a suit against the Joe Camel ad campaign under state false-advertising laws. And civil-rights precedents, though narrowed, have fared better than their national counterparts before a hostile U.S. Supreme Court.

The Bird court also was attacked for overturning voter initiatives. The Lucas court has been far more deferential,

Bob Egelko writes about legal issues for Associated Press in San Francisco.

upholding ballot measures to limit legislative terms, regulate insurance rates, restrict criminal defendants' procedural rights and limit local tax authority. It has also given a broad reading to the tax-curbing power of Proposition 13, the 1978 initiative that the Bird court upheld but interpreted narrowly. One notable exception to the Lucas courts' relaxed scrutiny of initiatives was its scuttling of efforts to revise two 1988 ballot measures restricting campaign contributions, a subject that will be back before the voters in November.

Another theme of the 1986 campaign was the need to restore public confidence in the court by removing it from politics — an odd goal of the most political campaign in court history, but one that seems to have been accomplished. Though Lucas court rulings were occasionally controversial, the court itself dropped out of the political spotlight. The justices have been routinely confirmed at the polls without a single organized opposition campaign, and their appointments have gone unmentioned in campaigns for governor and other state offices.

"Re-establishing the court as not such a politically polarizing court probably was the chief justice's main objective ... and it's the objective that he most clearly accomplished," says attorney and legal commentator Steven Lucas, a former law clerk to Malcolm Lucas, who is not related. "When you have a court that's affirming the death penalty regularly, you have a court that's of little interest to the public."

"They've gone a long way toward restoring confidence in California courts from an all-time low," says Kent Scheidegger, director of the pro-prosecution Criminal Justice Legal Foundation.

Not surprisingly, some criminal defense lawyers and civil-liberties advocates have a different perspective, viewing the Lucas court as politically oriented from birth.

Lucas "sat silently by" while his political patron attacked Bird, and thereafter became "the direct beneficiary of the politicization of the Supreme Court," says James S. Thomson, former president of California Attorneys for Criminal Justice, a defense lawyers' group. He says Lucas was just as activist in capital cases as Bird was accused of being, and was hypocritical in invoking the independence of the judiciary when his court later came under attack in the Legislature.

One change voters were probably not seeking, after removing three justices, was a high rate of voluntary turnover on the new court, dubbed the "turnstile court" by Santa Clara University law professor Gerald Uelmen. At least partly for financial reasons, and perhaps also because the court has become less prestigious and its death penalty-oriented workload less satisfying, justices have taken to retiring as soon as they were eligible for maximum pension benefits. Arguelles, Kaufman and Eagleson left after two, three and four years respectively, and Kaufman's successor, Armand Arabian, retired after five and a half years. Forty years ago, the average justice's tenure was 12 years, but since the early 1980s it has dropped to less than five years, Uelmen says. With Lucas' departure, only 83 year-old Justice Stanley Mosk, a 1964 appointee of Governor Pat Brown and the only Democrat on the court, remains from the original Lucas court.

With start-up time required for each new justice, the turnover has been disruptive and may be responsible for a decline in the court's output, to fewer than 100 rulings a year. On the other hand, it has brought in a new group of justices who are unconnected to the 1986 election and are a more diverse lot than the middle-aged white male business lawyers who made up most of Deukmejian's early appointees.

The court, which lost its first-ever female justice when Bird was removed, now has three: Deukmejian appointee Joyce Kennard and Wilson appointees Kathryn Mickle Werdegar and Janice Rogers Brown. Kennard and Wilson appointee Ming Chin are of Asian descent, and Brown is the court's first black member since 1991 and its first-ever black woman. There is a modest amount of ideological diversity as well: Kennard is a centrist and the court's most frequent dissenter after Mosk; the newly appointed Chin frustrated prosecutors as an appellate justice by striking down DNA evidence; and Werdegar and new Chief Justice Ronald George, while conservative by most definitions, seem more moderate than their Deukmejian-appointed predecessors.

In fact, the term "Lucas court" probably became a misnomer toward the end of Lucas' tenure. The chief justice clearly was the leader of the court in its early years, setting its agenda and writing some of its most important rulings: the 1988 decisions that barred third-party suits against insurance companies for bad-faith practices and severely limited suits by fired employees, and the 1991 rulings that upheld term limits and extended Proposition 13's two-thirds vote requirement to local agencies created to finance special projects. All those were split votes, with conservatives lined up behind Lucas. But by the last year or two of his tenure, he often could no longer command a majority in close cases.

The most striking example was the July 1995 ruling that banned sex discrimination at a private country club. The case would have been a tossup in the 1987 court, but this time Lucas was alone in dissenting from George's majority opinion, which later survived a repeal attempt in the Legislature. Lucas was again in dissent this May when the court ruled 4-3 that a landlady could not refuse to rent to an unmarried couple on religious grounds. That case almost certainly would have been decided the opposite way by the early Lucas court, which issued rulings weakening the state Fair Employment and Housing Commission and restricting the scope of the law that bans discrimination by businesses. (The spirit of those early rulings reappeared in last year's decision upholding some local anti-homeless ordinances.)

Lucas was among the majority May 4, 1996, in a 4-3 ruling by Mosk, upholding the state's never-enforced parental consent law for minors' abortions — the only victory for anti-abortion forces before the court, which repeatedly refused to reconsider a 1981 Bird court ruling maintaining Medi-Cal abortions for poor women. But before the parental consent decision became final, the majority lost Arabian and Lucas to retirement, and their successors, Chin and Brown, cast the deciding votes to grant a rehearing — a step that in the past has virtually always led to a reversal.

Another hallmark of the early Lucas court, its resistance to suits by employees, was undercut by recent rulings that allowed suits for wrongful demotion and for fraud in an employer's promise that induced a prospective employee to relocate.

If the later Lucas court proved more flexible in some areas of civil law, however, it stood firm in criminal law in general, and the death penalty in particular. Remarkably, the justices claimed to be applying much the same legal framework as their predecessors. They overturned only one major Bird court ruling, which required proof of intent to kill in most types of capital murder, and one lesser precedent, which prevented defendants from abandoning their case and asking the jury for death. The dramatic shift in results has been largely due to the court's expanded view of "harmless error," a flaw in a trial that did not affect the outcome.

The Bird court rarely found an error in a capital case to be harmless. In one case often cited by prosecutors, a man who had to reload his gun before each of several killings was given a new penalty trial because jurors had not been asked to decide whether he had intended to kill. The Lucas court, on the other hand, took harmlessness to its outer limits. One jury heard inadmissible evidence that a defendant had raped an elderly woman with a wine bottle; another jury wrongly found that a prisoner who killed a fellow inmate had also murdered a guard; one defendant's lawyer was drunk; a trial was conducted under the wrong version of the death-penalty law, and a defendant was prevented by the trial judge from telling jurors why de deserved to live. In each case, the court found that no reasonable juror would have been influenced by the error in sentencing the defendant to death.

How those rulings will ultimately fare in federal court is unclear; a pattern of early reversals by federal judges may be halted by a new law restricting U.S. court review of state rulings in criminal cases. But regardless of the outcome in individual cases, Lucas' effort to solve the court's death penalty problems was not wholly successful.

Despite a sometimes frantic pace, with 56 rulings in a single year, the court was unable to clear a massive backlog of capital cases. The number of death sentences each year usually exceeds the number of rulings, but the chief problem is a shortage of appellate lawyers; despite taking over lawyer recruitment and increasing pay scales, the court has been unable to find lawyers for 125 of the 440 death row prisoners, who now must wait three years or more for an attorney. It's getting harder to find private lawyers or firms who will undertake a commitment of many years with little hope of saving their client's life. The situation may have been aggravated by the recent cutoff of federal funds for death penalty resource centers, including the California Appellate Project, the backbone of capital defense in the state for a decade. The Legislature may respond by expanding the state public defender's office, whose 50 percent reduction by Deukmejian a decade ago forced the shift to private lawyers. Capital cases, meanwhile, continue to take up a considerable share of the court's workload. A commission appointed by Lucas early in his tenure recommended shifting portions of the cases to the appellate courts, but the proposal faded after the chief justice declined to endorse it.

Criminal-law issues outside the death penalty area were largely driven by two ballot initiatives, a 1982 measure curbing pro-defense rulings on evidence and increasing sentences, and a 1990 measure narrowing defendant's pro-

cedural rights in preliminary hearings and other pretrial proceedings. The Lucas court interpreted both measures broadly; whether the "three strikes" law, which cuts closer to the heart of judicial authority, will get an equally sympathetic reading remains to be seen. Individual rulings allowed convictions to be upheld despite coerced confessions, broadened the evidence of past crimes that could be used to prove guilt, and upheld police roadblocks for drunken drivers.

A few important rulings favored defendants by preserving the status quo: a refusal to expand murder prosecutions to cases of unintentional drug overdoses, preservation of a defense based on an unreasonable fear of harm, and a reaffirmance of the need for scientific consensus before DNA and other new types of evidence can be admitted — a Lucas opinion that affects civil as well as criminal cases.

Another area of significant change was damage suits. Plaintiffs' lawyers, long accustomed to enlisting the court's aid in bringing about social change, now were told to take their disputes elsewhere. Complaints about insurers' foot-dragging were referred to long ineffectual state regulators (whose increased powers the court was later to uphold in Proposition 103). Fired workers were told to trust in the marketplace. Crime victims who blamed property owners for lax security were redirected, in most cases, to police. Parents who blamed a church counselor for their son's suicide were reminded of the separation of church and state (a principle the court also cited in banning high school graduation prayers). And a little more than a decade after a more liberal court used the Lee Marvin case to allow an unmarried partner to enforce a promise of support, the Lucas court invoked the sanctity of marriage in refusing to let a man sue for emotional distress after seeing his lover killed in a car crash.

Some of the rulings were harder to pigeonhole: a 1990 decision allowing a medical patient to sue for lack of consent when an organ removed during surgery became the basis of a commercial product while but denying him a share of the profits; a 1993 ruling making it difficult for residents to sue for fear of illness from exposure to toxics, easing the standard when the pollution was deliberate or reckless. But the justices also made it clear that they preferred arbitration to lawsuits; a 1992 ruling made arbitrators' decisions virtually unreviewable.

One problem Lucas leaves his successor is relations with the Legislature, which were frayed by the 1991 ruling upholding term limits. In language that did not seem necessary to the decision, the chief justice wrote that the initiative was justified by the dangers of "an entrenched, dynastic legislative bureaucracy," and that it was "speculative" to claim that a 38 percent cut in the Legislature's operating budget would hurt the legislative process. Lawmakers briefly proposed cutting the court's budget by 38 percent and made it clear that they would be slow to forget. Though many have since departed as a result of term limits, George has some fences to mend as he seeks legislative support for increased state funding of trial courts, his top declared priority.

Yet Lucas' principal achievement may also have been in the political sphere: The court has won, if not acclaim, at least acceptance from much of the public. The justices can therefore expect some degree of political protection if the court, after swinging from left to right, is now starting to inch back toward the center. Making that shift possible would be a final, ironic part of Lucas' legacy. 🏛

The Next Wave

More juveniles are committing more violent crimes than ever before. Prevention has gained stature as an alternative to incarceration, but the age-old tension between punitive and rehabilitative justice hasn't gone away.

by Steve Scott

Reprinted from *California Journal*, March 1997

Every so often, as part of a "campy classics" film festival, one or another of the myriad cable television channels will roll out some vintage 1950s "hygiene" films designed to keep teenagers on the straight and narrow. "These," intones the stern-timbred narrator in such films, "are the telltale signs of juvenile delinquency." On the screen appear the denim-legged, slack-backed, pompadour-coiffed "delinquents," all looking like variations on Fonzie from "Happy Days." Their "crimes" usually consist of such indiscretions as underaged smoking, missing a bath every once in awhile, or snapping their gum in class. The films scarcely speak of drugs, guns, or violence, lest they implant the idea into some impressionable young mind.

There are some who argue that this relatively tame image of juvenile crime was always an illusion — that children have been committing crimes as long as adults have. But whether or not this perception was a fantasy in the 1950s, it is certainly a fantasy in the 1990s. On any given day, juvenile halls and detention camps are housing youths accused of crimes ranging from arson to armed robbery to rape to murder. Last summer, the combined ward population of the California Youth Authority's 15 facilities topped 10,000 for the first time ever. Virtually all of those wards were doing time for what might be termed "adult" crimes, and two out of three were committed for violent offenses.

This apparent explosion in juvenile crime has prompted policy makers to take stock of the state's juvenile justice system with an urgency that, by government standards, borders on panic. Three different major reports on juvenile justice in California have been released in the last three years — by the Little Hoover Commission, the Legislative Analyst,

and a blue-ribbon task force. All urge the common goal of heading off juvenile crime while it is still in the "gum-snapping" stage. But exactly how these criminals-in-waiting are intercepted on the way to CYA points to the central issue facing those who toil within the system: Should they be treated like children ... or like crooks?

"The subjects being dealt with are both children and criminals at the same time," said Peter Greenwood, who heads RAND's Criminal Justice Project. "Reconciling these competing demands is the most difficult task confronted by juvenile justice poilcy makers."

Confronting this task means taking a realistic look at the system's mission and objectives. For roughly a century, California's juvenile justice process has been predicated on the belief that all within it are "wayward youth," whose redemption was merely a matter of removing them from the bad influences. Unlike the adult corrections system, with its twin mandates of rehabilitation and retribution, the primary objective of the juvenile system was rehabilitation, at least in theory. The CYA housed not only the teenaged burglars and killers, but also the so-called "status offenders" — those arrested for non-adult crimes, such as repeated curfew violations, or excessive truancy.

As the juvenile arrest rate climbed and more children began to face trial in adult courts, the profiles of CYA wards began to look more like those of adult prisons. "At one time, the 'deep-end' [juvenile offenders] were the status offenders," said CYA Director Francisco Alarcon. "Now seven out of 10 are in for violent crimes. That's twice what it was 10 years ago." As the Youth Authority's "deep-end" got deeper, county juvenile halls and detention camps also got tougher. A one-day census of Los Angeles County's juvenile offenders showed that more than half of those being held in juvenile hall were accused of violent crimes.

"Because of our overcrowding, we have tightened increasingly over the past few years our detention criteria so that only teenagers who are accused of felonies will be detained while they're going through court," said Sue Cullen, an Orange County probation official who serves as president of the California Probation, Parole and Correctional Association.

Overcrowded as they are, these facilities, and the wards they house, represent the tip of a much larger iceberg. Nearly three out of every four juveniles arrested in California wind up being referred to probation — nearly 200,000 referrals each year. With politically popular programs such as law enforcement and the courts standing at the front of the line, probation departments have found themselves among the early casualties in fiscal downsizing. The result is that most juvenile offenders are released, and re-released without follow-up.

"What you have in a lot of counties is not probation — it's a paper system," says Alarcon. "There are no real consequences for young people in trouble... no supervision, no prevention."

None of this comes as a surprise to childrens groups and inmate advocates. Many of them argue that the system can never succeed unless it focuses the bulk of its resources on early intervention, prevention, and rehabilitation. What has surprised these activists, however, is the degree to which their voices are being joined by law enforcement and even victims-rights advocates.

Key to many of these proposals is the idea that the first arrest is the most important, and the one in which the consequences should be made the clearest.

"If you want to get control early, you intervene early with some certainty," said Steinhart. Defining the nature and scope of these interventions though, has caused many of the traditional adversaries to retreat to their respective corners and come out battling.

Children's advocates and probation officers and some youth corrections officials argue that sanctions should be accompanied by a "continuum of care," which is available to everyone from first-time shoplifters to hard-core CYA wards. "For the small percentage of kids that need to be locked up, you need to provide facilites that separate

them from the rest of offender population," said Dan Macallair, associate director for the San Francisco-based Center on Juvenile and Criminal Justice. "From there, you build down. Construct intervention on a continuum, based on needs of each kid [with] intensive follow-up services in community. Not just holding on to a kid, but getting into a kid's environment and working on the whole environment."

For many advocates, this continuum of care also implies a continuum of graduated sanctions, designed to bring home the message that society, as well as the delinquent youth, needs to be made whole. The term of art used to describe this approach is "balanced approach to restorative justice," and its backers say it is much more than just the "flavor of the month." The philosophy seeks to balance community protection, victim restitution, and rehabilitation and is at the heart of recommendations suggested by a two-year study of the juvenile justice system conducted by the blue-ribbon California Task Force to Review Juvenile Crime.

Those favoring a "get-tough" approach insist the key to combatting juvenile criminals is to target those most likely to become adult criminals. In Orange County, for example, research has concluded that about 8 percent of the juvenile population is committing about two-thirds of the juvenile crime. In a pilot program that state officials are looking to expand to other counties, law enforcement and social service agencies share information in an effort to identify which first offenders are most likely to become "Eight Percenters." These children are assigned a case worker, who attempts to resolve family and social issues which may lay at the heart of the criminal behavior. Early field testing of the program is encouraging — recidivism was cut in half among those who were part of the test.

Beyond early targeting, the "get-tough" approach suggests a system which removes those identified as "incorrigible" from society as quickly and permanently as possible. A 1996 report by the conservative Heritage Foundation concludes that "the best that state and local officials can do with the incorrigible juvenile [habitual offender] when the crime is serious is to try him as an adult, sentence him as an adult, and require him to serve at least 85 percent of his sentence...."

Lining up exactly where Califor-

nia policymakers will ultimately come down on the question of punishment versus prevention is still unclear. Last year, Governor Pete Wilson signed a bill co-authored by his legislative nemesis — Democratic Senate President pro Tempore Bill Lockyer (D-Hayward) — which will dole out $50 million in challenge grants to counties to help them re-tool their early intevention programs. Alarcon, a Wilson appointee, was a member of the blue-ribbon task force and is a strong advocate of the balanced approach.

On the other hand, Wilson also is drafting his own comprehensive juvenile justice program, which is expected to be unveiled later this spring. Indications are that the proposal will emphasize tougher penalties for violent offenders and gangs, increased information-sharing between agencies to help target the habitual offenders, and early intervention efforts like those under way in Orange County. There is also talk of stripping out the adult component of last year's unsuccessful bond proposal to construct new local jails and resubmitting it to voters.

With political leaders keeping a toe in both ends of the pool, some activists are pessimistic that the new focus on juvenile justice will generate much more than another round of finger-pointing. Macallair predicts the Task Force report will be added to the growing bookshelf of studies that are at odds with the urge to incarcerate, recalling a similar study of the adult system in the late 1980s. "They produced this great report, on a commission stacked with Deukmejian appointees," he said. "That report was put on a shelf and never saw the light of day."

Other activists are not so pessimistic. In fact, they see tremendous opportunity in new research techniques which will allow policy makers to more accurately gauge which is more effective — punishment or prevention. These techniques allow probation officers to track their cases better, quantify their results, and perhaps even answer the question of which works better — the carrot or the stick.

"Lawmakers are interested in prevention, but they want to get a bang for the buck," noted Steinhart. "Now, we're testing violence prevention programs to see if they deliver results. This is the new flag under which prevention programs fly. Do they prove themselves? Will they work?" 🏛

The Prison Dilemma

The California prison population, while still badly overcrowded, is slowing its precipitous growth. Does California need more prisons — or a different way of handling offenders?

By Sigrid Bathen

Reprinted from *California Journal*, March 1997

Franklin Zimring, a law professor and noted criminologist who directs the Earl Warren Legal Institute at the University of California, Berkeley, has been studying and writing about crime and punishment for more than 25 years. He is especially skilled at interpreting the Byzantine world of crime statistics — that bewildering array of comparatives and projections that has dominated state budget deliberations for the past decade, as the state prison population has taken a dizzying spiral through the budgetary roof.

State lawmakers, responding to public outcries against crime, and loathe to do anything that might make them look soft on criminals, have passed a plethora of tougher sentencing bills — including, but hardly limited to, the so-called "Three Strikes and You're Out" law — which have pushed the number of prisoners to the ragged edge of the state Department of Corrections' ability to house them, much less supervise their graduates on parole.

As voters and lawmakers alike begin to question how many more prisons California can afford — and whether the cost to other programs, such as education, is too great — experts like Zimring say there is some light, as well as considerable darkness, at the end of the corrections budget tunnel. And with increasing public sentiment for redirecting public funds to the juvenile prevention end of the system, those experts say this budget year could be pivotal in determining how the state's policy-makers appropriate public funds in the war on crime.

"One of the remarkable things that is happening about official sentiments now is the development of real enthusiasm for the front end of criminal controls," says Zimring. "What we're having now is an overstatement of the potential of front-end control. But there is an awful lot of enthusiasm, and the shifting of resources from the back end to the front end."

Critical to that realignment — if it goes beyond sentiment to widespread redirection of state resources — is the reasonable control of prison population and construction in a system where some institutions currently are running at 200 percent of capacity and tensions could easily explode, as in some instances they already have. "As between one new prison and 17 new prisons, my strong preference is for one," says Zimring. "Then you try and reduce populations. The worst of both worlds is to stuff in populations you don't have facilities for." Governor Pete Wilson has called for the construction of one new prison, largely with federal crime-control funds, in his proposed state budget, as well as initial planning funds for five new prisons. The corrections department has said it needs 17 new prisons to keep pace with growth in the immediate future.

Unfortunately for policy-makers, Zimring and others say, California's prison planning is predicated on growth. "It is the largest prison system in the free world," says Zimring. "California is England and Germany combined and still has room to accommodate a great deal of France...When you have a prison system that has grown as much as California's has, your principal activity is growing. Our principal prison industry in California is growth. Whatever energy and resources that are invested in governance and planning are invested in growth, rather than programs."

The numbers — both in human and fiscal terms — are staggering. Twenty-five years ago, some five years before the passage of the state's determinate sentencing law, California's prison population hit a low of fewer than 20,000 inmates. The department's 1971-72 budget was $127.4 million, and the system employed some 7,000 full-time staff. Fast-forward to fiscal 1995-96, and the population has mushroomed to 135,360 (as of June 30, 1996), with a budget of more than $3.3 billion and more than 35,000 full-time employees. The projections, which are slowing but still growing, are that the population, which is currently about 145,000 inmates, will rise above 150,000 by the end of fiscal 1996-97, with a state prison and parole budget of more than $3.6 billion. The governor's proposed corrections budget for 1997-98 is $3.8 billion.

And those figures are just for the grown-ups in prison. Administratively tied to the California Youth Authority under the aegis of the state Youth and Adult Correctional Agency (created in 1980 under the catchy acronym of YACA), the Department of Corrections houses adult inmates over age 18 in 32 prisons and 38 camps around the state, and supervises, by last count, more than 100,000 parolees in a swinging-door system with one of the highest recidivist (return) rates in the country. The average recidivist rate, according to the *Corrections Yearbook* published by the Criminal Justice Institute in South Salem, N.Y., which collects statistical data on prison systems throughout the country, is 34.7 percent, while California returns fully 56 percent of its inmates to prison within three years after release.

San Quentin mess hall, 1935. Courtesy of the Department of Corrections

The Lancaster prison under construction, 1991. Courtesy of Corrections.

Latinos and especially African-Americans are incarcerated in numbers far greater than their numbers in the general population, and whites in lesser numbers than in the general population — a common reality in prisons throughout the country and a major focus of critics who say the criminal justice system comes down harder on minorities and the poor. In California between 1974 and 1994, according to corrections, white male inmates dropped from 47 percent of the male institutional population to 29 percent, while Hispanic inmates jumped from 19 to 35 percent and Blacks remained relatively stable at 32 percent — still much higher than their percentage of the general population. Gangs in prison are rigidly divided along racial and ethnic lines, and overcrowding — with inmates two to a cell and double-bunked in available open space such as gymnasiums and day rooms — is exacerbated by the constant racial tension in prison. Add to that mix the high percentage — some place it as high as one-fourth of the inmate population — of mentally ill prisoners, and the results can be deadly, tragic and increasingly a target for expensive lawsuits.

"It's really dismal," says Donald Specter, an attorney who since 1980 has directed the Prison Law Office outside the gates of San Quentin in Marin County that has filed many of the landmark cases against the Department of Corrections. "At the same time the prisons are getting more and more crowded, the problems are becoming more and more serious. When you combine that with the tinderbox effect created by overcrowding, nobody will be surprised if it blows up."

Efforts to control spiraling prison costs increasingly focus on redirecting funds to early intervention in schools, communities and juvenile programs, where Zimring and others say there there have been astonishing successes but on a scale too small to make a major difference. In addition, lawmakers are looking at increasing funding for the huge population of criminals who are arrested and incarcerated — again and again, at huge public expense — for drug and drug-related offenses. Compared to other states and despite considerable data showing drug treatment to be effective in reducing inmate populations, California spends relatively little on reforming its drug-using inmate population, while incarcerations for drug and drug-related offenses continue to grow. Pilot programs, including those operated by the Department of Corrections at the R.J. Donovan Correctional Facility in San Diego and the California Institution for Women near Chino — and soon to be introduced at a new prison opening next fall adjacent to the existing prison in Corcoran — have demonstrated remarkable success.

Inmates who have completed the program have much lower recidivism rates, says Corrections Department spokeswoman Christine May — 27.6 percent after two years, which is nearly 30 points lower than the average state return rate of 56 percent. The program includes treatment in prison as well as intensive follow-up on parole. Although successful, such programs are a mere drop in the population bucket of the state prison system, but they have clearly piqued the interest of legislators searching frantically for some way to rein in the California prison budget without endangering public safety — or their own political futures.

The move toward redirecting resources seems, at least for the moment, to enjoy cautious bipartisan support — with somewhat different modes of getting there. Conservative lawmakers, while supporting more "front-end" prevention efforts, also want tougher sanctions on criminals while in prison and more exploration of proposals to turn over some prison operations to private industry. In a 1994 report on "Curbing the Cost of Incarceration in California," Senator Rob Hurtt (R-Garden Grove) suggested eliminating funding for "leisure-time activities" for prisoners and for inmate salaries in prison industry programs, as well as increased "privatization" of prison operations. Get-tough sentencing measures continue to be popular among legislators, although corrections administrators point out that tougher sentences generally translate into more people in prison for longer periods of time. And prison officials — not politicians — must figure out where to put them.

"Last year there was considerable discussion among [legislators] with some pretty wide-ranging philosophies who were in agreement that we needed to figure out how to control the spiraling budget of prison construction and operations," says Senate President pro Tempore Bill Lockyer (D-Hayward), who effectively blocked a prison bond —

strongly favored by Governor Wilson — from the November ballot by insisting as a caveat that a comprehensive plan which included alternatives to incarceration be more fully explored. "The essential problem, as I would define it, is that in six years of Wilson budget proposals, we've created 10,000 new jobs in the prison system and financed those jobs by cutting 10,000 positions out of the university and state college system. Everyone realizes that is a long-term mistake.

"Now, how can we take appropriate measures to protect public safety without spending excessively? There is no magic wand. There are a lot of small steps that will aggregate into major cost savings."

Those "small steps" include major expansion of drug treatment programs in and outside prison, as well as shifting non-violent offenders — many of whom have committed robberies or other property crimes to finance drug habits — to, as Lockyer puts it, "less expensive options." Those options generally involve more community placement of non-violent offenders, and shifting older inmates who may be incarcerated for long sentences but whose propensity for violence has decreased substantially with age, to less secure, less expensive facilities. The California Correctional Peace Officers Association, in a lengthy report on "Affordable Prisons," recommends construction of "mega-prisons" rather than expensive, smaller prisons, and suggests a major overhaul of inmate classification and detention systems, reserving expensive maximum security space for violent inmates and handling low-risk inmates in different ways.

Lockyer's SB 760, which was introduced last year and failed, included a mix of some construction, efforts to reduce recidivism — and more emphasis on drug treatment. David Panush, a fiscal adviser to Lockyer, says lower-level offenders, many of them drug offenders, are flooding the system. "They're in, often for less than a year, then they go out," he says. "They get very little treatment or intervention. Is it really surprising that they come back? Drug treatment is a little more expensive than doing nothing, but if done properly, the long-term savings are very significant." Panush also cites projected prison population figures that indicate a major "housing gap" in projections as lower-level offenders — who many experts say could more efficiently, and at considerably less expense, be handled in less secure community facilities — flood a system designed for longer stays and tougher security.

Lockyer and Senator Richard Rainey (R-Walnut Creek), a moderate Republican who is a former Contra Costa County sheriff, can again be expected to cooperate on joint legislation — as they did last session.

There is also talk of more extensive inmate work programs and job training — even a return to the "R" word (as in "rehabilitation") that fell out of favor in correctional jargon in the get-tough 1980s and early 1990s.

And Lockyer says the key concern for lawmakers is the juvenile system, which Zimring calls the one "bright spot" in the correctional quagmire. "The juvenile justice system," says Zimring, "ain't broke yet" — implying that it can still be fixed, perhaps in the process stemming the coming tide of youthful offenders expected to swell the ranks of adult prisoners as the babies of the baby boomers enter their crime-prone years.

Experts of varying political stripes attribute the drop in the crime rate, and the corollary slowing of the explosive growth in the state prison population, to a variety of factors — obviously giving certain factors more weight depending on their individual, endlessly debatable, views about the causes of crime. Some insist tougher sentencing laws like "three strikes" have slowed the crime rate, simply by "incapacitating" repeat criminals. Others say the crime rate has slowed in states with no such law, and that the law helps to clog the courts, jails and prisons. They say the drop in the crime rate is largely attributable to basic demographics — the aging of the crime-prone population — as well as to community-based policing and efforts to curb gun sales, particularly for cheap handguns.

Some say the state's switch to so-called "determinate sentencing" in 1977, severely limiting judicial discretion, has swelled the prison population to unnecessary levels and prompted an endless spate of get-tough sentencing laws.

"If anyone ultimately should be responsible, it is the [Jerry] Brown administration shifting to determinate sentencing," says Lockyer, "with specific legislative proposals, rather than the judiciary, making the sentencing decisions." While admitting that a return to indeterminate sentencing is not a particularly viable political solution, Lockyer says he sometimes longs for a return to the simpler days portrayed in '50s crime dramas like *Dragnet*.

"I love the old Jack Webb programs — you know, the ones that come on at 3 a.m., and at the end the hammer comes down and the voice announces the sentence, which is three years to life for *anything,* you name it...It was a whole different system which minimized the meddling of politicians." 🏛

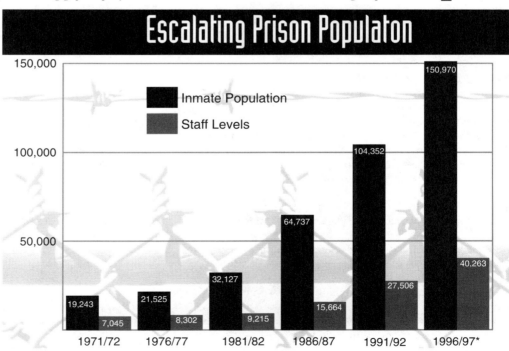

Escalating Prison Populaton

- Inmate Population
- Staff Levels

	1971/72	1976/77	1981/82	1986/87	1991/92	1996/97*
Inmate Population	19,243	21,525	32,127	64,737	104,352	150,970
Staff Levels	7,045	8,302	9,215	15,664	27,506	40,263

Source: California Department of Corrections and Governor's Budget

THE LEGISLATURE

California's Legislature is not much different from Congress and legislative bodies in other states in overall power and structure. It is, simply stated, the policy-making arm of government, restricted only by the federal and state constitutions and the governor's veto. Like Congress, it can also conduct investigations into almost any issue of public concern and impeach public officials. The Senate must ratify top-level, non-judicial appointments of the governor, while both houses have the opportunity to reject the executive's nominations for any vacancy among the state's constitutional offices. It also can ratify amendments to the United States Constitution. In recent years, there has been a trend toward the Legislature's appropriating for itself some of the appointive power traditionally given to the executive. Thus, it is not uncommon now to have a commission consist of both gubernatorial and legislative appointees.

Seats in both the 40-member Senate and 80-member Assembly are apportioned on the basis of population and under the 1991 reapportionment for the first time the court joined two adjacent assembly districts into one senate district throughout the state. (Until 1966, the Senate was apportioned by geography, like the United States Senate.) Assembly members serve two-year terms; Senate terms are for four years, with half the terms expiring every two years. Under the provisions of Prop. 140 of November 1990, term limits are now imposed on state legislators (3 terms, 6 years in the Assembly; 2 terms, 8 years in the Senate). Term limits were ruled unconstitutional by a federal court, but the decision was appealed and the limits remained in effect in the meantime.

The Senate and Assembly are organized differently, with power diffused in a committee of the upper house but centered in the office of speaker in the Assembly.

The Senate

The lieutenant governor is the president of the Senate, but this official has virtually no power. The lieutenant governor is entitled to cast a vote to break a 20-20 tie, but this is very rare. If the Senate can be said to have a single leader it is the president pro tempore, who is elected by a simple majority of his colleagues. The pro tem is charged with overall administration of the house, but the real power — committee appointments and assignment of bills to committee — rests with the five-member Rules Committee. The president pro tempore is chairman, and the other four seats are traditionally divided between the two major parties. In the past rural vs. urban, north vs. south or personal animosities created conflict. In recent years the divisions in the Senate have tended to be along party lines. David Roberti provided stable leadership to the Senate from 1980 to 1994 when Roberti was forced to leave the Senate because of term limits, the first state legislator in the nation to be forced out of office. The current President pro Tempore is Senator Bill Lockyer.

Aside from the Rules Committee, the two most important panels in the Senate are the Appropriations and Budget and Fiscal Review committees. The Budget and Fiscal Review Committee handles the budget. The Appropriations Committee hears any other bills with direct or implied state cost. Thus it can kill almost any major bill.

The Assembly

Until 1995 the Assembly had a form of government that might be called self-inflicted dictatorship. The speaker was elected by at least 41 votes (a simple majority) and thereafter wielded tremendous power; this officer appointed all committee chairs and named all committee members except for the Rules Committee. Control over committees amounted to the power to kill any bill. A bill defeated in committee could be brought to the floor by a majority vote of the full assembly, but this occured very infrequently. A vote to withdraw a bill from committee would be tantamount to a vote of no-confidence for the speaker. The speaker's control over legislation made whoever holds this office the second-most-powerful official in state government next to the governor. However, on occasion, the speaker had difficulty leading. Battles within majority Democratic ranks in 1979-80 between then-Speaker Leo McCarthy and challenger Howard Berman, each with his own faction, led to legislative paralysis in the lower house. In 1988 the "Gang of Five" (anti-leadership Democrats) openly feuded with Democratic Speaker Willie Brown over legislative matters in the Assembly. Though the five were punished by Speaker Brown (losing chairmanships, committee assignments, staff and office space) they refused to back down. For a time, the "Five" combined with the Republican caucus had a majority in the Assembly. However after the November 1988 elections, Democrats had 42 seats plus the rebellious "Gang of Five" who were no longer needed for a majority. The "Five" returned to the Democratic fold, and their transgressions forgiven.

However, a combination of term-limits-fomented-departures of veteran Democractic assembly members, the court-designed reapportionment of 1991, and a nationwide Republican surge provided the necessary ingredients for substantial Republican gains and corresponding Democratic losses in the Assembly in the 1994 general election. After the dust settled, 41 Republicans and 39 Democrats were elected to the Assembly. It appeared that Brown would lose his speakership, and that Republican leader Jim Brulte would replace him. However, it didn't happen—then. Rumors of Willie Brown's political death were exaggerated: Brown had an ace up his sleeve. Republican Assembly member Paul Horcher switched from Republican ranks to independent in early December 1994. On the floor he surprised his GOP brethren by voting for Willie Brown as speaker. This created a 40-40 tie and meant there was no immediate resolution of the leadership issue for the time being.

In January, Democrats and Horcher moved to oust Republican Richard Mountjoy from the Assembly. Mountjoy had been elected simultaneously to the Assembly and to the Senate in a special election in the 1994 election. Although Mountjoy fought to stay in the Assembly long enough to vote for Brulte, he was removed in mid-January 1995 on a 40-39 vote. (Of course, if he had resigned from his Senate seat, he could have remained in the Assembly.) With Mountjoy gone, Willie Brown was elected as speaker 40-39 (not with the customary 41-vote margin). And, Speaker Brown agreed to share power with Republicans. Of the 26 standing committees, 13 were chaired by Republicans and 13 were chaired by Democrats.

Angered by Horcher's defection, Republican Assembly leaders went on to recall him from office and elect a new Republican loyalist, Gary Miller, to the seat. In June 1995 Brown announced he would be running for Mayor of San Francisco (he won), and Democrats united behind maverick Republican Doris Allen electing her as the new speaker. Immediately Republican leaders sought to recall Allen, and several months later she resigned from the speakership. Allen, in turn, voted for her one Republican ally, Brian Setencich to replace her as speaker, again with Democratic caucus support. Republicans successfully recalled Doris Allen and she was replaced by Scott Baugh. Brown's departure from the Assembly and Miller's and Baugh's election to the chamber, allowed Republicans to depose Brian Setencich as speaker and elect their leader, Curt Pringle as speaker and Rules Chair. Speaker Pringle quickly "Brownized" Democrats by selecting Republicans to chair all committees (with one exception, Reform party member Dominic Cortese) and gave each solid Republican majorities. In 1996 the Democrats regained control if the Assembly and in December elected Cruz Bustamante Speaker by a 43-37 margin, the first Latino to hold the office.

Instability and turmoil will likely be the pattern in the Assembly for the forseeable future. Every two years a fresh new wave of 30-35 rookie legislators are elected. The grizzled veterans are members who have served for a term or two (a handful of exceptions include four members who once served in the Assembly before term limits and one Senator who decided to run for the lower house when his Senate service limit was reached). One thing is certain however: the immense power speakers such as Willie Brown once held is a relic of the past. Post-Brown speakers may retain the traditional legislative powers of the speaker, but will not be able to exert the all-encompassing influence of the past in the new term limits era.

Much of Willie Brown's power hinged on continuity (15 year as speaker and 31 as Assembly member); his ability to maintain the Democratic majority; and his success in wheedling large campaign donations from special interests (concerned about what passed or what was killed in the Assembly) and then divvying them out to Democratic Assembly members for their campaigns. This is gone. In the new term-limits era the Assembly Rules Committee may become more important in the Assembly in performing its various housekeeping duties: assigning bills to committee, setting salaries for legislative employees, determining offices for members and purchasing supplies. The Senate has become the more influential legislative house because the upper house has more experienced members. After all, most new senators have previously served in the Assembly.

Legislation

There are three basic types of legislation: bills, constitutional amendments and resolutions. These measures can only be introduced by legislators. The governor cannot introduce a bill, but he can ask a friendly member to put it in the hopper. Even the governor's budget carries the name of a lawmaker. In fact, however, very few bills are the direct inspiration of a legislator. Most bills come from interest groups, staff members, constituents, government officials, or a variety of other sources.

A bill is simply a proposed statute. It can be enacted by a simple majority vote in both houses unless it is an urgency measure or carries an appropriation, in which case a two-thirds vote of approval is required. Constitutional amendments are proposed changes to the state Constitution; a two-thirds vote of each house will place one of these measures on the ballot for voter consideration. Resolutions are merely statements of legislative viewpoint. They may be addressed to other governmental agencies, describe state general policy, or commend or memorialize someone. They are normally passed by voice vote. Constitutional amendments and resolutions, unlike bills, are not subject to gubernatorial veto.

Legislative process

When a member introduces a bill, its title is read and it is printed. Then it is assigned to a committee by the Assembly or Senate Rules Committee. The committee hearing is the most crucial stage in the legislative process, for it is at this point — not on the floor — that the fate of most legislation is determined. Following public hearing, the committee can kill the measure or send it to another committee (usually the fiscal committee) or to the floor as is or with recommended amendments. When it reaches the floor, the bill's title is read a second time, amendments are often made, and the legislation is placed on the agenda for debate. After debate, a roll call is taken. If the bill is passed, it is sent to the other house, where the same process takes place. If the bill is amended in the second house, it must return to the house of origin for acceptance or rejection of the amendments. If approved at this point, the bill goes to the governor for signature or veto. If the amendments are rejected, a conference committee of three members of each house is formed to compromise differences. This procedure is always followed on the budget and often used at the end of a session to speed the last-minute rush of bills (because a conference committee report can be produced more rapidly than a revised printed version of a bill).

A bill goes to the governor if both houses approve a conference committee recommendation.

In the Senate, roll calls are taken orally by the secretary of the Senate and aides. Once a roll call is concluded, members may not change their votes, and absent members cannot add their votes. The Assembly uses an electronic vote counter. Members push switches, and lights shine on a board — green reflecting aye; red, no. With the unanimous consent of the membership, members are allowed to change their votes the same day or add their votes if their actions do not alter the outcome.

Legislative modernization

Until 1966, the Legislature met for general sessions in odd-numbered years and for short budget sessions in even-numbered years. Legislators then received $6,000 a year, and their elective positions were not considered to be full-time occupations. In 1966, the voters approved Proposition 1a making each year's session unlimited, raising the pay to $16,000 and allowing lawmakers to give themselves cost-of-living increases of five percent a year. In the June 1990 primary election voters approved Prop. 112. While some of the provisions of this constitutional amendment established new ethics regulations, perhaps its key feature was the creation of a new Citizens' Compensation Commission. The reason this amendment was proposed was because the Legislature angered many votes when they voted to increase their salaries. To deflect this criticism the commission was established. In

December 1991 the new commission raised salaries of state legislators from $40,816 a year to $52,500. In addition, legislative leaders received extra compensation. Current salaries established by the commission are: legislator, $75,600; Speaker and President pro Tem, $90,720, and floor leaders, $83,160.

In 1972, the people approved another constitutional amendment. This one put the Legislature on the same two-year schedule as Congress, with bills remaining alive for two years. The Legislature now is in session year-round, with breaks for Easter, Christmas, part of the summer and during statewide elections. In addition to their salaries, legislators receive $109 a day for expenses and have use of leased automobiles, credit cards and district offices.

In addition to the standing committees, which consider the merits of bills, the Legislature also establishes two-house joint committees and one-house select committees to study specific problems (often of special concern to only one legislator, who becomes chairman of the committee). These committees can submit recommendations to the Legislature but have no direct power over legislation. Many of these select committees have been eliminated under the new budget strictures of Proposition 140.

Legislative staff

Each member of the Legislature has a personal staff plus the assistance of specialists assigned to committees and to the party caucuses. There are also three major independent bureaus with significant influence on the legislative process— the legislative counsel, the legislative analyst, and the auditor general.

• *Legislative counsel*, Bion Gregory, has a large staff of attorneys to provide legal advice to lawmakers and draft their bills and proposed amendments.

• *Legislative analyst*, Elizabeth Hill, provides advice to the Legislature on anything with a fiscal implication, which can cover virtually every major bill. The analyst annually publishes a detailed analysis of the governor's budget, which becomes the basis for legislative hearings on the fiscal program.

• *State auditor*, Kurt R. Sjoberg, conducts investigations of state agencies to determine whether they can be run more economically and efficiently, he reports directly to the Joint Audit Committee and to the Legislature as a whole.

In all, a staff of some 2,000 served the Legislature until the passage of Prop. 140 in November 1990 which mandated term limits for members and budget reductions for the Legislature. The Legislature's staff has been reduced to comply with the measure. In addition to the analyst, auditor, and counsel, there are sergeants-at-arms, secretaries, political aides, and committee consultants. The consultants are the most important element of the staff; they provide specialized knowledge for committees, gather information and provide independent evaluation of information obtained from interest groups, the governor and others.

Reapportionment

Almost nothing stirs the juices of a legislator — either at the state or federal level — as much as the prospect of his or her district being reapportioned. Redistricting takes place every decade and has the potential of throwing many legislators out of office. Every congressional, Senate and Assembly district in California must be redrawn after each census to ensure districts are equal in population.

California's Assembly districts have always been apportioned by population, but the state Senate has been apportioned under two systems. Prior to 1926, the Senate was also apportioned by population, but in that year the voters approved a "federal plan" devised by Northern Californians to keep control of the Senate from rapidly growing Southern California. This plan provided that no county could have more than one senator and that one senator could represent no more than three counties. As a result, the senator from Los Angeles at one time represented 440 times more people than the senator from Alpine, Inyo and Mono counties. This was the most severe apportionment imbalance in the nation. Such discrepancies were eradicated in 1966, when the U.S. Supreme Court's "one-man, one-vote" edict went into effect.

Redistricting can be simple if both houses of a legislature and the governor are of the same political party. The party in power merely divides the state to suit itself and gives the opposition party the scraps. The usual procedure is to offer some members of the opposition good deals so that a nominally bipartisan reapportionment bill can be passed. Actually, it is impossible to create good districts for one party without fashioning some just as good for the other. But the legislators doing the redistricting can usually pick and choose whom to favor among members of the opposition. In the 1980's reapportionment, although Democrat Jerry Brown was governor and Democrats had solid majorities in both houses, Republicans stymied the majority party's reapportionment plans by qualifying three separate referenda for the June 1982 ballot. Voters voted "no" against the three Democratic sponsored bills and forced the Democrats to make some adjustments to the district lines.

Under the state Constitution, the Legislature is empowered to reapportion all seats (52 in Congress, 40 Senate and 80 Assembly districts), subject only to a gubernatorial veto. Thus, when a governor is of a different party than the Legislature's leadership an impasse is apt to develop. In this case, either a bi-partisan plan is drawn favoring the incumbents of both parties, maintaining the status quo, or the matter ends up in the courts.

Republicans tried repeatedly in the 1980s to modify the reapportioning process. Their objective was to shift the decision making away from Democratic legislative leaders:

1) In 1982 Republicans joined with Common Cause and qualified Prop. 14 to establish an independent districting commission to do the reapportioning. Voters defeated the proposal.

2) In 1983 then Assemblyman Don Sebastiani qualified a new initiative which provided, he claimed, "fairer" districts than the one the Democrats had devised. This initiative was declared unconstitutional by the state Supreme Court prior to its being voted upon. The court ruled that reapportioning could take place only once each decade.

3) In 1984 Governor Deukmejian authored an initiative to have reapportioning handled by a panel of retired appellate judges. Voters rejected this proposal.

The 1991 reapportionment plans passed by the Democratic-controlled Legislature were vetoed by Republican Governor Pete Wilson. Because of the impasse, districts were drawn by the state Supreme Court with the help of "special masters."

CALIFORNIA LEGISLATIVE PROCESS

INITIAL STEPS BY AUTHOR

IDEA

Sources of bills: legislators, legislative committees, governor, state and local governmental agencies, business firms, lobbyists, citizens.

DRAFTING

Formal copy of bill and "layman's digest" prepared by Legislative Counsel.

INTRODUCTION

Bill submitted by senator or Assembly member. Numbered and read first time. Referred to policy committee by Assembly or Senate Rules Committee. Printed.

ACTION IN HOUSE OF ORIGIN

COMMITTEE

Testimony taken from author, proponents and opponents. Typical actions: Do pass; amend and do pass; no action; hold in committee (kill); amend and re-refer to same committee; refer to another committee; send to interim study. Committee actions are reported to the floor. Bills with any fiscal implications, if approved by policy committee, are re-referred to Appropriations Committee.

SECOND READING

Bills given do-pass recommendations are read the second time on the floor and placed on the daily file (agenda) for debate on a subsequent day.

FLOOR DEBATE AND VOTE

Bills are read the third time and debated. A roll-call vote follows. For ordinary bills, 21 votes are needed in the Senate and 41 in the Assembly. For urgency bills and most appropriations measures, 27 and 54 votes are required. If these numbers are not reached, the bill is defeated. Any member may seek reconsideration and a second vote. If passed or passed with amendments, the bill is sent to the second house.

ACTION IN SECOND HOUSE

READING

Bill is read the first time and referred to committee by the Assembly or Senate Rules Committee.

COMMITTEE

Procedures and possible actions are nearly identical to those in the first house.

SECOND READING

If cleared by committee, the bill is read a second time and placed on the daily file (agenda) for debate and vote.

FLOOR DEBATE AND VOTE

The procedure is identical to the first house. If a bill is passed without having been amended in the second house, it is sent back to house of origin for enrollment, then to the governor's desk. (Resolutions are sent to the secretary of state's office.) If amended in the second house and passed, the measure returns to the house of origin for consideration of amendments.

RESOLUTION OF TWO-HOUSE DIFFERENCES (IF NECESSARY)

CONCURRENCE

The house of origin decides whether to accept the second-house amendments. If the amendments are approved, the bill is sent to the governor. If the amendments are rejected, the bill is placed in the hands of a two-house conference committee composed of three senators and three Assembly members.

CONFERENCE

If the conferees present a recommendation for compromise (conference report), both houses vote on the report. If the report is adopted by both, the bill goes to the governor. If the conferees fail to agree, or if either house rejects the report, a second (and even a third) conference committee may be formed.

THE GOVERNOR

SIGN OR VETO?

Within 12 days after receiving a bill, the governor may sign it into law, allow it to become law without his signature or veto it. Bill is sent to Secretary of State's office and given a chapter number. A vetoed bill returns to the house of origin for possible vote on overriding the veto. It requires a two-thirds majority of both houses to override. Urgency measures may become effective immediately after signing. Others usually take effect the following January 1st.

TRANSITIONAL PRO TEM?

Bill Lockyer leads the Senate into the era of term limits

by Steve Scott

Reprinted from *California Journal*, November 1994

Earlier this year, as the state budget debate was approaching its end game, Bill Lockyer (D-Hayward) found himself in a familiar position: He was sur-rounded by reporters after a floor session. The rookie pro tem had just spent a fair bit of energy and time tamping down a fire that had erupted in the tension of the budget denouement. The battle was not the budget itself. Rather, it was an ugly public spat between Senators Dan McCorquodale (D-Modesto) and Steve Peace (D-Chula Vista). At one point, Peace, the Senate's loosest cannon, yelled across the floor that McCorquodale was "a nut case." When a reporter asked about the flap, Lockyer responded with a roll of the eyes that recalled similar expressions of exasperation one might have seen from his predecessor, David Roberti.

"When tensions arise in the Capitol," Lockyer shrugged, "these little blisters tend to arise."

There was a time in California political history when having both Peace and Lockyer in the same house would have been viewed as a sign of the coming Apocalypse. For much of his early career, Bill Lockyer didn't soothe blisters, he caused them. But times have changed, so much so that the 53-year-old Hayward Democrat has become only the third person in two decades to hold the post of president pro tempore of the Senate.

Lockyer's ascension comes at a time of great upheaval in the Legislature, and he faces challenges unimaginable to any of his predecessors. Term limits are likely to accelerate the arrival of bomb-throwers like Peace from the Assembly, where fiery partisanship is practically in the job description. Pressure will be on Lockyer to maintain the customary deliberativeness of the Senate while at the same time mollifying the more partisan members of his own caucus. Lockyer must also manage the surge of power and influence that most believe will flow into the Senate as a result of term limits, since the upper house will likely become the repository of the Legislature's institutional memory. On top of all that, Lockyer must also keep a check on his own partisan impulses, while at the same time following through on the one clear charge he's been given by his caucus: Keep the Democrats in power.

"David Roberti had a luxury Bill Lockyer will never have," observes Assembly Republican Leader Jim Brulte (R-Rancho Cucamonga). "Roberti had significant majorities to work with. Locker's strength or weaknesses will not be relational to his own abilities. It will relate to the solidification of his majority."

To the extent that Brulte is wrong, and ability is a factor,

the new pro tem certainly has the qualifications for leadership. For Lockyer, politics and the California Legislature has been, and remains, his life's work. Born in East Oakland in 1941, Lockyer grew up in the area he now represents, attending San Leandro High School. He earned a political science degree from UC-Berkeley, but his political activism was born not in the classroom, although as a participant in the Berkeley "Free Speech Movement" of the 1960s.

Already an activist in local Democratic circles, Lockyer worked for seven years as an aide to Assemblyman Robert Crown, and when Crown died in 1973, won the special election to replace him, using what were, at the time, unusual techniques. "At that time, a massive lawn-sign campaign, and campaigning to the reduced universe of likely voters were revolutionary ideas," he recalls. Lockyer quickly established himself as a young man in a hurry, but when the speakership beckoned ambitious lawmakers in 1979, Lockyer was content to wait his turn.

"From my observation of the speakership, it seems that half of the time is taken up handling the egos of the place," he said at the time. "Up to now, I've been one of the ones that's needed a temper calmed."

When he moved over to the Senate in 1982, Lockyer found himself serving on, and eventually chairing, the

Lockyer taking oath of office

girlie punch" at him. While still in the Assembly, Lockyer was threatened with arrest by Senator Alfred Alquist (D-San Jose) when he refused to leave a hearing room after Alquist had snubbed one of his bills.

Although he concedes this reputation is "part of my baggage," Lockyer insists such behavior is in the past, and that his detractors have to go back several years to find truly erratic behavior. "I think he has worked hard to get [his temper] under control," said Senator Robert Presley (D-Riverside). "It's a moot concern if you get it under control."

A "kinder and gentler" Lockyer was well positioned to step into leadership, and when the term-limited Roberti let it be known that he was going to run for statewide office, Lockyer immediately began lining up the votes to become pro tem. By getting out ahead of the curve, Lockyer insists he was able to get the votes he needed without making cutting individual deals for chairmanships or staff. Still, his mere acceptance of the job implied one huge promise to his Democratic colleagues: Don't lose control of the Senate.

After he took over for Roberti in late January, Lockyer moved to assuage early concerns that his leadership would be more par-

powerful Judiciary Committee, even though he was still attending law school at night. When he took his bar exam, there was, he recalls, "considerable press interest: 'Will the chair of Judiciary pass the bar?'" He did, and established himself as a master at the insider game. Lockyer was one of those who negotiated the infamous "napkin deal" altering the state's liability laws, which was worked out among lawmakers and lobbyists at Frank Fat's restaurant two days before the end of the 1987 session. Lockyer, in fact, displayed the napkin on the floor of the Senate the night the bill was passed.

Lockyer with Ken Maddy

While working his way up the legislative ladder, Lockyer's policy reputation was of someone who liked to push big ideas. In the Assembly, Lockyer introduced the first legislation to promote the concept of "comparable worth" for traditionally female occupations. Four years before it became a political litmus test, Lockyer introduced the first three-strikes-you're-out law for serious felonies. He wrote the first "Lemon Law" protecting automobile purchasers, and was an early advocate of legislation to keep large companies from filing harassing lawsuits against citizens. Lockyer's policy direction is informed by what he calls his "philosophical and temperamental sympathy for the rebellion in life," but he hastens to add that he does not share what he considers the more naive aspects of classical liberalism. "I'm much more sensitive to matters of history, tradition, and community."

Still, this rebellious spirit may have played a role in the development of Lockyer's more widely-known reputation — the one for temperamental instability. Stories of Lockyer's emotional outbursts are the stuff of Capitol legend. Tales include criticizing Senator Diane Watson (D-Los Angeles) during a committee hearing for "mindless blather," a pass he made at a UPI reporter which was followed by an attack on the "First Amendment scumbags" in the media, and a 1990 scuffle with a trial lawyer lobbyist whom he said threw "a

tisan than Roberti's. Senate Minority Leader Ken Maddy (R-Fresno), who had been one of the early skeptics about Lockyer's ability to tone down the partisanship, says he was satisfied with Lockyer's even-handedness in his first session. "He has tried very hard to accommodate everyone in the Senate, particularly the minority party," concedes Maddy. "He has attempted to keep most things status quo." Lockyer's handling of his first budget negotiations earned him points for being tough, but practical, and his more mercurial tendencies remained firmly in remission.

"He has been in total control of himself since the word go," says Senator Leroy Greene (D-Sacramento). "It was a relief to some of us who thought 'well, he's OK now, but what happens if he blows?' He didn't blow."

Keeping the Senate's traditional decorum intact didn't mean, however, that Lockyer had turned the house over to the GOP. As Roberti had during his first session as pro tem, Lockyer used the Senate's confirmation authority as a tool to establish his political *bona fides*. Two of Governor Pete Wilson's appointments — one to the UC Regents, the other to the CSU Board of Trustees — were shot down by Lockyer through his position as the chairman of the Senate Rules Committee. It was the first time in 111 years that a UC Regent appointment had been rejected by the Senate. While he kept the Senate from dissolving into a circus during the budget, Lockyer did engineer a show vote on an extension of a 1991 tax hike on the wealthy, and he says he was the only one of the "Big Five" who didn't want to "just get through the year."

Although he didn't make any wholesale changes, Lockyer is taking steps to put his own stamp on the administration of the house. His most controversial administrative step to date has been his decision to appoint the next session's committee chairs on the last day of this year's session. Lockyer moved some existing chairs into new roles, and elevated a number of less-tenured members into prominence. He also proposed creation of a separate Criminal Procedure Committee, comparable to the Assembly's Public Safety Committee, to take some of Judiciary's crime load.

Republicans charged that the committee assignments, and the decision to announce them early, point the way toward more partisanship from Lockyer in the future. "A lot of us were taken aback by it," says Senator Bill Leonard (R-Redlands). "He seemed like he was trying to solidify his leadership by keeping all parties in his caucus as happy as can be." Leonard says the appointment of Senator Tom Hayden (D-Santa Monica), an ardent environmentalist, to chair Natural Resources puts the Democrats "squarely at the far left end of the discussion" on environmental issues. For his part, Lockyer insists the move was simply aimed at insuring a smooth transition by giving prospective chairs a head start on organizing for the new session.

"The debate for me was simply one of whether to wait for January," says Lockyer. "Theoretically, you'd enhance your position [politically] by keeping everyone guessing."

Whatever Lockyer may have done for the organization and policy direction of the Senate so far, his biggest challenge as pro tem began in earnest when the session ended last month. Fourteen of the 20 seats up for grabs in the November election began the campaign in Democratic hands. Several have been, to varying degrees, contested. With the Democrats sitting at 22 by session's end, a loss of two seats could force him to cut deals with independents Quentin Kopp and Lucy Killea in order to retain power next year. "He's been handed a challenge that is almost overwhelming, with the number of races, the number of campaigns, the Republican surge, and the decline in voting by the Democratic base," says Hayden.

Lockyer began tackling that particular challenge even before he officially took over as pro tem. Throughout the 1993 interim, Lockyer worked six days a week on fund raising. When making his pitch in person, Lockyer brought along a stack of charts, *a la* Ross Perot, laying out the case for his party's continued control of the Senate. His chief target in these presentations was what he calls the "theocratic right," as personified by conservative GOP Senator Rob Hurtt (R-Garden Grove) and his Allied Business PAC. Lockyer has also made it his business to reverse what he sees as a tendency for contributors to favor the more flamboyant and well-connected Willie Brown's Assembly leadership caucus. "They develop some history with Willie, so it's almost autopilot," he says. "If they are going to contribute to Democratic races ... the Senate is entitled to equal treatment."

Even with all this effort, Lockyer faced an uphill climb to keep his numbers steady. Republicans say the narrow margin makes Lockyer's leadership tenuous at best. Any further narrowing of the margin would, according to Maddy "suggest all kinds of things for potential coalitions. There's

a group of Democrats that don't like Lockyer." Democrats insist Lockyer won't be weakened, even in the wake of possible election setbacks. "As long as Democrats and the independents control, he's fine," says Hayden.

"Serving as leader when so many Democrats are exposed is a particularly thankless job," adds Senator Pat Johnston (D-Stockton). "It's not credible to suggest that [Lockyer] was anything less than totally committed and quite successful in supporting our candidates."

Assuming Lockyer's still exercising functional power come next year, he faces an even more uncertain task: guiding the Senate into the term-limit era. "The power of the pro tem is probably going to be enhanced somewhat, and the power of the speaker will be reduced," offered professor Larry Berg, who directs USC's Unruh Institute on Politics. Berg's suggestion echoes an assessment shared by most in the Legislature, many of whom suggest the only thing keeping the Senate from rolling over the Assembly now is the experience and savvy of Willie Brown.

"The Senate will probably be the center of political stability and innovation in California," Lockyer says. "I have to, in collaboration with my colleagues, create a new, more dynamic Senate." That, in Lockyer's view, means taking steps to modernize the Senate technologically, keeping hold of the Senate's more experienced staffers, and doing a better job of controlling the flow of legislation. An early indication of how he will do might have come the last night of session: The Senate adjourned an unheard-of four hours *before* the midnight deadline rather than the more-typical four hours after.

Lockyer's Democratic colleagues see him as an excellent person to handle the transition to the new order. "He's indefatigable," says Hayden. "Those who've watched him for awhile know that he likes doing this. He'll go the extra mile." Greene says Lockyer's experience in both houses and as a player in policy issues give him the experience base to insure maintenance of an institutional memory. Johnston says Lockyer brings not only a good balance of policy and political skills, but also what he described as a "refreshing candor and directness" to the job.

Republicans offer a less flattering vision of the future. "The one thing that's more possible with Lockyer than with Roberti is an all-out war situation," says Maddy. "He's always volatile. You never know when he's going to blow up." Leonard says that, as long as the margin remains narrow, he sees coalitions in which the GOP teams with different sets of Democrats on different issues. "His [Lockyer's] will wind up being more of an administrative leadership," says Leonard.

Outside observers say it's still too early to predict how a Lockyer leadership will ultimately pan out, because the full impact of term limits likely won't be felt until 1996, when Willie Brown leaves the Assembly. Berg suggests Lockyer's ability to balance the conflicting impulses of stability and partisanship will say much about how the Senate moves into its new era.

"In leadership politics, the personality and skills of the individual may will be the critical factor," says Berg. "Bill Lockyer has a basic idea where he wants the institution to go. That is extremely important." If his words are any indication, Lockyer understands his role in shaping the future of the Legislative branch.

"I'm a transitional pro tem between the old Senate and what will eventually emerge as the new Senate," he says. "I think I have the appropriate combination of political and policy skills for that time." 🏛

The New Legislature

The Assembly's first Latino speaker confronts a caucus full of rookies, a lame-duck governor, and an ascendant state Senate, all with one eye on the term-limit clock.

By Steve Scott

Reprinted from *California Journal*, January 1997

Photos by Rich Pedroncelli

On the wall of the corridor which leads from the member's lounge to the side entrance of the Assembly chambers hangs a row of photographs which, depending on your perspective, constitutes either a Hall of Fame or a Rogues Gallery. The pictures are of every person who has ever served as speaker of the California Assembly. Under each photo is a small bit of engraving with the name of the individual and their term as speaker. For the first 145 years of the Assembly's existence, it was enough to indicate the speakers' terms in years: 1961-1969, 1976-1980, 1980-1995. But when you get to 1995, the methodology changes.

From then on, the dates are listed in their entirety — month, day, and year.

The new engravings provide graphic evidence of the dizzying instability that characterized the past two years. Between January of 1995 and December of 1996, five different individuals held the title of Assembly speaker. Three of those five held the title in 1995 alone. Among those five are the first woman speaker, the first freshman speaker, the first GOP speaker in a quarter century and the first speaker in 15 years whose name wasn't Willie Brown.

The individual whose photo will soon be added to the "Wall" of Speakers — Fresno Democrat Cruz Bustamante — also brings some historic significance. The milestone posterity is likely to append to his name is that of "first Latino Assembly speaker." Few deny that his ascension to the leadership post makes him one of the highest-ranking Latino elected officials in the nation. But Bustamante's enduring legacy may be in another milestone he carries — the first speaker whose entire membership was elected under term limits.

"He will define what a speaker is in an abbreviated period of leadership pre-determined by term limits," said Brown, who held the post for 15 years before leaving the Assembly last year to run for mayor of San Francisco. "He is the pioneer in that role."

Bustamante's election as speaker came less than a month after his party recaptured the Assembly majority it lost in the 1994 GOP tide. Many of the races which led to the Democrats' 43-37 majority were won by fewer than 1000 votes, and in districts where Republicans figure to be competitive again in 1998 (see *CJ*, December 1996). The Democrats' victory ended the abbreviated speaker-ship of Garden Grove Republican Curt Pringle, who took the reins in January (see *CJ*, April 1996).

Thanks to the 1990 term limit law, Proposition 140, the architect of the takeover — former Minority Leader Richard Katz — was denied the ability to enjoy the fruits of his success. But while term limits may have created Bustamante's opportunity, his rise to the key Democratic leadership post was not merely a product of timing. Bustamante worked his prospective colleagues, winning key early support from the likes of incoming liberal freshmen Kevin Shelley (D-San Francisco) and Don Perata (D-Oakland). Bustamante was also active in several primaries, in many cases helping Latino candidates against non-Latino opponents. "We [the Latino Caucus] did over 2.3 million pieces of mail," noted Senator Richard Polanco (D-Los Angeles), chairman of the Legislature's Latino Caucus. "It was a cultivation that occurred," said Polanco. "It wasn't an accident."

Despite his more moderate politics, Bustamante quickly embraced the liberal, non-Latino wing of his caucus. His leadership team is stocked with liberals, among them Santa Monica Democrat Sheila Kuehl, who campaigned for speaker before giving way to Bustamante. The new speaker also won enactment of new rules which re-integrated into the speaker's office the power that the GOP had parceled out to the Rules Committee. "This speaker has more power than Willie Brown ever had," said Assemblyman Bill Leonard (R-Redlands), one of five former members who have returned to Sacramento this year. Despite their suspicions, though, the GOP seems content to keep its partisan powder dry for the moment.

"We're willing to make sure we move forward and are not obstructionist ... but are people who are trying to work with [the process] and move it forward," said Pringle.

Over in the Senate, President Pro Tempore Bill Lockyer (D-Hayward) kept his majority intact, as well as most of his leadership team. During the 1995-96 session, Lockyer asserted his influence and that of his house, effortlessly turning aside a barrage of conservative legislation which flowed his way from the Republican Assembly. While Lockyer's dominance as a leader may have been enhanced by his unique position as head of the only arm of state government controlled by Democrats, there are many who believe the Senate will continue to be the place where most of the hard work of policy-making will take place. "The balance of power is still going to be tilted toward the Senate," said Tim Hodson, director of the Center for California Studies at California State University, Sacramento, and a former legislative staffer. "You still have a number of members of the Senate whose experience predates term limits. "That is simply going to give the Senate an advantage in many ways."

Irrespective of which house is dominant in the Legislature the road to success in any session invariably runs through the governor's office. Governor Pete Wilson finds himself in the same position as his immediate predecessor, facing a hostile Legislature in his last two years in office. While George Deukmejian's retirement was voluntary and Wilson's is imposed by term limits, the challenge is the same — getting lawmakers to view him as more than just yesterday's news. "There's going to be a natural incentive on the part of Democrats to not let the Republicans look too good," said Bruce Cain of the Institute for Governmental Studies at

University of California, Berkeley.

In 1997, that budget process will provide an early indication of how Wilson will approach the Democratic Legislature. A major feature of the budget this year will be the implementation of the new federal welfare reform law. Reducing welfare benefits has been a unifying theme of past Wilson budgets, and the ink was barely dry from the president's signature on the bill before the governor ordered benefits to illegal immigrants

Speaker Pro Tem Shelia Kuehl (L) and colleague Caole Migden

cut off. That order has since been stayed by a federal court. A hastily drafted implementation plan, followed by equally rushed public hearings, have left Lockyer accusing Wilson of trying to impose a solution. "When you construct a very complicated proposal in secret, it almost dooms the effort to failure," said Lockyer.

"I can't see how Sacramento is going to handle welfare reform without tremendous acrimony," said Cain. "Wilson has staked his career on these issues."

Welfare reform is hardly the only policy conundrum facing lawmakers this year. The Legislature will also be called upon to enact gambling regulation, reform the juvenile justice system, fund K-12 and higher education, explore ways to relieve pressure on the corrections system ... the list goes on and on. But every bit as daunting as these challenges will be coming to grips with the changing nature of the institution they inhabit.

It is possible that the 1990 term-limit law could be struck down by an Oakland federal court which is considering its constitutionality. The court held a hearing on the law in October and Judge Claudia Wilkin was outspoken in her discomfort with the law's lifetime ban. But term limits are only one of the factors which will affect the Legislature of the future. The 1996 campaign finance reform initiative, Proposition 208, will, if upheld, change the leader's traditional political function as chief fund-raiser for the party caucus. The new law bans fund transfers between candidates and restricts the size of contributions that can be made. There is also the overall uncertainty created by the 1991 redistricting, which increased the number of districts subject to election competition and will likely keep margins narrow in both houses.

Then there is that large rookie class. Even if term limits are thrown out, about three-fourths of the 80-member Assembly will enter 1997 with two or fewer years of experience. The Senate, meanwhile, is full of leadership prospects with their own eyes on the prize. If Proposition 140 is ultimately upheld, Lockyer will almost certainly face pressure to step aside early, especially if he follows through on hints of a run for attorney general.

Bustamante says he'd like to respond to the changes by better insulating the Legislature's staff from partisan changeover. "I do believe there are non-combatants," said Bustamante. "There needs to be more professionalization." Whether or not Bustamante follows through on his plans, it seems likely the Assembly — indeed the Legislature as a whole — will never run quite the same way it did before 1990. And that can only mean one thing.

The Assembly's Gallery of Speakers is going to get a lot more crowded. 🏛

Wheel of Fortune

The shifting legal sands and an array of disparate personalities has made the Assembly leadership crystal ball hazier than it has been since Willie Brown left Sacramento

By Bob Schmidt

Reprinted from *California Journal*, April 1997

Politicians are like the rest of us in one respect: Uncertainty makes them nervous. Nervousness is a normal condition for most politicians, given the capriciousness of voters, but they are especially nervous at the moment because the courts have also become involved in their political destiny.

Normally, politicians have to decide only if they *should* run, and the decision they make usually is based on whether or not they think they can win if they choose to run. But now they must first find out if they *can* run.

And that's where the courts come in.

California voters in 1990 approved Proposition 140, limiting the terms of most state elected officials, including members of the Legislature. As a result, 33 legislators were unable to seek re-election in 1996, and 27 more will be prevented from running for re-election in 1998.

Maybe.

Proposition 140 has been challenged in federal court, and a decision on the challenge could come at any time by U.S. District Court Judge Claudia Wilken. Most of the nervousness would disappear if Proposition 140 is held to be illegal.

But some nervousness would remain because of the campaign fund-raising restrictions imposed by Proposition 208, approved by voters last year and also awaiting a court ruling on challenges to it.

Proposition 208 not only sharply curtails the size of contributions that can be made, it flat outlaws fund transfers from one candidate's campaign to another's, meaning that the Democratic and Republican leaders in the Senate and Assembly can't go out and raise millions of dollars to spread around on candidates they favor.

The process of choosing party leaders in the Assembly and Senate is simple enough. The candidate with the most votes in each of the four caucuses wins. And the candidate with the most supporters gets the most votes.

But while the passage of Proposition 140 has not changed the process, it has changed profoundly the environment in which the process works, particularly in the Assembly.

If term limits do survive, members of the Assembly will have some new factors to consider when they choose their caucus leadership, including whether they want a "veteran" (meaning a member serving his or her second term) who can serve only one term or a freshman eligible to hold office for two terms.

It used to be that caucus leaders "emerged" after many years of toiling in the ranks and gradually acquiring the political acumen and chits needed to gather sufficient commitments to support a try for leadership.

But if Proposition 140 stays intact, ambitious aspirants in the Assembly will no longer have those many years to work their way to the top. With the limit of only three two-year terms available to newcomers, they'll have to begin separating themselves from the ranks almost immediately.

That is happening in the Assembly right now, as the more ambitious members maneuver to replace the two current leaders, Democrat Cruz Bustamante of Fresno and Republican Curt Pringle of Garden Grove, when their third and final terms expire in 1998.

Because of term limits, caucus members have two questions, one old and one new, to answer when choosing their leader. Question one, the old question, is, who can best lead us by increasing our number in the next election (and, not incidentally, help me get re-elected if I'm eligible)? Question two,

---

Bob Schmidt, retired Sacramento correspondent for the Long Beach Press-Telegram, *is a freelance wirter in Sacramento*

the new one, involves the choice between someone with experience but with only one term left, or someone with less experience who might provide stability and, with the additional time, stronger and more effective leadership.

Both Bustamante and Pringle say they are confident they, and people holding their jobs in the future, can be successful at providing assistance to selected Assembly candidates despite Proposition 208's strictures on fund raising and fund transfers.

And both said it was appropriate that candidates should have greater responsibility for their own fund raising than they had to have in the past, when the speaker and minority leader each had huge campaign war chests to distribute.

Although both Pringle and Bustamante are in their third terms, the situations facing the two Assembly caucuses are very different from each other, whether or not 140 survives.

If term limits are thrown out by Judge Wilken (and her ruling survives the inevitable appeal), Bustamante says he will seek re-election to a fourth term in the Assembly and to a second term as speaker.

Pringle, however, said he will not be a candidate for re-election if 140 is invalidated, and plans to step down as minority leader "at the end of this year" so his successor will have ample time to prepare for the 1998 elections.

"I will live by the intent of term limits," he said. "I think it will be a travesty if Proposition 140 is thrown out."

He said he does intend to stay in politics, however, and there are "three or four different options available to me, definitely including the congressional seat in my district [now occupied by Democrat Loretta Sanchez after her surprising ouster of Republican Bob Dornan last November], possibly a seat on the [Orange County] board of supervisors, and maybe even the state Senate, since my senator [Rob Hurtt] has not yet indicated whether he'll run again."

If Bustamante is given the opportunity to keep his speakership, that would probably terminate the reputed speakership aspirations of such "veterans" (meaning they're now in their second term) as Sheila Kuehl of Santa Monica, and Kevin Murray, Antonio Villaraigosa, and Wally Knox of Los Angeles, and put the speculated ambi-

tions of freshmen Don Perata of Alameda, Kevin Shelley and Carole Midgen of San Francisco, Carl Washington of Los Angeles, and Bob Hertzberg of Van Nuys, on hold.

If 140 is not overturned, Bustamante said, he'll "go back to cutting lawns" for a living. That's not entirely a joke. The 44-year-old Bustamante has worked in government all his adult life, and there doesn't appear to be a Senate or congressional seat open to him in the near future. Republican Ken Maddy's final term in the Senate ends in 1998, but Bustamante lives in the Senate district represented by Democrat Jim Costa, and Costa can serve until 2002. The Fresno area's two congressional seats are occupied by entrenched incumbents, Republican George Radanovich and Democrat Cal Dooley. Unless he receives an appointment or runs for a local office, Bustamante's career in elected office may be at an end.

In the Republican caucus, second-termer Tom Bordonaro, Jr. of Paso Robles seems to have distanced himself from other hopefuls as Pringle's successor. He acknowledges being a candidate, but says he will not actively seek the leadership position until Pringle decides to step down.

But, again, GOP caucus members will have to decide whether it's better to have Bordonaro (or some other "veteran") as their leader for one term, or give the reins to someone with two full terms to serve.

"I think there are people in the caucus on both sides of that question," Pringle said, adding that there are other members besides Bordonaro interested in the leadership job.

He declined to offer names, but other names heard in speculation about the top Republican office in the Assembly include second-termers Jim Battin of La Quinta and Keith Olberg of Victorville.

Among the Republican freshmen, Rico Oller of San Andreas and Rod Pacheco of Riverside seem to be attracting early attention. Bill Leonard of Upland and Tom McClintock of Simi Valley, both of whom have previous Assembly service, would also have to be considered in leadership discussions because of their experience. Leonard served in the Assembly from 1978 until 1988, when he was elected to the Senate. He ran successfully for the Assembly last year when he was termed out, and can serve until 2002. McClintock was elected to the Assembly in 1982

and served until 1992, when he left to run unsuccessfully for Congress. His 1990-92 service in the Assembly counts toward his term limit, however, so he can run for re-election only in 1998.

Earlier this year there was speculation that Pringle might be forced out as minority leader because he was at the helm when Republicans lost control of the Assembly in last November's elections, but that talk seems to have died down.

Senator Ross Johnson (R-Irvine), a former Assembly Republican leader, says he doesn't think Pringle is in any danger from within his caucus.

"I'm not aware of any unrest at all, absolutely none," Johnson said. "I think he did a heck of a job last year under not ideal circumstances. I think he has indicated he'll step down at some point, and I think it will be a point of his choosing." Johnson added that Judge Wilken's decision on term limits could have an impact on the partisan composition of the Assembly.

"For instance," he said, "if 140 survives, the seat now held by (Democrat) Debra Bowen in Los Angeles will be taken by a Republican. If 140 is thrown out, she could keep that seat. I think there are three or four other seats in the Assembly where the incumbent would be re-elected if 140 is thrown out, but if it's not, the other party could take the seat."

Ray McNally, a veteran Republican political campaign consultant, agrees with Johnson that Pringle can keep his leadership post "as long as he wants to."

"I just don't see a bloody coup happening," he said.

McNally added that he thinks the Republicans are in a better position in the Assembly than they've been in a very long time, despite their minority status.

"In the past, the Democrats always seemed able to outmaneuver Republicans on parliamentary matters, but they don't have Willie Brown and Phil Isenberg in their ranks anymore and I don't see anyone else with their smarts. I think the Republicans are actually better organized right now than the Democrats."

As long as the future is term-limited, being organized will pay dividends in the internal workings of the Assembly. If 1996 proved anything, though, it is that a well-organized caucus is no substitute for a well-organized, well-executed campaign. Term limits or no, it's still about winning in November of even-numbered years. 🏛

LOBBYING & INTEREST GROUPS

The Political Reform Act of 1974 helped reshape relations between lobbyists and legislators. Prior to enactment of this proposition, legislative advocates spent a great deal of time and money entertaining lawmakers and thus winning their favor (and their votes). But the 1974 act prohibited a legislator from taking more than $10 a month from a lobbyist, barred lobbyists from "arranging" for campaign contributions from their clients (this provision has since been invalidated by the courts), established extensive and detailed expense and income reporting requirements, and established the Fair Political Practices Commission to implement the law. The measure has been reasonably successful in cutting the entertainment tie between legislators and advocates and began modifying the way of life in the Capitol. Actually, the system had started to change in 1966 when the Legislature became a full-time body. Many lawmakers and lobbyists brought their families to Sacramento, reducing time available for socializing. In addition under the terms of the ethics measure, Proposition 112 of June 1990 members are: 1) barred from accepting honoraria (payments for speeches), 2) prohibited from receiving compensation for appearing before a state board or agency, 3) limited in the acceptance of gifts from special interests, 4) prohibited from accepting any compensation from lobbyists, 5) required to wait one year after leaving legislative sevrvice before filing as a lobbyist, 6) required to attend ethics training at the begining of each legislative session. In addition, the measure established the California Citizens Compensation Commission to set salaries for elected officals.

The system today is a far cry from the 1930's and 40's when the late Artie Samish boasted: "To hell with the Governor of California! I'm the Governor of the Legislature." And the state's archetypical lobbyist then was probably right. In his long reign, hardly a bill passed the Legislature without Samish's approval. He raised about $1 million over a six-year period from a nickel-a-barrel levy on beer provided by his biggest client and spent it getting legislators "elected and unelected," as he liked to put it. Until 1953 when he was convicted for income-tax evasion, Samish dominated Sacramento; other lobbyists were virtually powerless by comparison. Samish's downfall began when he was interviewed for Collier's magazine and posed with a ventriloquist's dummy he called "Mr. Legislature." The resulting embarrassment prodded the Legislature to pass a mild "reform act" regulating "legislative advocates" in Sacramento. But if the activities of lobbyists are not as blatant as in Samish's day, their power continues unabated. Indeed, the increasing costs of running for election — campaigning for a hotly contested Assembly seat can cost more than $1 million — has made lobbyists and the firms that employ them more important than ever. Moreover, the Legislature in recent years has been plagued with a new round of scandals set off by a "sting" operation run by the FBI and the U.S. Attorney's office. Four Senators were convicted for taking money to help secure passage of the FBI's phony legislative proposal, a bill that would have subsidized a shrimp-packing plant on the Sacramento River.

One Assembly member, a major lobbyist and several staff members were also convicted or pled guilty by mid-1994.

Types of lobbyists

The corps of advocates includes almost every interest group in the state. In 1996, 1092 individual lobbyists were registered. They fall into several categories:

• *Contract lobbyists.* These advocates will work for almost any client willing to pay their fee. The most successful of them charge high prices, make substantial campaign contributions and get results.

• *Corporation and trade association lobbyists.* These advocates work for one company and represent only the interests of their firms, although they often work in tandem with other lobbyists trying to reach the same goal.

• *Public agency lobbyists.* Aside from the associations representing public agencies, numerous cities, counties and special districts maintain their own representatives in Sacramento. And most state agencies have "legislative liaisons," though they are not required to register.

• *"Brown-bag" lobbyists.* These advocates represent interests seeking reforms in a variety of so-called public-interest fields. They include numerous organizations with budgets sufficient only for bag lunches.

Lobbying process

Lobbyists operate in several ways. They provide information and arguments on pending legislation in an attempt to win legislators to their point of view. This information function is a legitimate part of the Legislature's work as it helps define issues. Lobbyists also: have their memberships apply pressure; establish friendships with legislators and wine and dine them; and contribute sometimes substantial amounts to campaigns. Lobbyists also lobby the governor, the bureaucracy, regulatory commissions, the courts and the public.

Lobbyists succeed because there are a great many bills considered each year about which lawmakers have relatively little knowledge or interest, and a word from a lobbyist may tip the balance. A smart lobbyist knows he or she is wasting time trying to persuade a legislator who has a firm philosophical commitment to one side or another on an issue, and so focuses on the uncommitted lawmaker. All legislators are susceptible to persuasion by representatives of interest groups. But some are more attuned, for example, to corporate spokesmen, while others are more apt to go along with a representative of an environmental organization.

In the term limits era at the capitol it will be much harder for lobbyists to develop friendships with the turnstile-members. More of the lobby focus will likely shift to grassroots lobbying: letter writing or fax campaigns, plugging local members into candidates' campaign staffs, and bringing the membership to the capitol for meetings with elected officials and/or rallies and demonstrations. However, rookie legislators may need to look to veteran, savvy lobbyists for help. After all, there are no term limits for lobbyists. 🏛

"Astroturf lobbying"

Powerful (and not-always-popular) special interests influence the Legislature from behind the shield of others

By Bill Ainsworth

Reprinted from *California Journal*, November 1994

When state Senator Leroy Greene's (D-Carmichael) office received a barrage of calls this past April from senior citizens supporting a bill backed by oil companies, his staff wondered why so many Sacramentans were interested in such an obscure issue. But as the calls started tying up his phone lines, a seething Greene realized he was on the receiving end of an elaborate — and he says deceptive — public-relations blitz.

The lobbying campaign is one front in a war that oil companies are waging against California regulations requiring auto companies to sell electric cars. The industry spent hundreds of thousands of dollars to generate phone calls and postcards from ordinary citizens to create the illusion of grass-roots support for the bill.

The bill itself would have made it more difficult for utilities to service electric cars. But instead of broadcasting its own support for the legislation, the oil industry enlisted the help of a respected consumer group, Toward Utility Rate Normalization. TURN, which believed the legislation would prevent utility bills from going up, lent its name to a mass mailing that the oil companies quietly bankrolled. The bill itself quietly died before the end of the legislative session.

The oil industry's effort is just the latest example of an increasingly popular lobbying technique — termed "astroturf" by critics because the "grass-roots" are artificial. Three years ago the insurance industry spent $1.5 million encouraging citizens to write and call legislators to express support for no-fault auto insurance. During the past year, Philip Morris has spent hundreds of thousands of dollars to drum up small-business opposition to smoking restrictions. These efforts allow unpopular special interests to hide behind "white hat" groups — such as consumer activists, environmentalists, senior citizens and small business owners — whose motives are considered above suspicion. In some cases the public-relations firms hired by special interests actually create "grass-roots" groups.

As part of "astroturf" campaigns, the businesses fund phone banks, petition drives and mass mailings — methods refined by citizens' groups.

"Big business tries to make it look like they have a bunch of citizen support," says Ruth Holton, executive director of California Common Cause. "It's extremely deceptive." Such campaigns, Holton says, undermine efforts by genuine citizen activists. "How is a legislator going to tell the difference between a big business effort and a genuine effort?"

Assemblyman Terry Friedman (D-Los Angeles) first encountered "astroturf" campaigns while sponsoring anti-smoking legislation. His AB 13 banned smoking in all indoor restaurants and nearly all workplaces. Tobacco industry lobbyists decided that a lobbying campaign led by tobacco barons might not impress lawmakers. Instead, they decided to find ordinary, salt-of-the-earth citizens who also opposed the restrictions. The industry's high-powered, high-priced public-relations firm organized "grass-roots" small business owners and ferried some of them to Sacramento.

Meanwhile, Philip Morris already had experience creating and sustaining "grass-roots" groups. Three years ago, the tobacco giant hired the Dolphin Group, a Los Angeles public-relations firm, to form the California Business and Restaurant Alliance. Friedman calls it a front group for the tobacco industry. Located in the Dolphin Group offices, the alliance has recruited witnesses, published newsletters, and commissioned economic studies against local smoking restrictions.

Last year, when Friedman threatened statewide restrictions, the alliance turned its attention to Sacramento. Alliance members testified eloquently against AB 13 at a Senate Judiciary Committee hearing in April. Their opposition was especially helpful because the established restaurant group, the California Restaurant Association, supported the bill. One witness, Maurice Prince, told the committee that the anti-smoking bill would drive customers away from her popular Los Angeles eatery, Maurice's Snack & Chat. "I hate for you to tell me what I can do with my restaurant," she said. "I have worked day and night for my restaurant." Prince, who was later whisked from the hearing by a tobacco industry driver, said she was recruited into the effort by the Dolphin Group.

Tobacco lobbyists had shrewdly arranged for witnesses from key senators' districts. Prince, for example, owns a restaurant in Senator Diane Watson's (D-Los Angeles) district, while Rudy Martinez, another witness, owns a restaurant in Senator Art Torres' (D-Los Angeles) district. Both lawmakers are sensitive to problems faced by minority business owners.

After the testimony, Torres and

Bill Ainsworth is a Sacramento reporter for the San Francisco Recorder.

another Los Angeles-area Democrat, Charles Calderon, moved to gut AB 13 by allowing smoking in restaurants and wiping out tough local ordinances. Both senators said they were responding to the testimony by "grass-roots" opponents. "I'm concerned about [Martinez'] restaurant because that's in my district," said Torres at the hearing.

Torres later changed his mind and dropped his amendments after Friedman threw a fit. A candidate for insurance commissioner, he had been stung by criticism that he was hiding behind "grass-roots" opposition while actually doing the bidding of the tobacco industry.

Dolphin Group President Lee Stitzenberger, however, denied that his firm was running an "astroturf" campaign. "These aren't people made out of whole cloth. They are concerned business people who oppose smoking restrictions."

Friedman's bill eventually passed the Legislature and was signed into law by Governor Pete Wilson. It would be overturned, however, by the passage this month of Proposition 188, also sponsored in large measure by Philip Morris. The campaign to pass the initiative is being run by The Dolphin Group.

In its campaign against Friedman's anti-smoking bill, the tobacco industry created a new "grass-roots" opposition group. In another recent astroturf campaign, the oil industry exploited its alliance with an existing citizens' group — TURN. Earlier this year, TURN, which fights to keep utility bills low, sponsored legislation to make it more difficult for utilities to invest $600 million in the equipment needed to service electric cars. Under California anti-pollution regulations, by the year 1998, electric cars must make up 2 percent of the sales of major automakers. TURN argues that the investments are so speculative that utility company shareholders, not ratepayers, should bear any risk associated with them. Utilities and their environmentalist allies disagree, contending that the investments will help them manage their electricity more efficiently and eventually lead to lower rates.

Oil companies quickly realized that the bill had important implications for the future of electric cars. Without a large investment in charging facilities, electric cars cannot be driven conveniently. The Western States Petroleum Association, the oil industry trade group, wrote a letter to senators on the energy committee, arguing that the investments amount to an unfair subsidy to a competitor.

But the association's public-relations firm, Burlingame-based Woodward & McDowell, did not bring oil-company executives to Sacramento to testify for the bill in public. Instead, it organized "Californians Against Utility Company Abuses," a coalition including TURN, the California Manufacturers Association and other large energy users. Next, the firm sent 200,000 letters to taxpayers, urging them to stop a plan "cooked up" by utilities to "increase your gas and electric rates by $600 million to subsidize their profit-making ventures."

Warning that "powerful utility company lobbyists are already working behind the scenes to defeat these consumer-protection bills," the letter urged citizens to return postcards supporting TURN's legislation. It was signed by Audrie Krause, executive director of TURN, and Howard Owens, director of the Congress of California Seniors. The citizens who received the letter were not told that it had been written by the oil industry's public-relations firm and paid for by the industry.

Provoked by the alarming letter, 50,000 people returned postcards to Woodward & McDowell, which then forwarded the cards to legislators' offices. The firm then organized phone banks. It called citizens who had returned the postcards, and patched them in directly to the offices of their lawmakers. The phone banks targeted the 11 members of the Senate energy committee, which planned hearings on Senate Bill 1819. In this case, however, the campaign may have been too elaborate for its own good. Many citizens were confused by the calls from the phone bank. When they were patched in to government offices, some did not know whether they opposed or supported the bill.

Senator Greene said his district and Capitol offices took calls for two days from constituents who believed that his office was calling them. His staff members grew increasingly irritated. At the hearing, Greene and other senators were so angry that they forced the bill's author, Senator David Kelly (R-Hemet), to put it on hold.

Senator Steve Peace (D-Chula Vista) called the campaign a "sleazy tactic" because the mailing failed to mention oil-company funding. "You ought to make a public apology to every member of the Legislature," Peace told oil lobbyists.

Senator Tom Hayden (D-Santa Monica) said TURN's alliance with the oil industry had tainted the consumer group. "I find it to be the end of the independence of TURN," he said. Krause insisted that her group's association with the oil industry does not compromise its independence. She and oil industry representative Scott Macdonald of Woodward & McDowell defended their effort, arguing that it was a coalition, not an "astroturf" campaign.

"These are concerned citizens responding to an issue that is important to them," said Macdonald.

Both the tobacco and oil industry campaigns demonstrate the increasing sophistication of statehouse lobbying. It used to be enough for tobacco and oil lobbyists to strut around the Capitol, whispering in lawmakers' ears and making strategic donations. Now, however, these and other industries have found that their chances of success increase if they build coalitions with citizens' groups — even if they have to invent their own group. Critics charge, however, that the special interests are not only building coalitions with grass-roots groups, but using them — and hiding behind them — for their own selfish purposes.

"These guys should have built the Stealth bomber," said one supporter of Friedman's anti-smoking bill. "They are so good at disguising themselves."

Common Cause supported a bill by Terry Friedman this year that would have required more complete financial disclosure of astroturf and other lobbying campaigns. Under its provisions, clients of lobbyists would have had to itemize the money they spend on activities like economic studies, phone banks and public-relations campaigns.

"They shouldn't be able to hide their activities," Friedman said. "This is a sunshine bill."

At the end of the 1993-94 session, the California Manufacturers Association helped defeat Friedman's bill, arguing that it would have imposed burdensome record-keeping requirements. Although Friedman himself is leaving the Legislature to become a Los Angeles judge, Common Cause's Ruth Holton plans to seek a new author next year. She expects to see lobbyists rely more on public-relations experts to mobilize support for their clients' positions because term limits will weaken their relationships with lawmakers. 🏛

Third House Rising

In the ever-changing world of the term-limited Legislature, lobbyists, too, must change. No longer able to rely on long-term relationships, they may be called upon to spoon-feed institutional memory to neophyte lawmakers.

By John Borland

Reprinted from *California Journal*, February 1996

t's a campaign reformer's nightmare: A reporter calls a legislator's office with a question about a bill and is told to wait. The voice that replaces the staff member and answers questions is friendly and helpful enough. But it turns out to be that of a lobbyist working the bill, who just happened to be in the office when the phone rang.

This gaffe was only one particularly clumsy demonstration of the widening gap between lobbyists' and lawmakers' experience. By next year, nearly 75 percent of Assembly members will have served two years or less. New lawmakers will have at most 16 years in a state legislative career before being ushered out by term limits, and many observers fear that this rapid-rotation system is draining vital legislative knowledge out of Capitol offices — potentially dangerous in an environment where a good spin on the facts approaches the value of spun gold.

Proponents of term limits and some legislators downplay this diminution of institutional memory, saying it is more important for a lawmaker to be a quick study than to have first hand memories of a 10-year-old legislative fight.

"What I've found in one year is that most everything is learnable," says first-term Assemblywoman Sheila Kuehl (D-Los Angeles), noting that most new members bring some of relevant experience with them. "It's not like we're coming straight out of high school."

But others argue that unexperienced legislators' lack of history will lead them to accept and rely on biased information spoon-fed by lobbyists and the executive branch. "The reality is that if I know the policy area and you don't, I'm going to be able to influence you ... even if I play it completely straight," says Tim Hodson, director of the Center for California Studies at California State University-Sacramento and a former Senate staffer. "If the only information you're getting is from biased sources, how do you assess it?"

Lobbyists have no term limits, other than those imposed by a bad reputation or a poor sales pitch. But the now-perpetual legislative turnover nevertheless is forcing change in the third house. The friendships cultivated by long time advocates are disappearing with the legislative old guard. Lobbyists who founded lucrative careers on their access to powerful ears are being forced to rebuild their relationships with each new class of lawmakers.

"Those old relationships that were the mainstay of lobbyists are going to [disappear]," says Jack Gualco, head of the Gualco Group. "You've got to start new every two years."

The new working conditions are changing some of the third house's faces and tactics. "Some of the older lobbyists are saying, 'I don't know if I'm going to be comfortable in this new environment,'" Gualco says. "The big clean-out will be when the Senate really turns over."

While there has been no mass exodus from the profession, some older lobbyists may be thinking about speeding up their departure.

"I see a lot of veteran lobbyists who work on the basis of cultivated relationships having a hard time adjusting," says Barry Brokaw, a former Senate staffer who now lobbies for Sacramento Advocates. "You're seeing a lot of senior members of the third house retire in the last three to five years."

At the beginning of the career line, the ranks of lobbyists are growing, swelled increasingly by staffers disturbed by shifting legislative sands. "I've gotten calls from a lot of [staffers] looking for jobs," says one longtime contract lobbyist. "There's no stability over there."

Gene Erbin, now an employee with Nielsen, Merksamer, Parrinello, Mueller and Naylor, left his position as Democratic Assemblyman Phil Isenberg's (D-Sacramento) chief counsel earlier this year. "It was a combination of instability, restlessness and a good offer in my case," he said. "[The Capitol] is a different place than when I had worked there initially ... Are there other people who are growing frustrated and are anxious to change their position? Probably."

The number of lobbyists has been growing steadily since members of the corps first were required to register in 1974. But the rate of growth has jumped in the last decade, leaping from about 740 individuals in 1985 to nearly 1100 today. In 1975, by comparison, 616 lobbyists registered with the state.

Lobbyist spending, tracked quarterly by the Secretary of State's Office, also has risen sharply over the years. In 1975, companies and special interests spent $19 million to lobby state government. That figure rose to $74 million in 1985, and to $122 million in 1994, the last year for which totals are available. Even after adjusting for inflation, this is a 22 percent increase in the last decade, and a 150 increase in lobbyist spending over the last 20 years.

Faces and dollars aside, the rules in the advocacy game are essentially the same as always: Talk to the member and explain as best you can, as clearly as you can, why he or she should vote in the interests of your client. But the revolving slate of new members has made this task more complicated than in past years.

A lobbyist needs to win the trust of members and staffers in order to stand out as something more than a vaguely suspect face in a vaguely suspect crowd. This becomes more difficult because the size of the crowd is growing, even as opportunities to talk to the increasing number of new members become less frequent. "There is less personal contact," notes George Steffes, a one-time aide to Governor Ronald Reagan who has lobbied since 1972. "The old backslapping days are definitely going. ...There's more substance involved, but only because there is less personal contact involved."

Lobbyists say it is more essential than ever to know their issues and to be able to explain quickly and clearly why the member should feel a certain way, or care at all about the issue. "I don't have the time or [energy] for them to be too subtle," notes freshman Assemblyman Steve Kuykendall (R-Rancho Palos Verdes). "I need them to be specific, to put it into a big picture... Sometimes they become so ingrained in the process ... that they fail to do the fundamental sell on why we should do it at all."

"This does force us more and more into the sales ranks," Gualco says. The newer, more technically oriented generation of lobbyists "may be more marketing-savvy than people who have been around for a long time," he adds.

The relative scarcity of personal contact and relationships boosts the importance of other lobbying avenues. "Lobbyists will have to use a whole lot of other tools than the good-old-boy network," notes William Rutland, who works with Steffes' firm. These include talking to staff, preparing position papers for members and the media, forming coalitions with other interested parties, and eliciting vocal support for an issue from inside a member's district.

This latter "grass-roots" approach has generated a spate of publicity in recent years as public-relations firms have turned their attention — and the content of their pitches to clients — toward building constituent support. The idea is a persuasive one, especially to interests leery of becoming too identified with under-the-dome shenanigans: If constituents, who the legislator ultimately represents, can be persuaded to contact their representative, their voices will be more persuasive than that of lobbyists paid to represent a position.

Many long time lobbyists say this long has been a piece of their arsenal,

depending on the receptivity of the individual legislator. "I've always felt that the way to have a successful lobbying project is to do a number of things," Steffes says. Legislators always listen to people in their districts, he says, and the trick for a good lobbyist is to develop ways to communicate with those constituents. "The organizations that have large memberships in every district" — such as doctors, optometrists or trial lawyers — "are going to be better off than those that just have one company or factory."

Nevertheless, most note that this kind of constituent communication is no substitute for a face-to-face chat with the member.

"It has to be done in conjunction with a visit to the member here," says Beverly Hansen, a former assemblywoman now employed by Lang/Mansfield Governmental Relations. "Most people who visit the member in the district for the grass-roots ... don't explain the legislative process."

Lobbyists view their emerging position as the in-house repository of memory with mixed feelings. Some admit there are advantages to being the only ones who know what is going on. "On the dark side, there are tricks that would be laughed out of the building now, that can be dusted off and used again five years from now," says John Quimby, a former assemblyman and veteran county lobbyist. "It will be like a comedian working a new crowd in a new town."

But many bemoan the necessity of starting lobbying campaigns practically from the beginning with each new class. "It's going to be an absolute disaster," says Bill Bagley, the former legislator and current University of California regent who lobbies for the firm of Nossaman, Guthner, Knox, and Elliot. He cites work on the Freedom of Information Act, which took half a decade or more to reach the point of passage. "What you do is hammer away, achieve consensus.... With a six-year limit, it will be impossible to have legislative initiative."

"There is a flood of things headed our way with [federal] devolution," notes John White, a representative of several environmental groups. "If you add up all the talent that's leaving, and look at the flood of responsibility coming to the state, I wonder if we're going to be able to handle it."

The resurgence of labor

By Kathleen Les

Reprinted from *California Journal*, July 1996

Not long ago, big labor unions — representing the likes of auto and aerospace workers, truck drivers, farm workers, operating engineers, construction workers and their blue-collar brethren — exercised big political muscle. Aided by their mostly Democratic legislative allies, they pushed through friendly laws dealing with issues such as minimum and prevailing wages, worker safety, overtime pay and worker's compensation, to name only a few. Many of these laws were passed, despite fierce fights with California's business and manufacturing sector.

But those were during the halcyon days of the California economy — the explosive 1970s and '80s — when it seemed as though the good times would roll on forever and business could afford to cede an increasing share of an ever-increasing pie to labor.

By the 1990s, as a national recession edged its way onto the West Coast, California's long roll turned up snake eyes. The auto-manufacturing industry all but disappeared from California. The end of the Cold War brought severe cuts in military spending, which caused equally severe cuts in the aerospace and ship-building industries.

As a result, the state's economy began to change, moving away from dependency on the military and traditional manufacturing and toward high-tech, agriculture, finance and service industries. And as it changed, the membership in traditional labor unions waned. Politically, labor lost clout as its membership dipped. In addition, politicians began to pay closer attention to business interests who complained that government regulation in a wide variety of areas had made California an expensive place in which to operate. Republicans in the governor's office and in the Legislature joined with pragmatic Democrats in 1994 to pass, among other things, changes in the workers' compensation laws that labor seemed powerless to stop.

Business reached the apex of its political clout — at the expense of most unions — after the 1994 elections, when business-friendly Republicans gained control of the Assembly for the first time in 25 years. Among the items on the GOP's plate was roll-back of requirements that overtime wages be paid to those who worked longer than an eight-hour work day.

But there is some evidence that unions may once again be poised to regain some political clout, influence centered on new kinds of unions catering to groups such as janitors,

Kathleen Les is a California Journal *intern.*

hotel and restaurant workers, prison guards, state employees and others who work in the service industry or for government. The prototype for this new kind of union is the California Correctional Peace Officers Association, which muscled its way into the political consciousness during the 1990s by providing a steady stream of campaign cash to friendly — and mostly Republican — officeholders. The CCPOA also has been politically savvy on issues; for instance, recently proposing a scheme for cheaper prisons.

While overall union membership has actually held steady during the last 30 years, the slice of the work force that belongs to unions has dropped dramatically in both California and in the country. For instance, the number of union members in the state grew by 5 percent between 1977 and 1987 while the number of new jobs jumped by more than 30 percent.

At the same time, the state's socio-economic landscape was shifting like two geologic plates. During the 1980s, the Hispanic population grew by 70 percent; the Asian by nearly 120 percent. By 1990 non-anglos formed 47 percent of the total population. The new immigrants were overwhelmingly poor and uneducated and saw a $5-an-hour wage as a princely sum. Many found work in the expanding service industry, where the number of jobs increased 112 percent during the 1980s. They also provided fertile ground for union organizing.

"We've hit bottom and we're coming back up," said Tom Rankin, the main lobbyist for the California Labor Federation, AFL-CIO, and the man expected to become its president later this month. "Unionization has historically been a way into the middle class in this country."

Rankin admits that union leadership had grown lax in recent years but he now sees the chance to focus once again on labor issues — including a number of key ballot initiatives slated for November. Labor issues — those that affect a person's ability to earn a living wage — will be the litmus test by which all politicians will be judged, regardless of party, he says, envisioning a powerful network of educated voters who understand the link between actions in Sacramento and one's wallet. To back his claim that unions once again are becoming politically active, he cites two recent rallies by building-trades workers in Los Angeles and in Sacramento, centered around salvaging the prevailing wage. Money is another way to exercise clout in the political arena and the CLF intends to follow the lead of CCPOA and the California Teachers Association and spend on targeted legislative races.

It also plans to coordinate contributions among individual unions to increase the federation's overall strength.

And then there is person power, something unions traditionally have lent to politicians in abundance. The most recent beneficiary of union grass-roots visibility, according to some in the labor movement, was then-Assemblyman Byron Sher (D-Redwood City), who ran for the state Senate in a special election this past March. "When we walked with fellow union members door-to-door for Sher, it was clear we're right on the money ... with the issues," said Art Pulaski, head of the San Mateo Labor Council and slated to become CLF executive secretary/treasurer.

Pulaski also says overall union power is being enhanced by the growing strength of unions among factory workers, health-care attendants, non-profit employees, and those in the service and building trades. One example is the Los Angeles Manufacturing Action Project, which has its sights set on the largely Hispanic immigrants who hold down 700,000 low-wage factory jobs. Project Coordinator Peter Olney says "over the last 10 years, and the last six in particular, the most exciting and largest scale organizing taking place has been among low-income Latinos."

But low-income workers aren't the only targets. The largest growing sector of unionizing involves public employees. For instance, University of California employees, from lab technicians to various technical support staff and including faculty, have banded together under the University Professional and Technical Employees Union, founded in 1990. Within the next few years, UPTE is expected to reach 20,000 members. Other public-sector unions with growing membership — and clout — include the California State Employees Association, the CCPOA, CTA and California School Employees Association.

And then there is the Service Employees International Union, whose 300,000 mostly private-sector members make it the largest union in California. While the SEIU is home to every kind of worker — blue, pink and white collar — it has increased its ranks considerably by organizing those in the lowest job tiers through programs such as its "Justice For Janitors" campaign. It also has had considerable success organizing in health-care and some government workers.

"If the labor movement is to survive, we must be even more aggressive in our organizing and must pay closer attention to the interests of our members," said Eliseo Medina, executive director of SEIU Local 2028 in San Diego and president of the state council. In short, says Medina, "we have to radically restructure the way we do business to increase organizing and political action."

But translating union membership into union political clout takes coordination and educa-tion. Medina says SEIU, for instance, will work hand-in-hand with unions around the state to coordinate strategy and to ensure that every member in every precinct is contacted as part of a get-out-the-vote campaign. Although labor has traditionally been Democratic, SEIU is not beholden to a particular political party, says Medina. He cites the passage of the labor-opposed North American Free Trade Agreement (NAFTA) as a watershed that severed labor from its long-standing lock-step association with Democrats. Although that vote took place in the Congress, it means that all SEIU endorsements and donations will be based on a candidate's positions on labor issues — not party affiliation.

Chuck Mack, president of Teamsters Joint Council 7, says labor has been under attack by big business, multi-nationals and to a certain extent government over the last several years. "We've been under siege and we've withstood that," said Mack. "But NAFTA represented a bread-and-butter issue for us, and when we needed to count on the Democrats they said 'no'."

Mack cites minimum wage and maintenance of the prevailing wage as two litmus issues this fall, but they are not exclusive. Universal health coverage, overtime, collective bargaining, privatization and health and safety are other concerns. And although many in labor express disastisfaction with Democrats over NAFTA, Republicans at this point do not seem to provide a viable alternative on the breadth of labor issues. Elimination of prevailing-wage rules, for instance, has been a priority for Governor Pete Wilson, while congressional and legislative Republicans have been apathetic, if not outright scornful, of increases in the minimum wage. At the same time, Democrats have openly courted business over the past few years.

Still, business is wary of the re-emerging clout of labor. "If 1994 was the 'year of the woman,' then 1996 is the 'year of the labor union,'" says Jeff Gorell, a spokesman for the California Manufacturing Association. "They've definitely made a comeback by pushing economic emotional issues that will be pivotal in the next election." He points to the labor-backed minimum-wage initiative as an excellent ploy to get union members to the polls in November, and he forsees that most of them likely will vote Democratic.

Others in the business community also acknowledge labor's return on the political landscape. Kirk West, executive director of the California Chamber of Commerce, suggests that labor's new grass-roots strategy taps more heavily into its local base for political clout rather than relying on the CLF — much the way the chamber itself reorganized its political activity a few years ago.

"The days are over when a legislator only listens to the voice of major corporations and major labor unions," said West. "These days, legislators are more likely to hear from a local chamber and a local union on the same issue, and that is a healthy trend."

The biggest legacy of labor in the last 20 years is their success in unionizing public employees, particularly at the state level, according to Tom McClintock, a former assemblyman who now serves as a director with the conservative Claremont Institute. McClintock, who is back running for the Assembly this fall, blames labor for many of state government's economic woes. With public-sector unions came an enormous political clout over their working conditions and salaries. This, in combination with union-initiated laws to limit competitive pricing of government goods and services, says McClintock, has resulted in a bloated bureaucracy that has been the target of the GOP agenda for the last several years.

Unions will find themselves pushed into a corner, predicts McClintock, where innovation will be their only means to survival. He points to the CCPOA's recent proposals for a public-private management entity to oversee prisons as evidence that some labor organizations can be innovative.

With the oppression index pushed up for workers by an economy increasingly separating the haves from the have-nots, and with the minimum wage and prevailing wage under attack, labor unions surely have a role to play. This may once again be their time in history to insure a place for the masses at the table of economic prosperity and security. 🏛

Guardians of the Guards

The CCPOA and its aggressive leader have bulled their way toward the front of the line among Sacramento power players

By Noel Brinkerhoff

Reprinted from *California Journal*, March 1997

To hear California Correctional Peace Officers Association President Don Novey tell it, his involvement with the leadership of his union was inspired by "a feeling." "It was ... about setting an agenda for a profession that's been somewhat maligned and forgotten because they're behind the walls of these prisons," says Novey, who's been the head of the 25,000-member union since 1980. "I wanted to do something about it."

By any stretch of the political player's imagination, something significant is exactly what Novey has done over the past decade. Although it has yet to become as familiar a special-interest acronym among the general populace as say CTA (California Teachers Association) or CMA (California Medical Association), the letters CCPOA have firmly entrenched themselves into the political lexicon of lawmakers, campaign consultants and other insiders. More than just a union which looks after the interests of "a bunch of prison guards," CCPOA has transformed itself into a formidable political force whose campaign warchest can slug it out with the best white-collar PACs, be they teachers, doctors, lawyers or business

professionals. And in contrast to these other big-time players whose names may not always carry the same political attraction as their contributions, CCPOA brandishes a name that almost any campaign manager wants to stamp on their candidate's endorsement list.

"It's not just a union with a big check book," says Ray McNally, a Republican political consultant. "They are one of the smartest and most savvy groups in California, and their endorsement carries a lot of weight."

McNally's glowing critique of the organization might seem a bit parochial, given CCPOA's eight-year relationship as a client of McNally/Temple Associates. But the admiration with which McNally describes the union's abilities and presence can be found on the other side of the partisan fence as well.

"CCPOA is a very powerful political component and it's not just because of their money," says Gale Kaufman, a Democratic campaign strategist and consultant for former Assembly Speaker Willie Brown. "I can't think of a district — with the possible exception of San Francisco — where their endorsement is not sought out [by Democrats]."

Kaufman adds that, while they CCPOA does endorse Democrats, "they don't as much as I would like."

This tendency by the union to sometimes endorse and especially contribute to Democratic campaigns may come as something of surprise to those who view CCPOA as a Republican-oriented PAC. Such an assumption is understandable given their public safety constituency, which many associate as GOP property, and their well-known and generous financing of Governor Pete Wilson's gubernatorial campaigns.

During his first run for governor in 1990, Wilson received $1 million in political contributions from the correctional officers and another $500,000 for his 1994 re-election bid. And while the heavy dollar-sign bags deposited on Wilson's campaign steps may have prevented CCPOA from making Common Cause's top 10 PAC contributors list for legislative campaigns in both those years, the union managed nonetheless to shell out another half million to other candidates in both '90 and '94. And in presidential cycles, CCPOA has been anything but a stranger to the ranking of PAC bigwigs.

The 1987-88 period marked the

first time when CCPOA managed to shove its way into Common Cause's top 10 rankings, placing fifth with just over $500,000. Then in 1991-92, they moved up to second place with another $1 million in contributions, leaving them behind only the California Medical Association. It's too early to know where they will land once the 1995-96 findings come out, but it would be surprising if their $800,000 in campaign contributions doesn't put them somewhere amongst the finalists.

Apart from the stratospheric contributions to Wilson, the donor list plays both sides almost equally — both Attorney General Dan Lungren (a conservative Republican) and former Assembly Speaker Willie Brown (a liberal Democrat) tallied up $120,000 in contributions from CCPOA since 1992.

When Novey assumed the union's presidency in 1980, CCPOA was anything but a budding political force, having only 1,800 members and an unwanted reputation of being "the pest-control operators of public safety." To turn things around, Novey implemented a "master plan" which restructured the union's administrative design to make it more efficient and politically operable.

Novey — who often is referred to as the "man in the fedora" because of his penchant for men's haberdashery — is an impressive combination of prison guard moxie, wonkish intellect and unassuming charm. Having grown up in a blue-collar family that loves boxing — a sport Novey professes to have been his first love — the union leader learned early on about physical toughness before joining the military where he served as an intelligence officer.

In 1971, he joined the correctional officer ranks at the original Folsom Prison where he worked for 15 years, the last six while simultaneously running the union. Maintaining his post as a line officer, Novey insists, helped him keep his perspective of the rank-and-file membership who were less suspicious about dues increases and political activity knowing that one of their own was running things.

But that's not to say CCPOA doesn't have its dark side like any other political operation, sometimes being heavy-handed in its ways and seeking retribution against those who oppose its agenda.

Ten years ago, when the union first made its presence felt in political campaigns, CCPOA decided to let lawmakers know what they could gain by being on the right side of the prison guard agenda. Then-Assemblywoman Sunny Mojonnier (R-Encinitas) received a $10,000 honorarium in 1987 for leaving her hospital bed and casting an important floor vote approving a new prison in Los Angeles, while another $10,000 went to Senator Bob Presley (D-Riverside) "who we consider to be the godfather of public safety," according to Novey. The big checks were derided at the time as "political payoffs" and the payment of personal honoraria has since been banned for legislators. Still, Novey is unapologetic about the flap.

"We wanted to send a signal that these individuals had gone the extra mile," Novey said.

The correctional officers also made it clear a few years later what could happen when a lawmaker worked against their priorities. In 1990, then-Assemblyman John Vasconcellos (D-Santa Clara), who had received some modest union donations, helped lead an initiative campaign against a $450 million prison bond, which subsequently lost at the polls. CCPOA's payback came two years later when Vasconcellos, who held a safe Democratic seat, found himself facing a well-financed opponent in Republican Tim Jeffries. The union threw $75,000 into the losing GOP effort which saw Vasconcellos win re-election by 15 points.

Novey also has taken his lumps in the course of maintaining his political support of Wilson. During the 1991 labor dispute between the governor and state employees union, Novey led the effort within his organization to take a 5 percent pay cut to help balance that year's state budget deficit. And though the decision was ultimately approved by the union's voting board, Novey became the angry focus of those inside and outside CCPOA.

Despite CCPOA's generosity towards Wilson, Novey also wants it known that the union doesn't always get what it wants from the governor. One example is the ongoing push by Novey to have drug-addicted inmates housed in separate facilities from all others, allowing them to dry out before rejoining the other inmates.

"I've discussed this plan with three governors and none of them have gone for it," Novey explains. Other proposals the union has tried unsuccessfully to get passed are full background checks for corrections applicants, expanded academy training for officers, and the mandatory rotation of wardens and prison superintendents every four years.

If Novey is serious about implementing such reforms, his opportunity may come sooner than later. The union leader has found his membership being

Don Novey

called to account for accusations of abuse at Pelican Bay and Corcoran prisons. In the case of Pelican Bay, the union wants members of the prison's internal affairs unit — some of whom are CCPOA members — disciplined, claiming they coerced inmates into lying about attacks on convicted child molesters which were sanctioned by some correction officers. Novey claims the situation at Pelican Bay is representative of a larger problem with IA units in the Department of Corrections, saying they're "the worst of all law enforcement in the state."

Then there's Corcoran, an institution that's been under investigation for several years for alleged officer-staged fights between rival gang members, resulting in officer shootings of inmates after fighting got out of control, and the beating of new prisoners after getting off a bus. Most recently, correctional officers at Corcoran wore black masks and disguised their identities during a search of prison cells, during which an inmate's arm was broken. Novey says the mask-bearers are not representative of his profession, whose members he says are paid to "wear a badge and display...who we are." As for the shootings, Novey believes all were legitimate given the circumstances, and blames management for accusations that the abuses were covered up.

The controversies underscore, for some, the need to establish standardized training and job descriptions for the officers. Novey argues such training would reduce the potential for abuse and put California in the lead in professionalizing the ranks.

"Starting off with this peace officers' standards and training will be a big step that way," Novey says. Novey is working with other states' correctional unions to introduce Congressional legislation for standardizing the profession. If his hardball political style in California is any indication, Congress will soon know about the "man in the fedora." 🏛

PARTIES, POLITICS & ELECTIONS

Political Parties

By both design and tradition, political parties in California are exceptionally weak — especially when compared to the machine politics prevalent in some eastern states. The weakening of the party structure was engineered by Hiram Johnson and the Progressives starting in 1911 as a reaction to the machine politics of the railroad interests and San Francisco boss Abe Ruef. Parties were explicitly forbidden from endorsing in non-partisan contests and implicitly from making pre-primary endorsements in partisan contests for much of this century. All local offices and judgeships were made nonpartisan, and a unique method of running, called cross-filing, was instituted. Numerous provisions were written into the law for the express purpose of reducing party power, and many of these restrictions remain in the law today. An independent spirit was fostered in California, and even now there are parts of the state where the electorate pays very little attention to a candidate's party. It is these areas — notably the San Joaquin Valley and the rural districts that can hold the balance of power in state elections.

Under cross-filing, which lasted from 1914 to 1959, a candidate could file for the nomination of not only his or her own party but other parties as well (and until 1952, without any indication of party affiliation). This had the effect of weakening party structure and making pressure groups and the press more important. It also led to the election of popular candidates in the primary, when they won both the Republican and Democratic nominations. Generally, cross-filing helped Republicans more than Democrats, and it is probably significant that Democrats have done much better in elections since the system was eliminated in favor of traditional primaries.

California now has six official parties — Democratic, Republican, Libertarian, Peace and Freedom, American Independent, and the Green Party. A party can win official status by getting the signatures of one percent of the registered voters or by obtaining a petition signed by a number of voters equal to ten percent of the votes cast for governor in the previous election. To remain official, a party must get two percent of the vote for a statewide candidate and retain one-15th of one percent of registered voters. Loss of official status means that a party can run candidates by write-in only, a difficult assignment in an era of electronic voting.

Party organization

The party structure is spelled out in detail in state law, although some minor variations are allowed for Democrats and Republicans. These are the basic official elements of party structure:

• *National committee members.* These are elected by the delegation to the national convention and serve as the state party's representatives on the national committee of each party.

• *Delegates to national conventions.* Slates are developed by supporters of each primary candidate, and winning delegates — with alterations and additions — cast the state's votes at the quadrennial convention. The winner-take-all primary is used by California Republicans. State Democrats use a proportional representation system of delegates elected from congressional districts. California's primary and presidential primary will be moved ahead on the calendar to the fourth Tuesday in March 1996 to give California voters a greater opportunity to influence presidential nomination politics.

• *County central committees.* These committees, elected directly by the voters, are charged with directing party affairs in each county. In fact, however, these committees are weak, and the real power is held by the office-holders in each county.

• *State central committee.* This committee is comprised of about 1400 members in the GOP and 2500 to 3000 members in the Democratic Party. This committee is charged with electing party officials, managing and operating the party, and selecting presidential electors. An executive committee of the state central committee handles the day-to-day operation of the party.

• *State chairs.* In theory, the chair speaks for the party and develops election strategy in conjunction with the executive committee. With rare exception, however, the main leaders are the major officeholders of both parties.

As noted, Progressive reforms weakened party organization in the state. However, several developments may serve to strengthen California parties in the 1990s:

1) Because of court rulings in the 1980s, parties may now make endorsements in partisan primaries and in nonpartisan contests. Democrats have established detailed regulations for their party on their endorsing rules and format. Republicans have decided, because of potential divisions, not to endorse. Since 1988, (the first year that endorsing went into effect), endorsing has not been a major factor influencing the nomination or election politics of the Democratic Party, but it could evolve into a significant factor in the years ahead because of term limits and many open (no incumbent) districts.

2) Parties have democratized selection to State Central Committees. There are fewer appointments by office-holders, and more elections from the counties. Democrats have created Assembly District Caucuses in the 80 districts to choose 12 delegates per district.

3) Lastly, election by Democrats of Jerry Brown (former governor and ambitious elective office seeker) symbolized the growing importance of the state chair's position. Current state chairs are Bill Press for the Democrats and John Herrington for the Republicans.

POLITICAL PARTY ORGANIZATION

DEMOCRATIC PARTY ORGANIZATION

REPUBLICAN PARTY ORGANIZATION

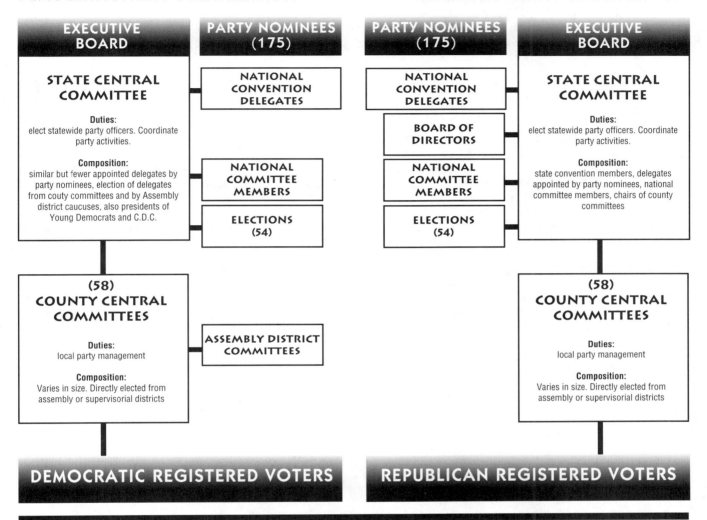

DEMOCRATIC PARTY ORGANIZATION

EXECUTIVE BOARD

STATE CENTRAL COMMITTEE

Duties:
elect statewide party officers. Coordinate party activities.

Composition:
similar but fewer appointed delegates by party nominees, election of delegates from couty committees and by Assembly district caucuses, also presidents of Young Democrats and C.D.C.

PARTY NOMINEES (175)

NATIONAL CONVENTION DELEGATES

NATIONAL COMMITTEE MEMBERS

ELECTIONS (54)

(58) COUNTY CENTRAL COMMITTEES

Duties:
local party management

Composition:
Varies in size. Directly elected from assembly or supervisorial districts

ASSEMBLY DISTRICT COMMITTEES

DEMOCRATIC REGISTERED VOTERS

REPUBLICAN PARTY ORGANIZATION

PARTY NOMINEES (175)

NATIONAL CONVENTION DELEGATES

BOARD OF DIRECTORS

NATIONAL COMMITTEE MEMBERS

ELECTIONS (54)

EXECUTIVE BOARD

STATE CENTRAL COMMITTEE

Duties:
elect statewide party officers. Coordinate party activities.

Composition:
state convention members, delegates appointed by party nominees, national committee members, chairs of county committees

(58) COUNTY CENTRAL COMMITTEES

Duties:
local party management

Composition:
Varies in size. Directly elected from assembly or supervisorial districts

REPUBLICAN REGISTERED VOTERS

Elections

A person may register to vote in California who is 18, a citizen of the United States and a resident of the county of registration for at least 30 days prior to the election (and who is otherwise not disqualified, such as in the case of certain felons). There are several types of elections in California:

• *State primaries.* These take place the first Tuesday after the first Monday in June of even-numbered years. At these elections, nominees for national, state and some local offices are selected. Usually, there are a number of propositions also on the ballot.

• *State general elections.* These take place on the first Tuesday after the first Monday in November of even-numbered years, and voters make their selections from among the nominees chosen in the primaries. The ballot usually contains more propositions.

• *Special elections.* These rarely take place on a state-wide basis because of high cost, although there was one in November 1973 when Governor Ronald Reagan put his tax-limitation initiative to a vote (it lost). Special elections are more often held locally to fill vacancies in Congress and the state Legislature. These are different from most other elections in that the voters are given a list of candidates of all parties. If no one candidate receives a simple majority, a runoff is held four weeks later among the top vote-getters in each party. In some cases, this means that candidates far down the list make the runoff while the candidate who finished second in number of votes does not.

• *Local elections.* Often, elections for local city council and special district-director posts are not consolidated with the primary and general elections and are held at various times during the year.

Political History

During the early years of state history, there were rapid political swings based on economics. When things went well, the big-business interests were in control. During a depression period in the 1870s, the Workingmen's Party under Denis Kearney of San Francisco came to power and managed to get much of its program enacted. When prosperity returned, the party disappeared. Economic and political power went into the hands of the "Big Four" — railroad magnates Charles Crocker, Mark Hopkins, Collis P. Huntington and Leland Stanford. Southern Pacific dominated California politics from the 1880s until the advent of the Progressives more than 25 years later.

The Progressives

Republican newspaper editors started in the first decade of this century to drum up opposition to the railroads and the boss of San Francisco, Abe Ruef. Disgruntled Republicans started the Lincoln-Roosevelt league, and graft-fighter Hiram Johnson became the group's candidate for governor. He pledged to kick Southern Pacific out of the Republican Party and out of California government. He won easily and immediately started enacting reforms such as the initiative, referendum, recall, cross-filing, civil service, and a multitude of other programs. Johnson went to the United States Senate in 1916 and was succeeded by another progressive, William D. Stephens. The movement lost its force in the 1920s as postwar prosperity produced political apathy. Until the next depression, the regular Republicans maintained control of state government.

The Great Depression resulted in the 1934 gubernatorial candidacy of muckraking author Upton Sinclair (his slogan: "End Poverty in California") with his radical plan for reforming the economic system. Republican Frank Merriam defeated Sinclair by about a quarter of a million votes. With the Democrats riding high nationally under President Franklin D. Roosevelt, the Republicans finally lost the governorship in 1938 to state Senator Culbert Olson.

Four years later, a new progressive era began under Earl Warren. Aided by cross-filing, the former Alameda County district attorney and state attorney general portrayed himself as a non-partisan official — an image he embroidered later as an activist Chief Justice of the United States. Warren's personal popularity was unprecedented in California political history. He was able to push most of his programs through the Legislature (with a compulsory health-insurance plan the notable exception). Warren was the Republican vice-presidential nominee in 1948 (with Thomas Dewey) and perhaps could have remained governor indefinitely. After 10 years as the state's chief executive, he was named U.S. Chief Justice by President Eisenhower in 1953.

The new governor was Goodwin J. Knight, who was reelected in his own right in 1954 but was unable to establish himself as leader of the Republican Party because he had to contend with two other major figures, then-Vice-President Richard Nixon and U.S. Senator William Knowland. In 1958, Knowland decided that for political and personal reasons —

he thought being governor was a better stepping stone to the presidency — he would leave his safe Senate seat to run for governor. Knight was pushed aside and virtually forced to run for Knowland's seat. Knowland embraced a right-to-work initiative, setting the stage for a massive Democratic victory led by the gubernatorial candidate, Edmund G. (Pat) Brown. Nixon, defeated in a 1960 run for president against John F. Kennedy, tried an unsuccessful comeback by running against Brown in 1962.

In his second term, Brown became embroiled in a bitter intra-party fight with the powerful speaker of the Assembly, Jesse M. Unruh, and elected to seek a third term rather than give his arch-rival a clear shot at his job. In the primary election, Brown's forces concentrated on shooting down the moderate Republican candidate, former San Francisco Mayor George Christopher, preferring to run against the conservative Ronald Reagan, a former actor. Somebody goofed: Reagan crushed Brown in the general by a million votes.

Democratic nominee Unruh tried to unseat Reagan four years later. Although plagued by limited financial resources, Unruh cut Reagan's victory margin in half. Reagan kept his 1966 pledge not to seek a third term in 1974, leaving the gates wide open. Twenty-nine candidates ran in the primary, with Brown's son, Jerry, and Houston I. Flournoy emerging from the pack to represent the Democratic and Republican parties in November. Brown won by only 179,000 votes, almost blowing his big early lead. Four years later, he rebounded with a 1.3-million-vote victory over the GOP attorney general, Evelle J. Younger.

In 1982 Jerry Brown continued the two-term limit tradition and ran for U.S. Senator (he lost to San Diego Mayor Pete Wilson, a Republican). Attorney General George Deukmejian won a tough primary against Lieutenant Governor Mike Curb for the Republican party nomination and squeaked past the Democratic candidate, Los Angeles Mayor Tom Bradley, in November.

In a repeat in 1986, Deukmejian trounced Bradley, winning by over a million and a half votes. Alan Cranston won re-election to a fourth term in the U.S. Senate, defeating Republican Rep. Ed Zschau.

Pete Wilson maintained Republican control of the state's chief executive position with his victory over Democrat Dianne Feinstein in November 1990. Wilson's non-ideological, pragmatic philosophy seemed to be more in the Warren, not Reagan, mold.

For the first time this century both U.S. Senate seats were up for election in 1992, the extra seat as a result of Pete Wilson's resignation from the Senate, and for the first time in the nation's history two women, Democrats Dianne Feinstein and Barbara Boxer, were elected the the U.S. Senate.

In 1994 Kathleen Brown, Pat's daughter and Jerry's sister, won the Democratic nomination for Governor. She was soundly defeated by Pete Wilson in November after leading by more than 20 points in the polls a year earlier. Feinstein was re-elected to the U.S. Senate after defeating Rep. Michael Huffington by a whisker in the most expensive election in U.S. history. 🏛

Dollars from the right

Conservative group is finding that even ideology has a bottom line

By John Borland

Reprinted from *California Journal*, September 1995

The first time anyone picks up a musical instrument, the results are more than likely to be horrendous. Ask any parent with a child in the school band. But there's a learning curve involved, and the passage of a few years and a little bit of practice will eventually produce something like a recognizable melody.

There's a learning curve in politics too, and the California Independent Business PAC — until very recently known as the Allied Business PAC — has reached the song-making stage. Formed by now-state Senator Rob Hurtt (R-Garden Grove), wealthy Orange County financier Howard Ahmanson and several other conservative businessmen in late 1991, the group immediately became the state's biggest benefactor of GOP conservatives and a lightning rod for liberal criticism. Their early efforts were marked more by purchasing power than political sense, but the PAC is learning the art of picking their battles and targeting their abundant funds to races they have a good chance of winning. There may be no immediate profit in campaign politics, they say, but it still requires business sense to succeed.

The four young women who do the PAC's day-to-day political version of heavy lifting present something of a stark contrast to the group of older businessmen donors. Executive Director Danielle Madison has been on board since the group's inception, performing the jobs of district analysis and the unearthing of suitable candidates. Madison reports periodically to the PAC's board of contributing members, now reduced to Ahmanson; Roland Hinz, a publisher of dirt bike and motocross magazines; Edward Atsinger, the head of a nationwide string of Christian radio stations; and Richard Riddle, owner of a box-manufacturing company. The recent name change was a way of codifying the withdrawal of Hurtt from day-to-day activities and of distancing themselves from the Christian right connotations attached to the Allied name, but the PAC's goals remain unchanged.

Rob Hurtt

The group denies, vigorously and repeatedly, that they are the banking arm of a monolithic religious right. "Religion has never been a prerequisite of the group," Madison says, adding that there are significant differences of opinion even within PAC ranks. She points to Ahmanson, the member most often accused of being the state Christian right's banker for his affiliations with conservative Christian organizations, and notes that he opposed Proposition 187 and does not support mandated school prayer.

"They're obviously religious people with strong feelings," says Ron Unz, the conservative Silicon Valley businessman who challenged Governor Pete Wilson in last year's GOP primary, and a former contributor to Allied's coffers. Through much of last year, Unz travelled to Orange County every month to participate in the group's board meetings, at which they discussed races and candidates. Religion was no more than a very small part of these discussions if it came up at all, Unz remembers. "Really a lot of it was political strategy," he says. "Can we win this district? What are the polls saying? Should we put more money into the district? Things like that ... It was never a question of discussing people's religion."

But opponents are far from satisfied with the group's denials. "They were formed to elect Christians to office," says Jean Hessberg, California director of the People for the American Way. She points out that several of the PAC donors have long had strong connections to Focus on the Family or other conservative Christian organizations. "Our complaint is that they're not representing to the voters what their real agenda is." Aside from that, Hessberg adds, the PAC is supported by only the four wealthy members, rather than by the broad-based groups many PACs represent. "That's not really what the political action committee process is about."

With total 1993-1994 political contributions by the PAC and its individual members topping $5 million, Allied far outstripped any other ideologically grounded group. But it is the rise of a business-minded, professional husbanding of its resources, as much as the incredible size of its pocketbook, that is allowing the PAC to have an increasingly visible influence on the makeup of the state Legislature.

The 1992 slate of Allied candidates tilted to the right like an upended Titanic, conservative enough on both fiscal and social issues to raise loud cries of an invasion by the religious right. The strategy worked well enough in the primaries, where the well-funded conservatives edged out a competing list of Wilson-backed moderates across the state. But it backfired badly in the general election, and a number of Democrats won in marginal seats that would have been more friendly for moderate Republicans. Allied bettered this record considerably in 1994, spending close to $2.8 million on state legislative races alone and winning 24 of 29 general election races, mostly in the Assembly.

"We didn't do thorough district profiles in 1992," Madison says. She points to the example of Brad Parton, the Allied candidate defeated by now-Assemblywoman Debra Bowen (D-Marina del Rey). "That was a case of trying to fit a square peg into a round hole." A more reasonable look at the district, in which nearly-even party registration should benefit Republicans,

calls for an entirely different kind of candidate, she explains. She notes that the district has recently elected four women as legislators: U.S. Senators Barbara Boxer and Dianne Feinstein, Representative Jane Harman and Bowen. "It looks like this district leans toward moderate women," she says.

The group no longer moves reflexively towards any candidate that fits their list of conservative issues. Before going into a race, Madison and her staff will commission a poll, developing a detailed profile of the district and its high-propensity voters. "We'll find out what the district wants," she says. "We'll look at the vote histories going back 10 years or so, and get a good sense of the history of the district."

The histories are particularly useful in deconstructing areas like the Central Valley, which has tended towards the more conservative over time. "We won't go to a district just because it has Republican registration," she says. "We go to districts with a history of voting Republican." Madison points to the PAC's support of Assemblyman Brian Setencich (R-Fresno) last year. "That district has Democratic registration, but their vote history is Republican." In 1992, voters there supported conservative talk-show host Bruce Herschensohn by a wide margin over Boxer, and the district was one of the few in the state to give President George Bush its solid support. "Everyone wondered why I was so adamant about going into that district," she recalls. "They're Reagan Democrats. They're looking for that independent Republican type. Setencich fits."

None of this means the group has moderated its picture of an ideal candidate. The PAC maintains a list of its positions on a number of issues, ranging from low taxes and decreased government regulation to school choice to the statement that "government should do whatever it can to discourage and restrict abortion." But Madison and the four families of contributors have realized that an eight-out-of-eight-point candidate will not fit every district, that there are marginal districts that, if they are to be won by Republicans, must be won with five- or six-point candidates that reflect district voters more than the PAC's positions.

In most cases, the PAC conducts interviews of potential candidates, looking for someone who fits their district profile. "We'll talk to people, look at

who we know, go through word of mouth, sometimes even call them cold turkey," Madison says. But the latter is only a last resort, in important districts that need a strong candidate. "Usually there are too many [candidates]. We need to weed them out, and find the people that fit the district."

Assemblyman Bruce Thompson (R-Fallbrook) interviewed with Allied before his 1992 race. The group did not end up officially endorsing him, but did contribute to his campaign. "They asked me what my positions on business issues were," he remembers. "They asked if I had problems that would surface during the campaign." The conservative social issues, while addressed, he says, were not as prominent as economics, crime and the year's hot topics such as three strikes and Proposition 187.

But not every candidate will go through these interviews. Assemblyman Bruce McPherson (R-Santa Cruz), a moderate for whom Allied produced an independent mailer during his 1993 special-election campaign, says he did not solicit the PAC's aid in any way. "I didn't even know it was coming until it was done," he says. And in his case, the help was not altogether welcome, given Allied's reputation for supporting only the most conservative candidates. "I thought that effort actually hurt me in the campaign," he says. "I don't need their help." He asked them to refrain from supporting him in his re-election bid, and they stayed away in 1994.

Another tool in the PAC's political utility belt is a series of training programs for candidates and campaign staff. The group funds a joint effort in late August with the conservative Young Republican Federation, featuring most of the state's major GOP consultants and a number of national strategists. "We do this because it's hard to keep good trained people on site," Madison says. "There are a lot of candidate training schools, but this is for the campaign team, one of the most important parts of the campaign." The weekend session solicits sponsorships of up to $2000, and charges $75 per attendee. Any funds left over will go to the Young Republicans, rather than back to the PAC.

Allied is one of the few donor organizations that does not explicitly lobby its candidates after getting elected, according to its supporters. Candidates supported by the group agree, saying that they have not had PAC staff knocking on their doors to ask for votes. "I'm surprised that they're not up here asking people to vote against the budget because of the abortion issues," says Thompson. But he recognizes, as do other observers, that the group primarily backs candidates that support its conservative philosophies. "If you go through and get good candidates, then there's no need for [lobbying them]," Thompson says.

Nevertheless, some do report feeling pressure, largely through the actions of Hurtt, one of the leaders of Allied until his election to the Senate. "[Hurtt] goes beyond the bounds of propriety in the way he tries to lead people around," says one Republican legislator, who asked to remain anonymous. This influence was particularly felt during the recent speakership battle, he adds. But the same legislator notes that Hurtt's actions are not necessarily seen as identical to the PAC's wishes. "It's not a monolithic group."

The PAC's recent name change has another sidelight. Traditionally focused on legislative races, the group now intends to begin playing on the local level, aiming at developing a "farm team" of candidates for future elections. The move comes both as a re-

sponse to the opportunities given by term limits and to frustration at past near-misses, according to Madison. "It's partly my frustration ... in finding people with local experience," she says. "It's vital in winning campaigns to have the pulse of the district. And no one does that better than elected officials."

A deep-pocketed group like Allied could be hugely influential in local elections, where candidates spend a fraction of the budget of a legislative campaigns. And the current volatility of local governments — fully half of state-wide county supervisory seats turned over last year — provides considerable opportunity for leverage. "It's a tactically wise thing to do," says Senate President pro Tempore Bill Lockyer (D-Hayward), who has kept a close watch on the group since its birth. "Anyone with mainstream or left-leaning candidates should be very concerned."

But local elections do have different rules. For one, the ballots are generally non-partisan. In addition, many municipalities have contribution caps limiting donors to $500 or less. And even if no limits exist, the usually tiny participating electorate in local elections may act as a brake on spending.

"The awareness level of voters in municipal elections to outside influence is much higher than in the 60 percent that vote in generals," says Tom Shortridge, a Los Angeles-area Republican consultant. "It becomes politically a little embarrassing if you're a councilman and you get $10,000 of your total $20,000 from Allied."

Democrats note the PAC's increasing success rate and widening scope with a wary eye. Lockyer has made it a point to keep a microscope lens trained on campaign expenditures made by both the PAC and its individual members, and loses no opportunity to publicly underline the group's extremely conservative agenda. Assemblyman Antonio Villaraigosa (D-Los Angeles), a member of the Assembly Democrats' 1996 campaign committee, agrees that information is the best way to fight back. "What will be the key is to show who [the PAC] is and who they're giving to," he says. He acknowledges that fighting candidates tailored to their district will be difficult. But PAC support is ammunition to link even a moderate to a highly conservative agenda, he says. "We've got to tie them to each other." 🏛

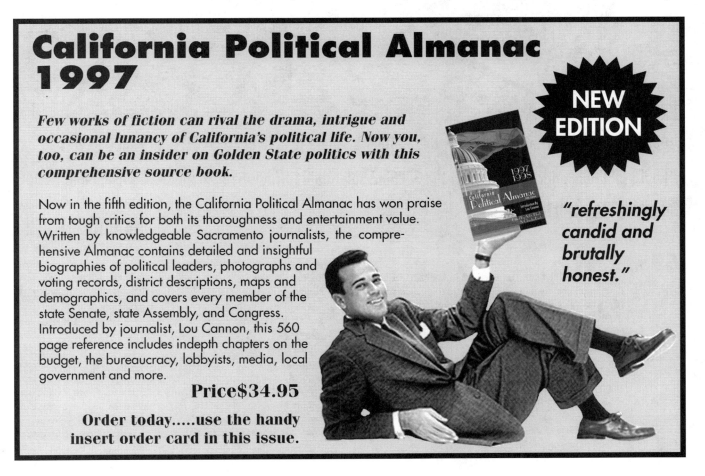

The Virtual Primary

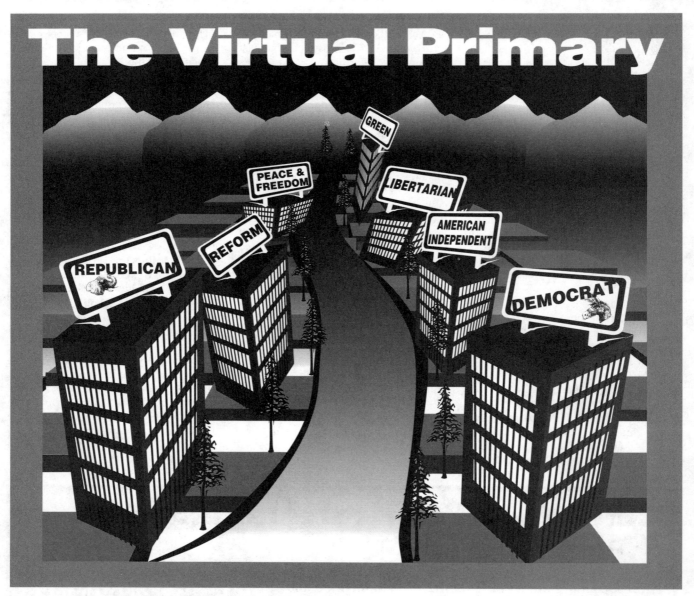

Proponents of California's proposed "open primary" want to give every voter the chance to vote in primary elections. But opponents of the scheme say it will further weaken political parties and allow "enemies" to skew the results.

By Charles Price

Reprinted from *California Journal*, November 1995

"Too often, the choice in the general election boils down to a Leon Trotsky-type Democrat versus an Attila the Hun-type Republican," lamented Richard Ferrari, San Diego Republican activist and co-author of the so-called "open primary" initiative, which has qualified for the March 1996 primary.

Ferrari's lament bolsters the notion that California's current "closed" primary system often produces candidates who represent the extremes of both major political parties. That system requires that voters who want to participate in a party primary must register for that party.

But Ferrari and his allies want to change that system with an open primary that would allow participants to cross party lines to cast their ballots. Instead of Democratic voters restricted to voting only for Democratic candidates, Republican voters for Republican candidates, and so on, voters would have the opportunity to vote for any candidate regardless of the office seeker's party affiliation. The party candidate receiving the most votes running for a particular

Charles Price is a professor of political science at California State University, Chico, and a frequent contributor to California Journal.

office would be listed as that party's nominee on the general election ballot. Republican and Democratic county central committee members, however, would be elected on a separate party ballot available only to their respective party voters.

At present, 11 states operate under some form of open primary. In eight of those states, voters are allowed to choose which party primary to vote in on Election Day. Currently in California, if a registered Democrat decided he wanted to re-register as a Republican in order to vote in the 1996 GOP presidential primary, he or she would have to complete the paperwork with election officials at least 29 days before the primary. Three states — Washington, Alaska and Louisiana — have what is called a "blanket primary," where voters may vote for the candidate of their choice regardless of that candidate's party affiliation. California's open primary initiative is patterned after those states. Louisiana's blanket primary has a unique twist: if a candidate running in the primary gets 50 percent-plus-one of the total vote cast for that office, he or she is elected automatically in the primary.

The current primary system in California dates to the early 20th century, when Progressive reformers successfully promoted it to undercut domination of the nominating process by party leaders and activists, who created party slates at state conventions. While most states have followed California's lead, a few Eastern states still cling to the old convention system. Thus, Ollie North received the Republican nomination for U.S. Senate in 1994 at a Virginia convention rather than in a primary. North eventually lost to incumbent Democrat Chuck Robb. With Progressive prodding, California also became one of the first states in the nation to elect rather than appoint delegates to the national nominating conventions.

Originally, California's primary featured an embellishment known as "cross-filing," which allowed candidates to file for a particular office in their own party's primary, and also in the "other" party's primary as well. The notion was that people had the right to vote for the best person in a primary regardless of party. Since a cross filer's party affiliation was not listed on the ballot when they entered the "other" party's primary, voters often did not realize they were voting for a person of the "other" party. They simply voted for the familiar name; usually, the incumbent. Candidates winning both party's primaries — sometimes as high as 70 percent to 80 percent of legislative races — were listed on the general election ballot as hyphenated Republican-Democratic or Democratic-Republican (depending on the incumbent's party affiliation); they had no major party opponent. On rare occasions, cross filers won the other party's primary but lost their own.

Republicans, for the most part, were able to take better advantage of cross filing because they had more incumbents, superior campaign financing and greater newspaper support. Because of its disastrous impact on Democratic Party fortunes, cross filing was modified via a Democrat-sponsored initiative in 1954 and completely abolished in 1959. Occasionally, however, a candidate may receive two different party's nominations for an office. Senator Jack O'Connell (D-Carpenteria) accomplished that feat as an assemblyman in 1990 when he won his own primary, then won the candidate-less GOP primary as a write-in. Assemblywoman Jackie Speier (D-South San Francisco) did the same thing after no Republican opponent filed against her in 1994. Both Speier and O'Connell received a sufficient number of write-ins from Republicans (at least one percent of the previous general election total).

In terms of objectives, the open primary and cross filing are similar, but the way they work are quite different. Instead of having a single, hyphenated candidate on the general election ballot with no major party competitor, under the "open" primary, each party's top vote-getter for a particular office becomes its nominee. This ensures competition on the general election ballot.

The open-blanket primary idea has been proposed periodically over the years by various "good government" reformers. Until recently, however, the idea failed to develop sufficient momentum. Open-primary legislation has been introduced in the Legislature before, but it always died in committee. In 1984 an open-primary initiative was filed, but proponents failed to get the necessary signatures to qualify for the 1986 ballot. Many of the activists from that failed effort are involved in the new initiative.

For the most part, the key activists who organized to promote the open primary initiative are moderate Republicans, including Republicans For Choice and the California Republican League. They launched their drive because they have become increasingly disenchanted with right-wing nominees who frequently win Republican primaries. A smattering of Democrats and independents provide some bipartisan balance to the initiative effort. For example, Trish Hooper, a Democratic activist of San Mateo County whose daughter is married to former GOP Congressman Pete McCloskey, is co-author of the initiative. State Senators Steve Peace (D-El Cajon), Ruben Ayala (D-Chino) and Lucy Killea (I-San Diego) also are supportive. And, United We Stand volunteers have been involved in initiative planning.

Any effort to qualify an initiative requires money. To that end, one of the open primary's chief legislative proponents, Senator Tom Campbell (R-Stanford), said that he persuaded David Packard, co-founder of Hewlett-Packard and one of California's wealthiest citizens, to offer a matching grant of $200,000 to the cause. William Hewlett provided another $25,000, and the Hewlett-Packard Corporation contributed $10,000. The early seed money from Packard was invaluable. Open-primary proponents hired attorney Peter Bagetellos, a specialist in initiative law-making, to draft the initiative, and American Petition Consultants, a professional signature-gathering firm, to collect the required signatures. The effort to qualify began in February 1994.

"The [open] initiative was not the easiest to qualify," said Bill Arno of American Petition Consultants. "Our solicitors had to spend a little more time explaining the measure. It wasn't nearly as easy to qualify as [Propositions] 184 [three strikes] or 187 [illegal aliens]. We had to pay our solicitors a little more per signature in order to collect all of our signatures." Arno said about 75 percent of the signatures were gathered by paid solicitors, with the remaining 25 percent brought in by volunteers.

Update

The open primary initiative (Prop. 198), was easily approved by voters in the March 1996 primary — 60% yes, 40% no. This initiative is currently under federal court review. If upheld, it will be in effect in 1998 when the next state primary is conducted.

Proponents of the initiative, such as Republican activist Susan Harding of San Diego, argue that their proposal provides three prime advantages. "First, it will increase participation in the California primary," said Harding, a Dean Witter executive and the measure's campaign coordinator. "Those registered as 'decline to state' will be able to vote ... in the primary, and this will increase their turnout. Second, it will reinvigorate the electorate by providing primary voters broader choices. Third, it will encourage parties to put forth stronger, more viable candidates."

Ferrari noted: "Those nominated in the Republican and Democratic primaries often have little in common with the great mass of voters. Our best officeholders tend to be mayors and supervisors — people who hold non-partisan office. Now, admittedly, many of these local officeholders are registered Republicans, but they're pragmatic Republicans like Mayor Richard Riordan of Los Angeles."

As moderate Republicans see it, conservative candidates tend to win GOP primaries because hard-core conservatives are more likely to vote in the primary. But these staunch conservative GOP candidates often lose to Democrats in the general. For example, moderate Tom Campbell lost to arch-conservative Bruce Herschensohn in the 1992 U.S. Senate Republican primary. Herschensohn subsequently lost to Democrat Barbara Boxer in the general. Cross-over Democrats voting in the primary for Campbell could conceivably have won him the nomination. And, it is possible that Campbell would have been a tougher opponent for Boxer in the general.

Open-primary advocates argue that most Californians live in legislative districts that are "safe" Republican or Democrat in registration. As a result, minority party registrants have no chance of influencing the legislative primary outcome and so often opt not to vote. Under the open format, their vote would have meaning.

Killea added that the open primary would "increase the opportunities for more moderate, less partisan candidates to get nominated. This isn't the complete solution to California's governmental problems, but it is one piece of it." Killea noted that moderate Republicans seem to be the prime instigators of the initiative because "they're suffering the most under the present system."

The prime opponents to the open primary are sure to be the Democratic and Republican parties and legislative party leaders. They argue that party registrants should determine party nominees, and the open primary will further weaken political parties in the state. "Our party hasn't taken an official position on the 'open' primary yet, but I suspect we will oppose it," said John Herrington, chairman of the state Republican Party. "Personally, I don't support it. It leaves room for a lot of mischief. The open primary would tend to blur the ideological lines between the two parties and more candidates would move to the center. That would be bad."

In a similar vein, Democratic consultant Bob Mulholland argued: "Would Lion's Club members invite Kiwanis members to vote in the election for the president of the Lion's Club? No way! I see the open-primary initiative mainly as a political agenda for David Packard to promote the candidacy of ... Tom Campbell."

Mulholland also argued that an open primary would encourage party raiding. "The open primary would work kind of like a special election, with all the candidates running on the same ballot. There would be all kinds of opportunities for Republican or Democratic party leaders to encourage their voters to switch and vote for the weakest candidate of the other party. We'll play under the rules that are adopted, but this would open the door to manipulation."

That fear has not materialized in other states, however.

According to political scientist Hugh Bone of the University of Washington, the blanket primary in his state has not led to organized party raids by one party against the other. Bone said there is no evidence to suggest that Washington voters have been more energized to vote because of the state's blanket primary.

Assemblyman Phil Isenberg (D-Sacramento) was skeptical of the benefits of the open-primary initiative and felt there was an "Episcopalian" impulse to it. The backers of the initiative are "the white Protestant, well-to-do, highly educated pillars of the community who always want to dictate to the rest of society their values. I can't guess what the ultimate consequences of the open primary might be — it's a leap into the dark. It would further weaken parties and could conceivably bring a kind of recall fervor to primaries."

Sharing Isenberg's negative assessment, Assemblyman Bernie Richter (R-Chico) said that he opposed it because he felt "it would significantly reduce the effectiveness of political parties in California. I think a much better institutional reform that would accomplish the same objectives of the open primary would be to guarantee no more political gerrymanders. Having a large number of marginal seats [where both parties are competitive] would force Republican and Democratic candidates in these districts to look beyond their core party constituencies."

Senate Minority Leader Rob Hurtt (R-Garden Grove), on the other hand, said he had "no problem" with the open primary for statewide elections, "but I do foresee trouble in legislative races at the district level where a few thousand votes can determine the outcome." Hurtt was concerned that in a high-registration GOP district, featuring a crowded Republican primary, Democrats could play a spoiler role by voting for the weakest Republican. He pooh-poohed the notion that electing more moderates to the Legislature might defuse partisan conflict.

Republican campaign consultant Wayne Johnson admitted that he had mixed feelings. "I like clear contrasts between the Republican point of view and the Democratic — the spirit of debate and the give-and-take. The open primary would lead to less well-defined, rich man's candidates running for office."

Johnson also scoffed at the notion that electing more Republican and Democratic moderates would promote more legislative harmony and effectiveness. "Not at all," he said. "The pettiness in the Legislature is not ideological; it's personality-driven. Willie Brown had the power to keep bills locked in committee at the behest of special interests and their campaign contributions. He didn't want floor debate on these bills." While Johnson admitted that the open primary could stimulate more turnout in primaries, he contended this would not automatically make it better. "To register independent means you skip the primary. It's a self-absorbed act. The voter is saying, in effect, 'I choose to be irrelevant.'"

What are the prospects for victory for the open primary? At this point in time, chances of success for proponents seem reasonably good. A Charlton poll done recently and an older Mervin Field survey indicate that about two-thirds of Californians favor an open primary, once it's been explained to them. And that explaining may be the fly in the ointment. Open primary is not a hot-button, emotional issue, such as term limits, three-strikes, illegal aliens, or the pending Civil Rights initiative to eliminate affirmative action. Thus, winning public approval requires a substantial educational campaign by proponents. The question is: Will anyone listen? 🏛

Taking Back Tinseltown?

Hollywood may be perceived as a political province of Democrats, but Republicans, too, are looking for cash and celebrity power among the entertainment industry's star elite.

by Susan F. Rasky

Reprinted from *California Journal*, September 1996

To be perfectly clear, nobody in Washington or Hollywood is predicting political realignment in an entertainment community whose hearts, souls and personal checkbooks have long been safe Democratic territory. Even political rapprochement would be an overstatement in describing the recent uptick in industry contributions to Republican congressional candidates.

But Sonny Bono's prosaic analysis notwithstanding, there is something that seems to be new and different going on between the nation's two most self-obsessed cities, and it probably bears watching.

The explanation for the improved GOP cash flow from Hollywood is simple enough. When Congress changed hands in 1994, studio political-action committees adjusted their contributions accordingly. Also at stake were two economic issues critical to the entertainment industry — a major overhaul of telecommunications law eventually approved by Congress in January 1996, and a trade dispute with China over the manufacture of pirated compact discs and videotapes.

Hollywood celebrities and creative types might shudder at the thought of cozying up to the foot soldiers in House Speaker Newt Gingrich's (R-Georgia) conservative revolution, but the Motion Picture Association's venerable lobbyist Jack Valenti, a former aide to President Lyndon Johnson and a lifelong Democrat, hasn't spent 30 years in Washington without learning his way to the Republican cloakroom.

So it was hardly surprising that Valenti early last year brought Gingrich together with a group of major studio executives or that he should, from time to time, remind the President Bill Clinton's White House that corporate Hollywood is interested in having allies on both sides of the political aisle. The Valenti fund-raising formula for individual political candidates is perfectly straightforward: The invitation goes out three weeks in advance, the contribution is $1000 — the legal limit — and the recipient, Democrat or Republican, is somebody in a position to be helpful to the industry.

More intriguing, however, is the getting-to-know-you waltz that seems to be going on outside Valenti's official orbit. The first public gesture came in September 1995 when Republican House members convened a "summit" in Beverly Hills with a handful of entertainment industry types to demonstrate Washington's good intentions. That was three months after GOP presidential candidate Bob Dole delivered what has since become known as "Hollywood I," a high-profile speech regarded by the entertainment industry as a blistering and unwarranted attack on the content of its films and television programming.

No matter that Clinton had offered much the same sort of moral tongue-lashing during his 1992 campaign and in subsequent presidential speeches. Clinton, after all, was an old buddy of television sit-com producers Harry and Linda Bloodworth-Thomason and a new buddy of Barbra Streisand. Dole, on the other hand, was a guy with a restive right-wing base to worry about. No telling what trouble he and the family values crusaders in Congress might cause.

Gingrich, ever the pragmatist and strategic planner where fund raising is concerned, sensed that repairs were in order — something Dole finally figured a few months ago in his more conciliatory "Hollywood II" speech — and that

Susan F. Rasky is director of California News Service at the University of California, Berkeley, Graduate School of Journalism and a contributing editor to California Journal.

at least on economic issues, free-enterprising Republicans and profit-conscious studios might have more in common than either side had been prepared to acknowledge. Gingrich by then had formed a 12-member entertainment task force with Bono as chairman and House Majority Whip Tom DeLay (R-Texas) as one of the members. The summit was to be its formal introduction to Hollywood.

Opinions in Washington differ as to whether Bono — whose star power was never exactly high wattage — or Gingrich was the originator of the task-force idea. But the specific parentage is beside the point. The inclusion of DeLay, an early and vocal opponent of the V-chip, of California Representative David Dreier (R-San Dimas), a close Gingrich ally and important GOP fund raiser, and of Representative John Kasich (R-Ohio), chairman of the House Budget Committee and a rising national figure in Republican politics, is an indication that the task force is meant to be more than window dressing. The reasons for including Representatives Andrea Seastrand (R-Santa Barbara) and Ken Calvert (R-Riverside) on the task force are somewhat harder to fathom, but then a speaker has to do what a speaker has to do.

In any event, the September 1995 Beverly Hills summit received passing attention in several industry publications and more respectful coverage in the *Washington Times*, a paper known for its attentiveness to conservative Republican causes. A variety of entertainment industry participants — none of Hollywood's "A List" actually attended — was quoted as saying polite things about the "positive attitude" displayed by members of the task force. It took *The Washington Post* another month to notice, at which point the paper ran a somewhat bemused piece in its financial section focusing on Bono and not-

ing that Valenti seemed to think trade and copyright matters were perking along just fine, thank you very much, without the ministrations of the entertainment task force.

By year's end, with legislative work on the telecommunications bill nearing completion, assorted studio types ventured to Capitol Hill for meetings, including another get-acquainted session with the task force. The *Washington Times* again obliged with positive coverage, this time in a lengthier article for its Sunday magazine, *Insight*. Here, at last, the Hollywood contingent bared its soul, or more precisely, David Horowitz did.

Horowitz, a '60s leftist turned conservative activist, runs a Los Angeles outfit known as the Center for the Study of Popular Culture, a sort of think tank for, well, deep thoughts about popular culture. During the Reagan years, he knocked around Hollywood trying without great success to coax reluctant Republicans out of the political closet.

"We are at the opening of a window for golden opportunities," Horowitz told *Insight* following the Capitol Hill meetings. "The conservative movement is, as we all know, truly radical and progressive in its goals. The party of Newt Gingrich is the party of small entrepreneurs and lean government, and that speaks to artists everywhere. The message that the new leadership is sending out, which supports greater respect for the First Amendment and free expression, coupled with a plea for a greater moral and communal responsibility, resonates with people here."

Hollywood and Washington do share a certain special appreciation for the importance of atmospherics, and Republicans in Hollywood have certainly made themselves more visible in the past four years. Horowitz can take some credit for that. Following the 1992

elections, he and producer/director Lionel Chetwynd founded an *ad hoc* discussion group known as the Wednesday Morning Club, which has become something of a forum for Hollywood's nascent conservative movement and a speaking venue for conservative politicians looking to tap into it.

In February of this year, Horowitz's center in conjunction with the National Review Institute sponsored a conference at Paramount Studios that brought together a cast of bona fide celebrities from both the entertainment and the political world for a "dialogue" on images of Washington and Hollywood. That, in turn, generated a more serious wave of press attention, and by March the articles were flowing. How much money was the GOP really generating in Hollywood? Which household-name celebrities had climbed aboard the Republican bandwagon?

The answer from the Democratic and Republican fund raisers who troll Southern California for dollars is that, by and large, the fundamentals are unchanged. Studio money, like that of any major business, follows the national political currents, which means for now that higher profile Republican congressional candidates or those with seats on key committees can count on solid contributions. But the basic fund-raising rules hold true — Republicans find their California money in Orange County and Democrats find it in Hollywood.

Republican political operatives do detect a greater willingness of Hollywood compatriots to publicly be identified with the party, a change, they say, from a climate in which actors in particular feared they would risk jobs if their true political affiliations were known. Democratic political operatives insist that the bias was more imagined than real and that closet Republicans were simply unwilling to appear "different" in a community that remains overwhelmingly Democratic.

As for celebrity firepower, Republicans are still confined to trotting out the likes of Charlton Heston, Arnold Schwarzenegger, Sylvester Stallone, Bruce Willis and Tom Selleck, while the Democrats retain the advantage of a more dazzling and diverse superstar lineup. It's image, not money, here that counts, and Hollywood GOP activists like Chetwynd say that at the very least Gingrich and some of his congressional Republicans seem to understand that. 🏛

Campaign consultants
view Election '96

Yes, Latino voters had an impact on selected races. But some Republican polling failed, precinct walking wasn't what it used to be, attack ads backfired, consultants had to raise money rather than just spend it, and the conventional wisdom about high-propensity voters got turned on its head. Other than that, 1996 was a normal year on the unicycle.

By A.G. Block

Reprinted from *California Journal,* January 1997

The toxic glow cast by Election '96 finally has dimmed. And although voters and the general population may breathe a sigh of relief, the campaign consultants whose livelihoods depend upon these biennial upheavals are sifting through the embers, seeking to understand the nature and personality of the recent bonfire. It is a necessary task, for therein may be found clues about how to maneuver through the next election. And after all, the first sparks of Election 1998 already are smoldering (see story, page 12).

It ain't easy being a political guru these days. The job entails enough day-to-day uncertainty and enough variety to make campaign consultants seem like jugglers on unicycles. So, what did all that juggling teach us in 1996? To answer that question, we sought out more than two dozen consultants involved with a variety of '96 efforts, from congressional and legislative races to statewide initiatives to local bond measures. Was 1996 unique, and what happened last year that could signal a trend?

At the outset, Latinos made a difference in selected races — a view that has been well documented in the media (see district-by-district analyses, *CJ,* December 1996). But beyond the Latino factor, what else happened?

Many consultants focused on turnout, and on the conventional wisdom about who is and who is not a high-propensity voter. In years past, it was assumed that Republicans held the edge among likely voters, but that equation seemed to turn on its head in 1996 as GOP campaigns complained openly about low turnout and the fact that a large chunk of its base simply stayed away from the voting booth. Reasons for the fall off varied. Some blamed demographics, others the party itself.

"The nature of the electorate has changed for Republicans," said GOP consultant Dave Gilliard of Sacramento, who managed 14 races last year. For the first time, said Gilliard, Republicans had a hard time motivating many of the "young Yuppies" who migrated to the party during the Reagan years. "Their lives aren't impacted by government," he said. "They are detached from government and involved with their families."

At the same time these baseline Republicans were detaching, Democrats were joining the ranks of high-propensity voters. "It's the aging of the baby boomers," explained Jeff Raimundo of Townsend Raimundo Besler & Usher of Sacramento. "And boomers tend to be Democrats."

Gilliard agreed. "The traditional Democratic electorate is aging," he said. "And older folks tend to vote. Democrats now are older voters and easily communicated with on issues like social security and medicare." This, said Gilliard, represents a long-term problem for the Republican Party. "We had success getting young people into the Republican Party," he warned, "but now we must motivate them. When Republican turnout falls to 60 percent, it kills us."

But other Republican consultants said the party's problems went beyond mutating demographics. Wayne Johnson of Sacramento blamed what he called "a dearth of ideas coming out of the national [Dole] campaign" and the attempt to stifle conservative elements within the GOP. "There was just a lack of Republican ideas," said Johnson, who won five of the eight legislative races he managed. "Instead, we campaigned on three strikes and Proposition 13 and other long-in-the-tooth issues."

More significant, said Johnson, the GOP "carpet-bombed its base." "There was a conscious attempt to mute the distinctives," he complained. "In some ways, there was out-and-out hostility. If, for example, the Republican Party mutes its support for the pro-life position, nobody shows up to man phone banks or walk precincts. Or to vote. A large part of the Republican base didn't believe in the national party." By contrast, Johnson noted, "Democrats don't repudiate folks in their base, even though they disagree with them."

On the other hand, Republican Sal Russo of Sacramento blamed GOP fall off on the cumulative effects of 16 years of negative campaigning. He harkened back to the 1980 elections when Republicans knocked off such high-profile Democratic U.S. senators as Idaho's Frank Church and Indiana's Birch Bayh by hammering each with an unprecedented series of attack ads. "It was the first time that the negative campaign became effective," said Russo, adding that it changed the conventional approach by the targets of such ads. Instead of ignoring attack ads, as Church and Bayh attempted to do, the targets responded in kind. As a result, "each cycle has become more and more negative."

Today, said Russo, voters have grown weary of nonstop nega-tive campaigning because all they hear are candidates attacking one another. They rarely hear about vision or programs. Echoing Gilliard, Russo said that "voters no longer see the political system as relevant to their lives. So, they have little stake in an election."

This detachment hits the GOP harder at this point than it does Democrats because it applies more to younger voters; older voters nearing retirement nearly always feel vested enough in

Illustration by Christopher

government to vote. The result: no shows among younger GOP voters.

Turnout also was affected by voter lifestyles. The economy was improving. The country was at peace. Life was good. As a result, many voters simply never tuned into the election until very late in the game. And when they did tune in, they may not have liked what they found.

One critical campaign tactic affected by changing lifestyles in 1996 was precinct-walking. "The best way to get a vote," said Los Angeles Democratic consultant Larry Levine, "is to look a voter in the eye, shake a voter's hand and ask for a vote. But today, a lot of people aren't home. It used to be that, at the worst time of day, you'd find 40 percent of the people home. Now, you're lucky if you get 40 percent at the best time of the day."

But even that 40 percent was barely focused on elections until late October, as evidenced by the large number of undecided voters showing up in poll after poll all through the fall.

"It was very difficult to get the voters' attention," said GOP consultant Ray McNally of Sacramento. "We felt like we were playing to an empty concert hall."

"The electorate largely fell asleep on Labor Day through late October," said Lee Stitzenberger of the Dolphin Group.

Wayne Johnson blamed the long period between the March primary and November election for much of the public's ennui, and for complicating the running of a campaign. "It threw the timing off," said Johnson. "Some campaigns tried to run through the summer and ran out of money. Others tried to shut down and then to revive, which was tough for on-site people."

Stitzenberger added that the confluence of a long campaign season and short voter attention span made allocation of campaign resources more critical. Mistakes were amplified, as many consultants noted regarding supposedly safe Republican Assembly districts that eventually went Democratic. "Republicans failed to devote the money and effort to nail down those districts early in the campaign," said one observer, referring to races in the 26th, 43rd, 56th and 78th districts (see *CJ*, December 1996). "They let Democrats back into the game."

Because voters dropped in late, they were treated to the election's final frenzy when most campaigns involved in tight races went highly negative. Result: more alienation.

Some in the trade believe, however, that the universe of nonstop negative campaigning may have run its course, and that 1996 was the watershed. Tupper Hull of the PBN Company thinks the political awakening by California's well-heeled high-tech community signaled a change in the atmospherics. "This is a revolutionary change in California," said Hull. "They understand that government has an impact on their operations, and they understand the need for the high-tech community to be smart and involved and engaged in the process over the long run." According to Hull, high-tech, which largely financed the $40 million effort to beat Proposition 211, has enough financial clout to force campaigns to focus on issues rather than on personalities or candidate-bashing.

The high-tech community, Hull said, does not view politics as an end in itself but as a means to an end, and it takes a dim view of politics as a game. "The Silicon Valley," explained Hull, "is not partisan. They are very problem-solving oriented, and they view problems within the government sector as problems that can be solved."

In the short run, however, consultants were divided over whether 1996 saw the beginning of the end of negative campaigning.

McNally, for instance, was among those who felt that negative campaigning still was king. "It worked again this year," said McNally, who said that two of his state Senate candidates — Phil Hawkins in the 27th District and Richard Rainey in the 7th — were targets of relentless and misleading ads about their positions on gun control and tobacco. Rainey won, but Hawkins lost to Democrat Betty Karnette.

"It's as bad as I've ever seen it," agreed GOP consultant Alan Hoffenblum, referring to negative campaigns run against his clients — deposed U.S. Representative Bill Baker of Walnut Creek; Republican Dan Walker, who lost to Democrat Debra Bowen in the 53rd Assembly District; and Lynn Leach, who narrowly won in a heavily Republican 15th Assembly District. "Veracity is no longer a cogent word."

Phil Giarizzo, a Democratic consultant who ran a bevy of legislative races, said the negative or attack ad still has its place in the campaign arsenal. "Politics is a war of ideas," he said. "And you have to point out people's records. And pointing out record, ideology and what I would consider 'bad' candidates for the right reasons is a public service." But Giarizzo said that attacks must be accurate and what consultant Stephen Sheldon of the REX Company in Los Angeles called "believable."

Yet other consultants noticed signs that the era of negative campaigning is coming to an end.

"There was a hunger among voters for a focused, positive message and with a plan," said Harvey Englander of the Kamber Group in Los Angeles. "There had to be more than 'the other person is awful.'"

Democratic consultant Parke Skelton of Los Angeles saw negative ads backfire when used against his candidates, especially Adam Schiff, who defeated Republican Paula Boland in the 21st Senate District. "They never established any positive story about Boland," he said. "All they did was slime Adam, and they destroyed their own campaign."

Skelton cited a survey, taken in mid September when Boland had five pieces in the mail and Schiff but one. "The poll showed that Boland's own negative material made folks less interested in supporting her by a two-to-one margin," Skelton said. "That shows me that something was wrong."

Raimundo, too, cites evidence that negative ads actually helped the target of those ads. In one of his campaigns, the target was then-Assemblyman Byron Sher (D-Palo Alto), who was running in a special state Senate election last March against Republican Patrick Shannon. "Shannon was closer to Sher when he campaigned on the issues," Raimundo recalled. "But when he went highly negative, the gap widened dramatically. It had the opposite effect Shannon wanted."

Polling, long a fundamental tool of political campaigns, also proved a problem for some consultants. Tracking polls especially came under fire for two reasons — accuracy for Republicans and proliferation for Democrats.

"One of the unusual things about '96 was the unreliability of polling data," said Wayne Johnson. "The problem was methodological: Nobody is answering their phones. Seventy percent of the people are screening their calls, which limits the universe of respondents to the point that you can't count on representative samples."

Pollsters, however, took a different view. "[Johnson's] old arguments have been around for years," said Gary Lawrence, a GOP pollster based in Orange County. "The resistence rate, the hang-up rate, the refusal rate still is within acceptable margins. Most people participate once they know they won't be sold something."

If Republicans had a problem with polls, said Lawrence, it stemmed from assumptions made about the data. "We no longer ask, 'What did the polls say?' Instead, we ask, 'Which turnout model did we run the data through?' Because the number of voters turning out is declining, we need to find out who will turn out to vote. In some elections, we use 10 or more turnout models."

Lawrence also agreed with an assessment made by Democratic pollster John Fairbank of Los Angeles, who indicated that Republicans may not have done enough polling in critical legislative races where large numbers of undecided voters lingered in the equation until late in the game. "One of the ideas behind polling early and often," said Fairbank, "is to try to create a profile of the undecided voter. In many legislative races, you have to poll early and often to watch the movement of voters. Many Democrats and independents moved late, and we were able to help the Assembly caucus target those undecideds with a message they wanted to hear."

But that "early and often" strategy, although helpful, caused problems. According to Democratic consultant Gale Kaufman of Sacramento, every group with two nickels to rub together commissioned its own tracking poll before it would part with even one of those nickels. "Everybody and their mother was doing polls," she said, referring to large special-interest donors such as teachers, trial lawyers, labor and business groups. "It's one thing to have informed folks reading those polls, and another to try to educate people who are not used to what the numbers mean. It was difficult to make a case for a client when all this data was floating around, and when you didn't contract for the data or have any say in reading it."

Kaufman also said that the sheer number of people performing tracking polls in critical districts sometimes conflicted with her candidates' phone operations. "On any given night of the week," she said, "we couldn't get through with paid phoning [phone banks] because of all of the folks doing polling. In one week, there might be three polls in one district by three different entities — none of whom were the [Assembly] candidate."

Because the polls themselves were used by special interests to help determine where to put their resources, the burden of getting a share of those resources often fell to consultants in 1996 — another change from years past, especially for Democrats. "In previous campaigns," said Kaufman, "I just spent the money. I never had to get it. High-profile campaigns never had to worry about being funded, but this time I had to spend time selling my clients" to lobbyists and special interests with big money to contribute. She said uncertainty in Assembly Democratic leadership fueled a freelance system of campaign funding — and begging. "You had no assurance that you would get funded until late in the game," she said. "So, you ended up hustling ..."

Finally, several consultants pointed to the unusually large number of close races for Congress and the Legislature, and to the number of "clustered races" spread across the map. According to as yet unofficial results, 15 district races were decided by less than 5000 votes. All but two of those races also overlapped with high-stakes races for some other legislative body.

"California could be entering a permanent era of marginality," said consultant Don Solem of San Francisco. "The closeness in that number of legislative races is unprecedented, and in could also be true in supervisorial races. Convincing [legislative] majorities could be a thing of the past." 🏛

DIRECT DEMOCRACY

In California government the people have three tools that make them very powerful participants in the decision-making process. The initiative, referendum and recall were instituted by Governor Hiram Johnson and the progressives in part to break the hold of the railroad interests on state government in the early 1900's. With all three of the direct democracy devices, a simple majority of those voting determines whether the proposal passes.

• *Initiative.* The initiative gives the people the right to place local or state measures on the ballot if they obtain the required number of signatures. It has also been used by governors, legislators and special-interest groups to get what they want after the Legislature has rejected or been unable to meet their demands. To qualify for the ballot, a statewide constitutional initiative requires signatures equal to eight percent of the vote cast in the last gubernatorial election; initiative statutes require five percent.

After the 1994 gubernatorial election the number of signatures required is:

Constitutional initiative - 693,230
Statutory initiative - 433,269

Today, a powerful and sophisticated initiative industry has developed: signature-gathering firms, pollsters, political lawyers, and campaign management firms specializing in the qualifying and passing of ballot measures.

• *Referendum.* This is a procedure that can be used by the public, if they can gather sufficient signatures, to block a state statute or local ordinance pending a popular vote on the issue. It is not used often, but the threat of a referendum occasionally has the effect of blocking enactment of legislation. This procedure cannot be used to stop urgency bills, and for this reason emergency measures require a two-thirds vote rather than a simple majority in the Legislature. The referendum procedure was used successfully at the state-wide level to place four measures the Peripheral Canal and three reapportionment plans — on the ballot in June 1982.

The number of signatures required is the same as for a statutory initiative.

• *Recall.* The third of the Johnson direct-government reforms establishes a petition procedure for placing on the ballot the question of removing any elected official or officials from office. Recall elections are common in local government and have increasingly been used to target state legislators. Former President Pro Tem David Roberti in 1994 and Assembly member Paul Horcher in 1995 had to face voters in recall elections.

California's system of direct democracy does not stop here. The Constitution and local-government charters can be amended only by a vote of the electorate. Neither the state nor any local governmental agency may incur a general-obligation debt without prior approval of the electorate (although revenue bonds can be sold without such approval). At the state level, a simple majority vote is sufficient to approve bond measures for such purposes as higher-education construction, park acquisition and development, the Cal-Vet farm and home program, and water-pollution plants. But at the local level, all bond proposals — even school bonds — require a two-thirds majority.

In recent years, the potency of direct democracy in California has grown. This power was demonstrated by the far-reaching tax revolt, which started with Proposition 13, the Jarvis-Gann property-tax initiative in 1978. This was followed with the "Spirit of 13" spending-limitation measure enacted in 1979, a successful Jarvis-sponsored income-tax indexing proposal in June of 1982, the successful Gann Legislative Reform Initiative of June 1984 and a number of other Proposition 13 follow-up measures thereafter. Proposition 140 imposes term limits on California elected officials, plus it mandates a 38 percent cut in the legislature's budget. Proposition 164 imposes term limits on our U.S. Senators and Members of the House of Representatives. In 1994 two initiatives were at the center of state political debate: The "Three Strikes" (Prop. 184) and illegal aliens (Prop. 187) initiatives. In 1996 the much ballyhooed Civil Rights Initiative abolishing affirmative action programs is likely to be *the* issue of the year. The number of measures qualifying for the ballot shows no sign of abating in the near future.

With these tools, there is hardly any aspect of state government that cannot be controlled by the people. 🏛

initiative reform

Is it time to return to the "indirect" initiative?

Illustration by Mike Tofanelli

By Charles M. Price

Reprinted from *California Journal*, April 1994

I f public attitude toward state government was a radar screen, the little blip marked "confidence" probably has disappeared from view. And the reasons for it are myriad. Corruption unearthed in an FBI sting operation conducted inside the Capitol ensnared legislators, lobbyists and staffers. The economy has been blistered by defense cutbacks, an unemployment rate higher than the national average, a tidal wave of illegal aliens, a never-ending series of fires, floods, drought and earthquakes, and human maelstromes such as

Charles Price is a professor of political science at California State University, Chico, and a frequent contributor to California Journal.

the Los Angeles riots. When dealing with all of this, political institutions often seem mired in gridlock and unable to cope.

Thus, the public took matters into its own hands, using a process of "self-government" established more than 80 years ago — the initiative. Beginning with Proposition 13's overhaul of the property tax system in 1978, voters systematically restructured state political institutions and changed forever the way state and local governments funded themselves. They also put a cap on the amount of time state elected officials may serve in office.

But a growing number of critics feel that the initiative process, set up to curb the influence of special interests on government, has become instead a tool for those interests. Critics also feel that the laws that emerge from the initiative system are flawed. And they want the process overhauled.

The initiative — together with its cousins, the referendum and the recall — first saw the light of day in California back in 1911 when Progressive Governor Hiram Johnson led the charge to write them into the state Constitution. Initiatives allow voters the right, via the petition process, to propose and enact laws and constitutional amendments, and, by so doing, bypass the Legislature and/or governor.

Initiative critics, including elected officials and academicians, point to a number of problems with the current system.

• Initiatives are often authored by special interests or by ambitious politicians, not by average citizens, as Johnson intended.

• These measures are filed and approved for circulation without any in-depth analysis. Although the attorney general makes sure proposals don't violate the constitution, many slip into circulation with drafting errors or are flawed in other ways that must later be sorted out in court.

• Most initiatives qualify for the ballot through the work of professional petition firms rather than the efforts of volunteer citizens.

• Initiative propositions are laden with legalistic jargon, making them difficult to understand for the average voter.

• So-called "counter-initiatives" — two proposals on the same subject and the same ballot — often complicate the voter's ability to sort among conflicting measures.

• Initiatives add to the length of the ballot and number of decisions facing voters.

• Propositions are packaged into deceptive campaigns by slick professional campaign consultants.

• Finally, initiatives, once approved by voters, are amended with great difficulty.

Beyond these problems, a succession of fiscal initiatives have severely hampered the governor and Legislature's ability to provide fiscal leadership — or even craft a budget. Included in this group are Proposition 13's 1978 property tax relief; Proposition 4 of 1979, which imposed government spending limits; Proposition 6 of 1982, which abolished property and gift taxes; Proposition 62 of 1986, which required a two-thirds vote before cities may raise taxes; and Proposition 98 of 1988, which mandated a minimum funding level for K-14 public schools.

Finally, voter adoption of Proposition 140 in November 1990, the harsh term limits and legislative budget reduction initiative, was for many legislators, especially Democrats, the "last straw."

Thus, over the last several legislative sessions, various Democratic legislators have proposed "reforms" to stem the initiative tide: raise the filing fee from $200 to $1000, require that signatures be collected in a specific number of counties, increase the percent of signatures needed to qualify an initiative or require that the percent be geared to registered voters not to the total vote cast for governor at the last election, the current requirment. This proposal would double the number of required signatures (currently 615,958 for a constitutional amendment and 384,974 for a statute). Yet, none of these proposals passed even though Democrats had secure majorities in both houses.

Restrictions on the initiative process fail for a number of reasons. First, conservative Republicans are wary of under-

cutting a process they often have used with great success. Term limits, for instance, was proposed by former Assemblyman and former Los Angeles County Supervisor Pete Schabarum — a Republican conservative. Second, polls repeatedly show that the public supports the initiative process. And although that support has declined over the last several decades, it still is backed by more than 60 percent of the electorate, according to *The Field Poll*. Third, an alliance of interests united to help protect the initiative during the 1991-92 legislative session. This "Initiative Coalition" included political watchdogs such as Common Cause and the League of Women Voters, environmental groups such as the Planning and Conservation League and the Sierra Club, and conservative anti-tax groups such as the Howard Jarvis Taxpayers Association, People's Advocate (founded by the late Paul Gann), and Paul Gann's Citizen Organization. The coalition opposed restricting the initiative process because its members had successfully sponsored initiatives and were reluctant to see the process dismantled. Moreover, the Jarvis and Gann groups have used the initiative process as a money-making tool to help fund their activities.

One significant initiative reform emerged from the 1991-92 session, however — Democratic Assemblyman Jim Costa's ACR 13, which established a 15-member Citizen's Commission on Ballot Initiatives to study the process and propose possible remedies. Under ACR 13's provisions, the governor, Assembly speaker and Senate Rules Committee each selected four members, with appointees a reflection of the state's diverse population. The commission also included a designee of the secretary of state, attorney general and president of the County Clerk's Association. Retired Legislative Analyst A. Alan Post, one of the most respected former officials in the state, was selected to chair the commission.

The commission met periodically during spring 1993 to listen to various initiative experts recommend initiative reforms and to formulate a proposal. Two experts in particular played key roles in framing the commission's deliberations: attorney Robert Stern, former counsel to the Fair Political Practices Commission and author of "California's Fourth Branch of Government;" and Floyd Feeney, a University of California, Davis, law professor and co-author of "Improving the Initiative Process: Options for Change." The "Initiative Coalition" also provided input.

In the end, the initiative process gained a vote of confidence from the commission, although there was substantial consensus that it had some problems. As Post commented, "I don't think that commissioners felt the initiative process should be constrained nor that it was overused. The intent was to make it a better instrument." Post and his colleagues agreed a comprehensive package of initiative reforms was needed and, in January 1994, they presented their recommendations to the Legislature. Costa packaged these recommendations into an omnibus initiative reform bill introduced in February 1994.

The most dramatic change proposed by the commission involves reinstitution of a modified "indirect initiative." Currently, initiatives that qualify go "directly" to the next statewide ballot. The commission would detour those measures by requiring that qualified initiatives first go to the

Legislature for evaluation.

Under an "indirect" system, sponsors of an initiative would have 180 days (30 more than under the current system) to circulate petitions and gather enough signatures to place their proposal on the ballot. But instead of going before voters at the next statewide election, the proposal instead would be sent to the Legislature, which would have 45 days to act on it. Lawmakers would hold hearings where proponents and opponents could testify. Lawmakers also would negotiate with sponsors to iron out flaws or correct drafting errors. Sponsors then could amend the measure as long as the amendments were consistent with the "purposes and intent" of the original proposal. Each house would vote on the initiative and — if the Legislature passed and governor signed it — it would become law without going before voters. The governor and Legislature also could adopt their own law on the same subject, and proponents could choose to withdraw their proposition if satisfied with the effort. If, however, the governor and lawmakers reject a qualified initiative, it automatically would be placed on the next statewide ballot, where it would become law if approved by voters. If a statute, the Legislature subsequently could amend it after three years by a two-thirds vote of each house. Constitutional amendments could not be amended by the Legislature.

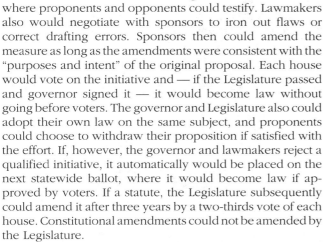

There are advantages to this approach, the commission argued. For one, proponents would have a little more time to qualify their petitions, and this might encourage more volunteer rather than paid signature collecting. More important, it would provide a mechanism for revising initiatives after they have been filed. Today, qualified measures go on the ballot, period. The commission's plan, however, would allow for hearings, complete with bill analyses, review and amendments. Oversights, ambiguities and gaffes in the initiative text could be corrected. For example, opponents of Proposition 165, sponsored in 1992 by Governor Pete Wilson to reform welfare and the budget process, focused on one significant drafting error: Although the proposal gave the governor emergency fiscal powers, the Legislature was not given the power to override his decisions. George Gorton, Governor Wilson's initiative campaign manager, admitted to the drafting flaw but contended the courts would take care of it. This could have been avoided had the commission's format been in force because Wilson would have had the opportunity to amend his proposal.

There are problems with the commission's recommendations, however. Hiram Johnson sought a procedure that would bypass a gridlocked or special interest-dominated Legislature. The proposal puts the Legislature back in the loop. Also, from 1911 to 1966, the California Constitution included both a direct and an indirect initiative, but the latter device was rarely used. Finally, *The Field Poll* reported in 1990 that 50 percent of Californians opposed the indirect initiative, while only 41 percent favored it. Also, if initiatives never reached the ballot, it would mean less money-making opportunities for campaign consultants.

In addition, opponents often want proposals killed, not amended, and see their best chance at the ballot. In this vein, they might not want to tip off proponents to drafting errors

at a legislative hearing but would rather spring these shortcomings on proponents later in the campaign.

The Post Commission also included a smorgasbord of other fine-tuning reforms, including additional contribution disclosure statements, improved signature-verification procedures, better ballot design, and full disclosure of the top five contributors to the proposition.

The commission, however, did not deal with the role of money in the initiative process. Court rulings mostly have preempted the subject. Powerful groups like the California Teachers' Association or the tobacco industry are in a better position to qualify their proposals than is, say, an animal rights' group because wealthy organizations can spend a lot of money on professionals to collect the required number of signatures. The U.S. Supreme Court ruled in 1988 in *Meyers v. Grant* that states can not prohibit paid petitioning because the ban limits free speech.

Clearly, the side with the most campaign money, particularly if it's by more than a two-to-one or three-to-one margin, has a better chance of winning at the ballot box. This advantage is even more enhanced in the 1990s because the "fairness doctrine" — which once required radio and television stations to provide some free air time to proponents or opponents of propositions with modest financial resources — is, at present, dead. Yet courts also have ruled that attempts to set contribution or expenditure limits also violate free speech.

The contemporary initiative process seems to work. Since the 1970s, only about 20 percent of the filed initiatives actually qualified for the ballot. Of these, only about one-third were approved by voters. If "too many" initiatives get on the ballot, or if initiatives are too lengthy or complex, voters tend to play it safe and vote "no." Thus, in effect, the initiative process already has a self-correcting mechanism.

For his part, Costa has pushed ahead with plans to author legislation to implement some commission recommendations. At the end of February, the Fresno lawmaker introduced AB 3181, which incorporates those recommendations that received unanimous support from the commission. Among the bill's provisions are the requirement for legislative hearings on proposed initiatives, a procedure for proponents to amend their measures, an extension of the circulation period, an improved signature-verification system, and provisions for additional campaign statements.

Costa also introduced ACA 40, which puts provisions of AB 3181 before voters. Both bills are headed for their debut before the Assembly Elections and Reapportionment Committee. Randall Henry, a senior consultant to Costa, expressed guarded optimism about the fate of the two bills, saying that Costa packaged only those recommendations that had been given unanimous approval by the commission, with its varied representation.

Still, Costa's success could depend on how lawmakers perceive declining public support for the initiative, legislative anger over term limits and support from the Initiative Coalition.

Meanwhile, the public seems to be in for a breather — the June 1994 ballot contains only one initiative.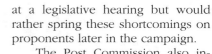

In the shadow of Jarvis and Gann

Citizen initiators tilt at the electoral windmill

By Charles M. Price

Reprinted from *California Journal*, April 1995

Seventeen years ago, a singular success turned their names into household words, made them instant inductees into the grass-roots hall of fame, secured their places in California political history and launched a movement that even today has the power to turn normally forthright, sane and otherwise stalwart politicians into quivering mounds of Jell-O. One was a cantankerous Southern Californian, the other a gentlemanly Sacramentan, and prior to their success, they had a somewhat checkered history as authors and proponents of ballot initiatives. Both separately and together, they had logged a record of failure that might have caused ordinary mortals to develop a more rewarding hobby.

But these two had the kind of genuis that comes from the dogged pursuit of a singular goal. Or, maybe they just had blind luck, for in 1978, Howard Jarvis and Paul Gann hit paydirt, nirvanah, the promised land. They offered up a property tax relief initiative that captured the imagination of beleaguered taxpayers, who endorsed their proposal — known then and forever as Proposition 13 — and made it the law of the land. From that day forward, Jarvis and Gann became mythical practitioners of initiative politics.

Jarvis and Gann scored a huge success, but many less-successful promoters push their ideas just as doggedly — often in the face of defeat after defeat.

Take, for instance, Robert W. Wilson, a Southern California artist and initiative proponent whose motto might well be, "If at first you don't succeed — try, try again." In 1964 Wilson qualified a ballot initiative that would have set up a statewide lottery — Proposition 16 that year. Voters, however, rejected it.

"I was 20 years too early," Wilson lamented, adding that Nevada gambling interests and California horsetracks poured millions of dollars into the effort to derail his initiative because they feared the competition for gambling dollars.

Embittered by his experience, Wilson in 1965 filed a new initiative that would have allowed casino-style gambling in Adelanto, a small San Bernardino County community in the Mojave Desert a few hours drive from Los Angeles. It also would have provided for extended pari mutuel wagering on horse racing. The initiative was a less-than-subtle swipe at the enemies of Proposition 16, but Wilson failed to gather enough signatures to qualify it for the ballot. Undaunted, Wilson has resubmitted his Adelanto gambling measure 25 times since 1965. It has yet to qualify.

Wilson and his band of allies remain undaunted. "Do you realize that Californians spend over $3.5 billion yearly gambling in Nevada?" asked John Brown, an Oxnard attorney who co-authored Wilson's 1994 gambling proposal. "That's why Nevada doesn't have to have a state income tax. Hang Nevada."

Brown may be correct, and a whole bunch of Californians may agree with him. But the act of qualifying

---

Charles M. Price is a professor of political science at California State University, Chico, and a frequent contributor to California Journal.

an initiative requires more than an idea whose time may have come. It requires big money. Thus far, Wilson and Brown have been unable to find the financial backing needed to hire professionals such as American Petition Consultants to secure the needed signatures. If they ever do find a bankroll, they might just qualify their idea. And given the mood of the electorate, it might pass. After all, that's precisely what happened to those old men of myth — Jarvis and Gann.

Meanwhile, Robert W. Wilson symbolizes the potentials and pitfalls of the initiative process. In a nutshell, the process that has so enmeshed Wilson goes like this:

A person or group drafts an initiative idea — whether a statute or constitutional amendment — into the proper legal form. Generally speaking, politically savvy proponents rely on experienced attorneys to put their proposals into proper legalese. Others may request drafting assistance from the legislative counsel if the request is accompanied by the signatures of 25 voters. The Legislative Counsel's Office lends this assistance as time permits. The proponent then submits the initiative proposal to the attorney general, along with a $200 deposit for processing costs that will be refunded if the measure qualifies. The Attorney General's Office gives the proposal a title and summary, after which it is sent to the Secretary of State's Office, which sets the deadline for turning in enough valid signatures to qualify for the ballot — currently, 432,945 for statutes and 692,711 for constitutional amendments. In addition, a fiscal analysis is prepared by the Department of Finance and Joint Legislative Budget Committee. Finally, if a sufficient number of valid signatures are collected by the deadline, the measure goes on the next statewide ballot where voters approve or reject it.

Over the last 30 years, initiatives have increasingly occupied center-stage in California politics. Among the most prominent were Proposition 4 — the Political Reform Act of November 1974; Jarvis-Gann's Proposition 13 of June 1978; Proposition 140 and its imposition of legislative term limits in November 1990; Proposition 174's school-voucher proposal of June 1993; and Propositions 184 and 187 of 1994, better known as the "three strikes" and "illegal immigration" initiatives. Already approved for the March 1996 primary election is an "open primary" initiative that would allow voters the right to vote for any primary candidate regardless of party label. In addition, another school-voucher bombshell is in the works, also aimed at March 1996, while a measure to abolish the state's affirmative-action laws could land on the November 1996 ballot. All three promise to have substantial impact on the elections of 1996. Overall, since 1964, nearly 650 initiatives have been filed in California, approximately 17 percent have qualified for the ballot and about 7 percent approved by voters.

Initiative qualifying may have crested in the 1987-90 period when some 36 made it to the ballot. Of these, 15 were approved. Since 1990, the number of proposals qualifying for the ballot seems to have slacked off despite a continued stream of petitions circulated for signatures.

What sort of people file initiatives? Essentially, there are three types: elected officials, executives of financially powerful interest groups and private citizens. Most initiatives that qualify for the ballot are authored by the first two groups. These proponents are politically astute and often have the financial wherewithall necessary to promote petition drives. They nearly always hire professional firms to guarantee their measures make the ballot.

Elected officials have introduced a fair share of initiatives over the past three decades as well. In particular, conservative Republican officeholders such as John Schmitz, John Briggs, Pete Schabarum, Floyd Wakefield, Don Rogers, Frank Hill, Bill Dannemeyer and Ross Johnson have put forward ideas and, by so doing, have sought to bypass the Legislature, which has been controlled for the most part by liberal Democrats.

Not that Democrats, too, haven't felt compelled to use the ballot. The likes of former Assemblymen Lloyd Connelly and Dick Floyd and Senator Tom Hayden and former Senator Alan Robbins have filed initiatives. A more recent trend has been for major statewide officeholders or candidates to propose initiatives as adjuncts to their campaigns. John Van De Kamp, Leo McCarthy, George Deukmejian, Pete Wilson and March Fong Eu are examples. Interest-group leaders such as John Henning of the AFL-CIO, Kirk West of the Chamber of Commerce and Carol Lee of the California Medical Association have been active initiative proponents as well.

Even political insiders frequently fall short in their signature-qualifying efforts, however. For example, no one is more keenly aware of the problems in collecting sufficient valid signatures in the right amount of time than the secretary of state. Yet, former Secretary of State Eu failed to qualify her "Dimes Against Crimes" initiative in 1987.

It was average citizens like Robert Wilson, not political insiders, whom Progressives wanted to empower when they first placed the initiative procedure into the state Constitution not long after the turn of the century. After all, elected officials and lobbyists had access to the formal institutions of lawmaking — Legislature and governor. The initiative was designed for those outside the regular process.

Who are these average Joes and Janes? And why are they willing to plunk down $200 for their initiative idea? How do they hope to collect the hundreds of thousands of signatures needed to place their measure on the ballot?

Some private-citizen initiators believe strongly in their issue but have little appreciation or understanding of the costs of printing thousands of petitions and coordinating a massive signature drive. For example, builder Norman Bedford of Healdsburg was the subject of several expensive lawsuits. Bedford became angered by what he considered to be excessive costs for attorneys, and he filed an initiative to limit their fees.

"I thought I would receive financial support from the insurance industry with my proposal," Bedford admits. But, the money never appeared. He has filed seven initiative proposals over the years, but none has ever qualified.

In 1973, in a one-week period, Patrick O'Shaughnessy of San Francisco filed 20 separate initiatives on a wide variety of subjects. None qualified, and O'Shaughnessy was out $4000 for his trouble. And, in 1994 one proposed initiative on "Forfeiture of Office" listed an all-time high of 57 co-authors. It, too, failed to make the ballot.

Some citizens launch initiatives aware that qualifying them will be difficult but do so to get media coverage for their measure, or to give their issue legitimacy. For example, Barton Gilbert, in the 1970s and '80s, and currently Jack Herer have promoted efforts to legalize marijuana under certain circumstances — an issue the Legislature has been reluctant to take on. None has ever made the ballot.

Said Robert Wilson, "I didn't even try to qualify many of my [gambling] initiatives. I kept reintroducing them because this was my idea — my way of maintaining a kind of patent on the idea."

A fair number of private-citizen initiatives are filed because particular interests such as doctors, lawyers, teachers or insurance companies have a virtual veto over hostile legislation. Thus, to circumvent the power these groups hold over the Legislature, proponents resort to initiatives such as single-payer state health system, school vouchers or "pay at

Illustration by Mike Tofanelli

the pump" no-fault auto insurance.

Some citizen initiatives promote non-traditional approaches to government. Some of those filed over the last two years:

Matt Dillon proposes a 24-hour-a-day, 365-days-a-year telephone voting system on propositions submitted to voters.

Former Alaska Senator Mike Gravel would allow California citizens a chance to participate in a world constitutional convention to establish global governance. It appropriates 25 cents per California resident from the general fund to help finance the effort.

Cheryl Fort wants to amend the preamble to the state's Constitution.

Norman Bedford wants to implant facial identifying numbers subcutaneously on released violent felons.

Robert Bell proposes that California secede from the Union and become an independent nation.

Eurica Californiaa wants laws on nudity to apply to males and females equally, bare chests and all.

Occasionally, initiatives sponsored by private citizens have qualified. In the 1970s Ed and Joyce Koupal, after failing to qualify a recall of Governor Ronald Reagan, left Sacramento and moved to signature-rich Los Angeles. Activists — mainly students and housewives — were organized into the People's Lobby, a petition-sponsoring group that promoted

liberal causes. With minimal financial resources but dedicated volunteers and a no-nonsense approach to gathering signatures, they succeeded in qualifying several of their initiatives. Ironically, one novice who learned at their knee was Howard Jarvis, himself a right-wing ideologue.

And then there were Jarvis and Gann. Prior to Proposition 13, Jarvis and Gann had failed to qualify any of their six initiatives. After Proposition 13, they jointly or separately succeeded in qualifying a number of measures, with several winning voter approval. They also established two organizations that promote conservative causes via the ballot box.

The most-recent heir-apparent to the Jarvis-Gann legacy is Mike Reynolds, a Fresno native whose 18-year-old daughter was murdered by a paroled felon after she refused to give him her purse. Reynolds labored for years to pass stiffer penalties for violent felons, only to see his effort crushed in a Democrat-dominated Legislature. In 1993, Reynolds went the initiative route — his cause helped when Petaluma 12-year-old Polly Klaas was kidnapped and murdered by an ex-con with a history of violent crime. His proposal became the "three strikes and you're out" initiative of 1994 — Proposition 184.

In addition, public-interest lobby groups with modest financial resources — for example, Common Cause, the American Cancer Society, Campaign California and Californians Against Waste — using mostly dedicated volunteer signature collectors have sometimes been able to qualify petitions. Another, the California Planning and Conservation League, has enlisted high-powered and high-paying allies to fund its initiatives, mostly by writing shares of the spoils into the initiative on behalf of those it seeks as co-sponsors. This "Christmas tree" approach has succeeded in qualifying and passing ballot measures in the 1990s. In addition, the Ross Perot-inspired United We Stand, led by state chair Kirk McKenzie, attempted to qualify four separate initiative proposals in 1994 but failed.

Much of the criticism concerning ballot-box lawmaking — use of counter-initiatives; paid signature-gathering; partisan game-playing; and expensive, duplicitous campaigns — can be tied to elected officials and financially powerful interest groups who seem able to buy their way onto the ballot at a whim. But it is the Howard Jarvises, Paul Ganns and Robert Wilsons of the world — underfunded grass-roots citizens or groups with altruistic, irksome, wacky, innovative, naive or even unconstitutional proposals — that more closely reflect what Progressives had in mind when they advanced the initiative process nearly a century ago. 🏛

Paying the tab for recall elections

Assemblyman Mike Machado was the target of a recall election in 1995. The attempt failed, but the Linden Democrat wants the state to pay the nearly $1 million it cost Machado to defend himself.

By Charles M. Price

Reprinted from *California Journal*, June 1996

Mike Machado seems an unlikely target for Republicans. A conservative Democrat from the rural San Joaquin Valley, Machado now and then breaks with his Assembly Democratic colleagues to throw his lot in with the GOP on policy matters. Only this past April, for instance, Machado was the lone Democrat to vote in favor of Governor Pete Wilson's proposed 15 percent tax cut.

But a year ago, Machado was very much in the GOP's crosshairs because he was the wrong guy in the wrong place at the wrong time. The setting was the speakership wars which wracked the Assembly following the 1994 elections. Machado had voted for his own party's nominee as speaker — then-Assemblyman Willie Brown Jr. (D-San Francisco). And that vote gave Republicans the pretext to employ a little-used tactic to try to oust Machado from office — the recall election.

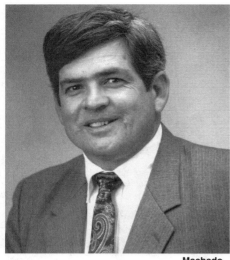

Machado

The recall effort against Machado ultimately failed. But the Linden lawmaker was not one to forgive and forget. If the recall itself was rare prior to 1995, Machado's subsequent action was even more extraordinary: He asked the state of California — through the Board of Control — to reimburse his campaign for the $889,000 cost of defending himself against the recall. Machado and his allies contend that the state constitution provides for the reimbursement, and that it is fair that he be made whole after voters turned back the recall effort. Critics of his action argue that the notion of reimbursement, if upheld, might deter recall efforts against other officials.

Machado found himself at the heart of this controversy because he was caught up in recall mania — the "string 'em up" attitude fostered by Assembly Republicans who sought revenge on two of their own members: Republican-turned-independent Paul Horcher of Diamond Bar and Doris Allen of Cypress. In separate incidents, the pair had deprived Republicans of the speakership after the GOP had gained a 41-vote majority in the lower house during the 1994 elections. First, Horcher voted for Democrat Willie Brown Jr. for speaker. Then, Allen took the speakership for herself with the help of Democratic votes, a maneuver also engineered by Brown.

To punish the dissidents and keep other potential malcontents in line, Assembly Republican leaders applied the seldom-used recall procedure. Under this process, recall activists collect sufficient signatures from registered voters in a member's district within a stipulated time period, and the member is forced to stand for election. If a majority of those voting in that election opt for recall, the member is removed from office immediately and is replaced by whichever candidate receives the most votes from a slate of hopefuls who run in the same election. Both Horcher and Allen met this fate and were replaced in the Legislature.

But Machado was targeted for a different reason. On the surface, Republicans said that Machado ought to be removed because he had promised during his 1994 election campaign to exercise independent judgment when voting for speaker. Then, these Republicans claimed, Machado had the audacity to vote for his *own* party's choice — Willie Brown Jr.

But the real reason that Republicans went after Machado is more simple and more crass: They thought he could be had, and his removal would provide personal gain for the recall leaders — Assemblyman Larry Bowler (R-Elk Grove); Dean Andal, a member of the Board of Equalization who formerly represented Machado's district in the Assembly; and Senate Minority Leader Rob Hurtt (R-Garden Grove), who provided seed money for the recall's signature drive.

Machado was viewed as vulnerable because his 1994 margin of victory was only a few hundred votes. In addition,

had the recall succeeded, Bowler would have been well positioned to challenge Senator Pat Johnston (D-Stockton) in his 1996 re-election and thus provide Republicans — and Hurtt — with another vote in a closely divided Senate.

But the plan misfired. As Republican political consultant and recall expert Tony Quinn noted, "In Horcher's and Allen's Southern California, high Republican registration districts, there was intense opposition to Willie Brown and those Republicans who collaborated with him. In Machado's Stockton district, Democrats turned the tables on the Republicans. They argued that Southern California politicians were trying to tell them who their assemblymember should be. It was a very effective message."

Even some Republicans thought the Machado recall effort was unwise. For example, Assemblyman Bernie Richter (R-Chico) considered the Machado recall wrong. "It was an attack on the validity of the election results," he argued. "That's banana republic."

Using the recall to oust a state legislator still is a rare event, although less rare today. Prior to 1994, only three had had to fight off such a threat in the 83 years since the recall was first placed into the state constitution in 1911. Since 1994, however, four members have faced recalls — Horcher, Machado and Allen in 1995 and former Senate President pro Tempore David Roberti (D-Van Nuys) in 1994. Roberti successfully defeated an effort launched by gun enthusiasts angry over his sponsorship of a ban on assault weapons. Although the Allen recall last December was the last in the current spasm of recalls, the successes against recalcitrant colleagues suggest the procedure could be used again as a disciplinary tactic.

But the spate of recalls also has renewed a long-standing debate over their value. Critics contend that recalls are too easy to put on the ballot, are costly to local governments and taxpayers, foster "down and dirty" campaigns, poison the already bitter mood in the Legislature and should be used only as a last resort, not to discipline measures or to reverse the results of a close election. Proponents, on the other hand, say that the threat helps keep public officials attuned to their constituents. Citing the godfather of recalls, Progressive Hiram Johnson, they argue that the recall was never intended as a last resort but as a "precautionary measure to remove recalcitrant officials."

"The original idea for the recall was to reduce the power of the political boss and party machine," noted Quinn. "Progressives were angry with elected officials who did whatever their boss told them to do." According to Quinn, the recent GOP-inspired recalls were aimed at overthrowing the formerly, all-powerful speaker, Willie Brown, and very much in the Progressive tradition.

But one facet of the recall law has yet to play itself out. Article 2, Section 18, of the California Constitution reads, "A State officer who is not recalled shall be reimbursed by the State for the officer's recall election expenses legally and personally incurred." Evidently, it was placed in the constitution to discourage capricious use of the procedure. Incumbents who were vindicated in a recall would have their recall election expenses paid.

This reimbursement feature applies only to state recalls, not to local efforts. Nor is it a feature in any of the other 14 states that provide for recalls of state officials. To date, only three California legislators have beaten back recalls and thus were eligible for reimbursement: James C. Owens in 1914,

Roberti in 1994 and Machado. Neither Owens nor Roberti filed a claim. Roberti said that he considered requesting a reimbursement for recall expenses but decided against it.

"I didn't apply for reimbursement because this recall provision is very vague," Roberti explained. "The major problem is you'd have to establish the fact that the money you're requesting was your's personally and not the campaign's. Also, it's a very long process. The claim has to go to the Board of Control and, if they approve, to the Legislature and governor. There would have been a lot of public debate about whether I deserved the money." For Roberti, it wasn't worth it, and now his one year statute of limitations has run out.

Machado, on the other hand, is pushing forward. He thinks the amount he should receive "should be defined as the total amount of money I spent to defend myself, $889,000." Machado has promised that if his request is approved, he will give San Joaquin County $150,400 to pay for half of the cost accruing to the county to conduct the election.

"I think that Larry Bowler and Dean Andal ... should put their money where their mouth's are," Machado said. "They should offer to pay the other half of San Joaquin County's expenses for the recall." For his part, Bowler tried with House Resolution 18, designed to compensate San Joaquin County for conducting the recall election. The measure died in Rules Committee.

Machado's reimbursement claim has been submitted to the State Board of Control by his attorney, Joe Remcho. The board is responsible for governing claims against the state for money or damages. After input from its staff and Department of Finance consultants, and following a public hearing on the matter, the three-member board will make its decision. The board currently is made up of Democratic state Controller Kathleen Connell and two appointees of Governor Pete Wilson — Chairman and Director of General Services Peter G. Stamison and a public member Bennie O'Brien. If they recommend reimbursement, the Machado claim, along with other civil claims against the state and victims of crimes claims, will be incorporated into an omnibus bill introduced in the Legislature. If the board rules against Machado or recommends an amount of compensation less than what Machado believes is fair, he may take the matter to court. In the Legislature, the Board of Control's claims bill goes to the two houses' fiscal committees for approval, floor votes, and then submission to the governor for is signature or blue pencil.

Given the fact that Machado's request for reimbursement is unprecedented, and because the constitution is vague on this point — "expenses legally and personally incurred" — and due to the highly charged partisan nature of the three speakership-related recalls, how much money Machado will receive is very much in doubt.

Not surprisingly, some are contemptuous of Machado's request. "We view this as a publicity stunt," said Bowler Chief of Staff Don Ediger. "It's not a legitimate claim. He's trying to manipulate the media and portray himself as a victim. ...Why should state taxpayers have to fund Machado's recall expenses when he displayed zero restraint in spending on the race? Should we reward financial mismanagement?" Ediger argues that the reimbursement feature was designed when a recall campaign's total budget might be a few hundred dollars — most of it being the incumbent's own money. "But it was never intended to cover the [incumbent's] total expenses in a modern recall campaign." Echoing this sentiment, Quinn said, "I think this reimbursement feature is a bad idea. Why don't we just reimburse everyone who wins an election for their expenses?"

Richter, on the other hand, thinks "[reimbursement] a good idea, although it should be made crystal clear in the constitution exactly what expenses should be reimbursed."

Besides being compensated for his recall expenses and providing San Joaquin County money for conducting the election, Machado has one further objective in pursuing this quest: to quell what he believes is abuse of the recall process for partisan advantage.

"Progressives put the reimbursement feature as a protective mechanism," said Tim Riordan, Machado's chief of staff. "By providing a reimbursement, some people may think twice about pursuing a frivolous recall in the future."

But Assemblyman Phil Isenberg (D-Sacramento) doubts that reimbursement will deter future recall efforts. "Machado will be reimbursed by state taxpayer funds, not [by] the people leading the recall drive," he said. "The people you want to deter are those using the recall as an election technique or strategy."

Machado himself has introduced AB 2782, which would require the state — not local governments — to pay for the costs of recalls aimed at state officials.

Update

In 1997 the three members Board of Control rejected Assemblyman Mike Machado's requests to recieve reimbursement for his expenses in his winning recall effort. The Board ruled that the state constitution stipulates that only those recall expenses "personally and legally incurred" qualify for compensation. Machado had neither.

Meanwhile, his unusual request for reimbursement adds yet another wrinkle to a recall saga that already has changed the face of the Legislature. 🏛

Charles Price is a professor of political science at California State University, Chico, and a frequent contributor to California Journal.

LOCAL GOVERNMENT

One reason why Californians have so many elections and frequently such long ballots is that the state has a complex system of local government. Every citizen in the state probably is a resident of a dozen or more units of local government, among them:

Counties. The state has 58 counties (counting San Francisco), some of which are governed by general state law and others by charters (similar to constitutions) voted by the people.

Cities. Most Californians live in one of the state's 470 cities, but some live in unincorporated areas in which municipal services are provided by the county and special districts. General law cities (384) operate through a structure established by state law. Charter cities have more flexibility in their structure and procedures.

City-county. San Francisco is a combined city and county operating under a charter.

School districts. Public schools from kindergarten through 12th grade are operated by independent districts with directly elected governing boards. There are about 1200 school districts in the state.

Community college districts. Directly elected trustees also run community colleges, which provide freshman and sophomore courses.

Special districts. These can vary from large regional districts such as the Metropolitan Water District in Los Angeles to a local mosquito-abatement district. There are more than 3400 special districts formed to provide specific services for a defined area. Most directors are elected by the public.

Local Agency Formation Commissions. Each county has a commission that serves as clearinghouse for annexation of territory by a local agency and for formation of new cities.

Regional governments. There are no all-powerful regional governments in California, but there are numerous limited-purpose regional agencies such as the Bay Area Air Pollution Control District, Rapid Transit District and Sewer Service Agency. Efforts have been underway for years to enact a powerful regional government for the San Francisco area. There are several voluntary associations of local governmental agencies designed to help resolve regional problems; these include the Association of Bay Area Governments and the Southern California Association of Governments.

City and county government

Counties are run by boards of supervisors elected by the public, usually by district. In most counties, the board appoints an administrative officer to supervise the details of county government. Counties also have other directly elected officials, such as the district attorney, the sheriff and the assessor.

Cities are operated under a variety of systems. Under one basic arrangement not widely used, the strong-mayor system, the mayor is the chief-administrative officer of the city, and policy is set by the council. The more common system establishes the mayor, who may be elected either by the people or by the council, as the ceremonial chief of the city and puts the administration of municipal affairs under the control of a powerful city manager or administrator. The council has the power to appoint and remove the manager. Under this council-manager form of government, the council is supposed to be limited to the setting of policy, but there have been a few cases in which a mayor, by virtue of a strong personality, had been able to run the city government, relegating the manager to the role of errand boy.

More frequently, however, the manager, by virtue of the fact that he is a full-time employee with a large staff, plays a role as large as or even greater than the council in establishing policy.

Special districts are usually administered by a superintendent, general manager or other executive selected by the governing board. 🏛

Counties
in crisis

Problems assailing Los Angeles and Orange counties once again raise questions about the relationship between state and local governments, and the need to pay for increased services with diminished resources.

By Laureen Lazarovici

Reprinted from *California Journal*, November 1995

Lassen County no longer has a department of animal control. If any critters get out of hand, residents have to call the cops. "In egregious cases, a deputy goes out," says county administrative officer William Bixby. In the Sacramento County suburb of Elk Grove, the special fire district is considering charging homeowners $500 dollars to put out a blaze. Los Angeles County came only days away from virtually shutting down its public health-care system, and Orange County has the dubious honor of being the largest municipal entity in the nation to declare bankruptcy.

Why are California counties in a seemingly continuous state of crisis — and what are leaders trying to do about it?

Observers agree that the 1978 passage of Proposition 13 and the property tax shifts in the early '90s from municipalities to the state are the root causes of the counties' woes. How to solve these problems yields less agreement, however. Liberals argue for more taxes, while conservatives focus on privatization of services. Transcending ideology is a larger debate over a total overhaul of the relationship between state and county government.

Southern California this year provided stark case studies of counties' dire straits. In Los Angeles, years of stop-gap measures to balance the budget and of increasing demands on services — one in five residents receives some sort of public assistance — resulted in a $1.2 billion deficit. County officials considered closing Los Angeles' largest public hospital, raising the specter of people literally dying in the streets. Plans for only slightly less drastic closures of other public-health facilities were drawn up as alternatives. Only after President Bill Clinton came up with $364 million in federal funds to rescue and restructure the ailing county health-care system was a complete meltdown avoided (see "Washington Perspective," page 40).

Neighboring Orange County, meanwhile, struggled to climb out of bankruptcy. During the 1980s, then-Treasurer Robert Citron leveraged the county's investment pool into risky and exotic investments. No one raised an eyebrow as long as the financial markets were going his way. At one point, up to one-third of the county's budget came from interest income, making up for losses from other sources. But then the market started going the opposite direction than the way Citron bet, resulting in $1.7 billion in losses. Creditors couldn't be paid, and the county sought protection from the bankruptcy court. Under pressure from an emergency chief administrative officer, county supervisors reluctantly placed a sales-tax measure on the ballot to pay for the shortfall. It failed miserably. But in the closing days of the legislative session, relief came in the form of funds shifted from transit, flood control, park and redevelopment agencies.

Both counties have solvency in sight — for now. But as California State Association of Counties deputy director Dan Wall points out, "What brought Orange County to the edge of the cliff were the same forces that brought L.A. — and other counties — to the edge. The underlying circumstances are identical." Moreover, he adds, "None of the fundamental relationships have changed with these patchwork solutions."

Those underlying circumstances and fundamental relationships can be traced back to Proposition 13. That taxpayer revolt initiative capped property taxes and shifted revenue-raising authority away from counties and to the state. But counties still retained the responsibility for providing services. Proposition 13, in effect, delinked raising revenues from providing services. In the post-13 environment, the state government cushioned the blow to counties by taking over some of their health and welfare programs and by returning some property tax money to them. That worked — as long as the state could afford it. When the recession hit statewide, Sacramento in effect told the counties, "We want our money back." In 1992 and 1993 the state budget shifted tax money away from the counties and into the schools. For a large county like Los Angeles, that meant a loss of $1 billion. The legislative analyst's office cites the shift as one of the primary reasons for Los Angeles' budget crisis.

Proposition 13 changed the relationship between the counties and the states. The property tax shifts merely papered over, but didn't change the structure of that relationship. "The root problem is county boards have control over neither revenue nor expenditures," says Wall. On the revenue side, counties can't raise property taxes at all. They are allowed to raise general taxes with a majority vote of the people and special taxes with a two-thirds vote — a requirement recently upheld by the State Supreme Court. On the expenditure side, counties are bound by state and federal mandates, and much of their spending is indexed to ever-growing caseloads. Ten years ago, 15 percent to 20 percent of a county budget was discretionary. Now, it's down to 5 percent to 7 percent.

Liberal critics look at the revenue side of the equation. "Ultimately we're going to have to reform Prop. 13," says Lenny Goldberg, executive director of the California Tax Reform Association. "One simple sentence would do it: 'Non-residential property shall be assessed at market value,'" he says. Simple, but politically explosive. Ending Proposition 13's protection of commercial property has been a non-starter for years. Other tax measures have passed — notably 1993's Proposition 172, which permanently extended a special half-cent sales tax for public safety — but most don't fare well. This year, Los Angeles County sought the authority to tax alcohol and tobacco, but bills allowing that authority didn't even come close to getting out of the Legislature, although some officials now talk about a statewide ballot measure next November to that effect. Orange County's bankruptcy relief tax flopped by a wide margin at the polls.

In contrast, conservative critics focus on the expenditure side of the ledger. Early in Orange County's bankruptcy crisis, for example, the all-Republican legislative delegation introduced a carload of measures to privatize county services and relax state mandates on services. The bills went nowhere, but they did dramatize the difference in approaches to fixing county financing.

Tinkering with taxes and mandate relief within the current structure is just a shell game, according to those trying to look at the big picture. The Constitutional Revision Commission, empaneled to examine a whole range of state dysfunctions, has drafted an ambitious plan to bring together local governments — county, cities, special districts — in community charters to consolidate local services. Both general and special local taxes would be subject to majority votes, and property taxes would be allowed to be raised with the consent of two thirds of the voters.

Other reformers are examining the relationship between counties and the electorate. "A board of supervisors is a 19th century institution," says Peter Detwiler, former consultant to the Senate Local Government Committee. "A board blends legislative and executive responsibilities, and it doesn't do either well. The California Constitution ought to separate these functions and reduce the size of districts, increasing the number of supervisors. There should be a directly elected county mayor and reduce the number of directly elected department heads." The fact that some counties can't solve crises within their own governmental structures is proof of the need for reform, says Detwiler. "Why did L.A. appoint a health czar?" he wonders, referring to former Assemblyman Burt Margolin (D-Los Angeles). "We have to do extraordinary things when ordinary things don't work."

Many political pitfalls stand in the way of reform. Not the least of them is a large gulf of distrust and rivalry between state and local elected officials. Orange County Supervisor Marian Bergeson has a unique perspective on that issue, given that she was a Republican state senator for 16 years before taking her current post. "Until I actually served as a supervisor, I hadn't realized the damage Sacramento had done, especially in terms of mandates," she says. Lawmakers trying to solve the Los Angeles and Orange county problems were constantly laying blame on one another. Orange County legislators chastised the board of supervisors for dragging its feet on coming up with a recovery plan. Los Angeles legislators said supervisors got themselves in the mess, while supervisors shot back that it was their own delegation that went along with the devastating property tax shifts. When Los Angeles state officials finally put together a plan authorizing a loan from the local transit agency to the county, supervisors snubbed them by turning it down.

Any type of reform would necessarily trample on turf and gore some sacred cows, including police agencies. "No one is talking about the inefficiencies in law enforcement," says CSAC's Wall. "Why do we need city and county departments? Why not consolidate? It's politically taboo. It's about turf."

Perhaps the starkest political reality is that counties serve politically powerless constituencies: those on welfare, those who use public hospitals, those going through the court system. They are not the ones going to the polls every time a special tax is on the ballot. "Our clients are not the ones who show up for fund raisers," observes Bergeson ruefully.

Increasingly, voters are asking themselves not which governmental entity ought to be providing these services but whether government should be providing them at all. This larger question haunts the debate over reforming counties or even doing away with them altogether. "What kind of Hobbesian choices are we going to have to make?" asks Dave Oppenheim, senior legislative analyst for CSAC. "The safety net that everyone depends on — the courts as well as health and welfare — is in jeopardy. The service responsibilities don't go away. Doing away with counties doesn't get to the real problem." 🏛

Breaking up

Los Angeles

by Sherry Bebitch Jeffe

Reprinted from *California Journal*, August 1996

A mega city with mega problems, the state's biggest metropolis is beset by disgruntled citizens who want to shatter it into diverse pieces.

Humorist Mort Sahl once called Los Angeles "a hundred suburbs in search of a city." These days, a more apt description might be "a hundred suburbs looking to flee the city." Well, not exactly a hundred. But there are rumblings of dissatisfaction — with the size, the distance and the unresponsiveness of city government — that have led communities from the Harbor area in the south to the San Fernando Valley in the north to contemplate the idea of leaving Los Angeles.

What has triggered this flirtation with secession? Is Los Angeles fraying? Has it become too large geographically? Too unwieldy politically? Too diverse? Has government become too indulgent to some at the expense of others? Or are Angelenos just in a cranky mood?

In a word, yes. Said Los Angeles City Councilman Hal Bernson, who represents a Valley district: "I think there is an attitude problem. I don't think we think as a city any more."

Some would argue that the biggest "attitude problem" is the San Fernando Valley's. The union of "the Valley" and the City of Los Angeles was a shotgun marriage to begin with, driven by San Fernando's need for water — which began flowing from the Owens Valley Project to Los Angeles in 1913. Inevitably and grudgingly, Valleyites acceded to the city's demand for annexation in exchange for water. Today,

Sherry Bebitch Jeffe teaches at the Claremont Graduate School and is a contributing editor to California Journal.

the Valley is a 222-square-mile area, separated from the rest of Los Angeles by the Santa Monica Mountains. It comprises about 35 percent of the city's population and is the heart of its "middle class."

The Valley also is home to growing agitation to seek a divorce from Los Angeles. Secession proponents argue that the Valley doesn't get the services — or the attention from distant civic leaders — it deserves. Activists have rallied around legislation (AB 2043) authored by Assemblywoman Paula Boland (R-Granada Hills) that could make it easier to secede. The bill would nullify the City Council's veto over secession and allow communities the right of "self-determination" at the ballot box. Argues Boland, "Eight people [on the Los Angeles City Council] from over the hill shouldn't control the lives of 1.3 million people." The Boland bill, however, goes beyond process to the question of what Los Angeles will become as it enters the 21st century. Will its various parts spin off into homogenous enclaves and abandon the notion of a diverse world city?

A *Los Angeles Times* Poll taken in June showed that, despite an uptick in the Los Angeles economy and a downturn in crime statistics, dissatisfaction with city government and institutions persists. Angelenos are generally pessimistic about the direction city life is taking. And the frustration and anxiety that many feel have given increased impetus to break-away talk.

Throughout history, secession movements have been

driven by common themes: the desire for local control and a smaller, closer, more responsive — and less costly — government. For example, tradition has it that in 1850, the Mother Lode town of Rough and Ready declared itself a new nation in reaction to a mining tax that enraged the locals. But, said writer Charles Hillinger, the residents "soon tired of being an independent republic and after 12 weeks threw in the towel" and rejoined California and the union. More recently, secession movements have popped up in the borough of Staten Island in New York City, and in conservative, middle-class West Seattle, Washington. And last year, after decades of battling over whether the French-speaking province of Quebec should leave Canada, Quebec separatists narrowly lost a divisive referendum on independence.

The modern Valley secession movement began in 1975 with the formation of the Committee Investigating Valley Independent City/County (CIVICC), which claimed "Valley Taxpayers Don't Get Their Fair Share." It was stoked by a council redistricting that secessionists felt diluted the Valley's voice in City Hall, and by the threat of mandatory busing to suburban schools.

The Boland bill was first introduced three years ago but was quickly withdrawn. Faced with strong opposition by Democrats, who controlled both houses of the Legislature, Boland opted instead to concentrate on legislation to ease the way for dismantling the gargantuan Los Angeles Unified School District (LAUSD) — which had become a symbol of bureaucratic failure and urban deterioration. That legislation, which had its genesis in the Valley-based anti-busing movement in the 1970s, passed last year — with an assist from Senator Tom Hayden (D-Santa Monica), whose district contains pockets of the Valley. Currently, disgruntled parents and politicians throughout the city are urging the break-up of LAUSD into smaller, more locally accountable units. So far none of these break-away attempts have come to fruition. But that doesn't mean this latest debate should be ignored. It can help us understand the psyche of Los Angeles.

First of all, reports of the city's imminent geographical demise are exaggerated. Asked how they felt "in general ... about communities seceding from the city of Los Angeles," only 35 percent of the respondents to the *Times* poll supported a community's right to break away; 47 percent opposed it. And the poll indicated only "lukewarm support" for Valley secession, specifically. Even if the Boland bill were law, secession would not be a slam-dunk. The poll showed that only 45 percent of Valley residents — well below the required majority — would vote to secede if the election were held today.

Support for splitting up the city is strongest among Anglo and more affluent Angelenos — who happen to live predominantly in the Valley and on the city's upscale Westside. Opposition is greatest among African-Americans and Latinos, who are more likely to be found in the urban core of southern and central Los Angeles. On the matter of the Valley's secession, 61 percent of blacks and 56 percent of Latinos were opposed, compared with only 38 percent of the Anglos. The geographical split underscores the dynamics of race and class that infuse the issue of secession.

Valley residents, in particular, see themselves as "short-changed" by city government. And 57 percent of Valley poll respondents said they paid more in city taxes than they got back in services (only 30 percent of all respondents agreed with that perception).

It is not only the Valley secession movement that defines a discontented city tugged by class and race on issues of governance and policy. There is a parallel thrust to dismantle LAUSD that also traces its geographical roots to the Valley and shares the suburbs' anti-bureaucracy, pro-local control philosophy. Some insist the success of Boland's school district break-up bill gave new impetus to the Valley secession movement. And poll data on attitudes toward the school district break-up show similar divisions on the basis of race and class.

Among Anglos, the percentage of respondents to the *Times* poll who favored dismantling LAUSD was 66 percent. Conversely, only 32 percent of African-American respondents and 35 percent of Latinos support a school district break-up. There was also greater support for decentralization among affluent respondents and Westside and Valley residents. Less well-off respondents and residents of Central and South Los Angeles were more opposed to dismantling the school system.

Equally revealing are attitudes of Angelenos toward their most visible leaders: Mayor Richard Riordan and Police Chief Willie Williams. Williams, the LAPD's first African-American chief, came on board in 1992 — in the aftermath of the Rodney King verdicts — to help heal the wounds of a divided city and restore trust and confidence in a police department under attack for racism and brutality. Early on, Williams rode high in the estimation of Los Angeles' citizens. Then a series of ethical and leadership questions began to dog him and put him at odds with Riordan and several members of the City Council.

The June poll numbers showed Williams' city-wide job approval rating (56 percent) higher than that of the mayor (46 percent) and City Council (34 percent). But both Riordan and Williams appear to be suffering from their lengthening tenure in politics and government. The mayor's job rating has slid 13 points since 1994; the chief's has tumbled 17 points (from a career high of 73 percent in 1994).

It appears the longer both men serve in a system that is seen by Angelenos as dysfunctional, the more they are perceived as part of the problem. Therefore, the less they are trusted to solve it.

Beyond a growing negativism toward their leaders, Angelenos' attitudes toward Riordan and Williams differ — yet again — by race and region. Mayor Riordan's approval rating among Anglo respondents to the *Times* poll was 60 percent, but only 30 percent among African-Americans and 34 percent among Latinos. Riordan's approval rating is highest in the affluent Westside (60 percent) and lowest (37 percent) in the inner-city south area. On the other hand, Williams' approval rating is highest among blacks (68 percent) and Latinos (62 percent) and in the urban south (65 percent) and central (64 percent) areas. It is lowest among Anglos (49 percent) and in the Valley (50 percent) and on the Westside (42 percent).

These figures suggest that the future of Williams could become a hot issue in the 1997 election year. Under police reforms enacted in response to recommendations by a citizens commission in the wake of the King beating, Williams' contract is up for renewal next year — at the end of his first five-year term. Overall public opinion is split over his rehiring, according to the *Times* poll (44 percent in favor and 43 percent opposed). However, African-Americans solidly supported Williams, with 72 percent favoring renewal and only 19 percent opposed.

What does this pattern of perception mean for the future of Los Angeles? For attempts to reinvent its government? What solutions are being offered to assuage the frustration and division highlighted by the secession debate?

Most reforms aim to blunt the impact of Boland's bill and keep the city intact. "Neighborhood" — as in control, empowerment, governance — appears to be the operative buzzword. In his annual State of the City address last April, Riordan called for a "neighborhood convention" that would bring residents from throughout Los Angeles together to discuss their concerns and expectations. "It is up to the neighborhoods to solve their problems," Riordan said.

Riordan borrowed his plan from Valley Councilman Joel Wachs, who first proposed it during his unsuccessful run for mayor in 1993. In the wake of renewed interest in Valley secession, Wachs has refloated his proposal, which would create 103 "neighborhood councils" to advise the city's elected officials on matters ranging from planning decisions to community policing. The nebulous plan is already being attacked by some Valley activists as unresponsive to demands for more local control over government decisions.

Hayden has entered the fray with his own proposal "to decentralize power throughout Los Angeles to neighborhood levels" through "democratically elected neighborhood representatives taking part in decisions concerning zoning, growth and the environment." A charter amendment incorporating his plan would be placed on the city ballot next year — just in time to offer Hayden a convenient platform for a possible mayoral run.

Another Valley councilman, Arthur Alarcon, has suggested examining other alternatives to Valley secession, including the "charter school model" of local control over decision-making and the creation of community improvement districts to allow a community to raise "revenue that can only be used in that community."

Councilman Mike Feuer, whose district straddles the Santa Monica Mountains, has embraced a proposal by a group of influential Valley business organizations, community and civic leaders for a Charter Reform Commission to revise Los Angeles' 71-year-old, 694-page charter. The citizens' group would be empowered to garner public opinion on restructuring city government and then create a new charter to be put on the ballot for voter approval.

City Council members appear to be embracing this plan. After all, it could take at least three years to complete the process — long enough for them to defer difficult decisions and wait for term limits to kick in or the political winds to shift.

The reforms that have come out of the current secession debate may address geographic distance between citizens and their government. But they do little to address the chasms of class and race that separate Los Angeles communities. In the dispersion of governance to the city's neighborhoods, there is further potential for balkanization.

The "quick fixes" and palliatives that have begun to surface in the wake of the Boland bill offer no silver bullet that will end the frustration, anxiety, alienation and divisiveness that mark life and governance for many Angelenos. In the end, the risk is not that Los Angeles is too big or too unwieldly. It is that its citizens can't — or won't — agree on what it should be. And that its leaders, unable to muster consensus, simply continue to punt.

Perhaps the most chilling insight into the psyche of Los Angeles came at a Valley meeting on the Boland bill. "We got money and they don't," someone growled. "Screw 'em." 🏛

Managed care struggles to come of age

After more than a decade of explosive growth, HMOs find themselves at the core of a controversy over their priorities. Are they driven by the corporate urge to make money, or by the societal ethos to provide quality health care? And are the two compatible?

By Mary Beth Barber
Reprinted from *California Journal*, April 1996

anaged care as a concept has been around since World War II, when a multi-faceted steel and ship-building conglomerate run by the late Henry Kaiser provided its own doctors to workers and their families. But the benchmark year for managed care is 1982, for that is the year that the Legislature pushed the concept for those who depended on government for health care — thrusting the world of medicine firmly into the competitive marketplace.

"Managed care" actually is an umbrella term for a number of health plans that try to control costs through preventive care and "capitation" of costs — establishing a set annual fee per enrollee, regardless of the level of health care that ultimately is provided. Its most common manifestation, the health-maintenance organization (HMO) also is varied, although most consumers think of the giant Kaiser Permanente — the current incarnation of Henry Kaiser's program — where doctors are employed by the organization.

But Kaiser actually is the exception. The more common forms are:
• contract HMOs, that deal with one medical group;
• network HMOs, that work with a handful of providers; and,
• independent practice association HMOs (IPAs), that contract with doctors who also serve non-HMO patients.

Managed-care programs didn't begin to spread, however, until after California started to feel fiscal pressure in the wake of Proposition 13 — the 1978 property tax-slashing initiative. Faced with shrinking government revenues, especially at the county level, the Legislature in 1981 found itself in a difficult position when it came to that part of the population that depended on

---

Mary Beth Barber, a former assistant editor of California Journal, *is a freelance writer in San Francisco.*

Steve Thompson

Quite simply, profits accrue and premiums are reduced if less care is rendered. The for-profit HMOs are in the business of making money.

— Thompson

government for health care — basically, those who were too poor to afford their own medical services and who were served through the state's MediCal program, which draws funding from federal, state and county sources. The state could either serve fewer MediCal patients or spend less money on each. The state chose to control costs.

Historically, most insurance companies and federal programs have reimbursed doctors and facilities on a "fee-for-service" basis. Patients could see the qualified doctor of their choice, or go to the most convenient hospital or clinic, and those doctors, hospitals and clinics — known as "providers" — charged a wide range of fees for each service rendered to a patient. Insurance companies, or the government, then paid the fee. For a variety of reasons, including the increased costs of more sophisticated technology and the influx of additional money through federal programs such as Medicare and Medicaid, inflation hit the health-care field, increasing costs at nearly three times the national rate of inflation by the early 1980s. The cost of health insurance skyrocketed as insurance companies passed on their increased costs to the folks who paid for that insurance — namely, individual consumers and employers. Employers, in particular, complained to the Legislature.

But it took a MediCal budget near $5 billion to spur lawmakers to action in 1982. The state's solution, as health-care expert Soap Dowell points out, was to inject market-place competition into health care by contracting with doctors who offered favorable rates — rather than by turning the MediCal population loose to see any doctor or hospital. The rates themselves were negotiated and bids were competitive. According to Dowell, the Legislature then was persuaded to give private insurers the same authority that had been given to MediCal, extending marketplace competition to the private sector as well. It also helped insurers compete more adequately with the few HMOs because it freed them from the requirement that their clientele be able to choose any physician or hospital and allowed them to contract with an entity known as a Preferred Provider Organization, or PPO. Rather than charge a capitated fee like an HMO, PPOs negotiate fee-for-service rates that are fixed for a given period of time.

If 1982 marks the birth of managed care, then the system now is entering its teen-age years. Like all teen-

agers, it occasionally requires a stern guiding hand. Sometimes, the system behaves responsibly toward its enrollees; at other times, it displays a contemptuous side that often is highlighted by the media. Although it still is growing, managed care is trying to decide what it's going to be when it matures — with doctors, executives and government as mentors tugging it in different directions.

"Managed care is causing a revolution in the way medical care is provided in this country," said Dr. Arnold S. Relman, editor-in-chief emeritus of the *New England Journal of Medicine*. Because the traditional one-on-one doctor-patient relationship has been replaced by medical networks of physicians and other providers, "it erodes the bond between the individual and doctor," said Relman. "The doctor has two masters now: the patient and the company."

Reminding the medical establishment that someone has to foot the bill is not necessarily a bad thing, said Byron Chell, executive director of the California Medical Assistance Commission, the state agency that oversees MediCal hospital contracts, who adds that preventive medicine is the best way to reduce the cost of providing medical care. "I like the idea of a group of doctors working as a team for my health."

Most HMOs created in the early '80s were simply health-insurance companies that converted to a "capitated

model," one that limited physicians and encouraged primary, preventive care. Kaiser, the only major HMO to survive the '70s, was thriving and growing, and nearly all HMOs at that time were non-profit — a situation changed by a proliferation of HMO conversions from non-profit to for-profit over the past 10 years. Currently 13 non-profits exist, including Kaiser. There are 23 for-profit plans available, eight of which once were non-profit.

Exactly how the for-profit factor affects health care is at the core of the current debate over managed care. Profit motive is nothing new in health care. "Since the days of Florence Nightingale, there has always been a for-profit motive in health care," said Kurt Davis, a spokesman for Foundation Health, a for-profit organization.

Yet consumer studies have shown that patients really don't like the notion of a company making money off their health. Myra Snyder, executive director of the California Association of HMOs, pointed out that health care was initially supplied by missionaries as charity. "I don't think we can ever in the United States have ever shed that belief," she said. But whether a company is for-profit or non-profit has little to do with the health care they provide, she contends. "These are not monetary titles, but rather how they are structured. Some non-profits make money, and some for-profits go bankrupt."

The California Medical Association, however, doesn't see the differences as structural. "Quite simply, profits accrue and premiums are reduced if less care is rendered," said Steve Thompson, CMA vice-president for legislative affairs.

"The for-profit HMOs are in the business of making money."

Relman is especially critical of the percentage of profits that go for administration and into stockholders' pockets. Non-profits typically dedicate around 10 percent for non-medical costs; similar costs for for-profits can vary anywhere between 15 to 30 percent.

CMA has been pushing legislation to discourage non-profits from converting to for-profit. Doctors feel their judgment and control over patient care is jeopardized by the profit motive; HMOs charge that doctors bear a grudge because their incomes are dwindling and because many medical specialists are finding themselves squeezed out by organizations that rely more and more on general practitioners.

Government officials like Chell disagree that for-profits can't provide good medical care at low costs. "If they provide the service, who cares?" he said. "You don't have to be dishonest or unethical to make money in health care."

Consumer groups tend to disagree. "The concentration on the bottom line is not what health care needs," said Harry Snyder of the Consumers' Union. He and others cite numerous horror stories to show that HMOs are concerned primarily with the bottom line, at the expense of sound patient care and treatment.

The place where these disagreements are sorted out tends to be government, where managed-care organizations are regulated. But even here, the trail of regulation can be confusing. The law most directly affecting HMOs is the Knox-Keene Act, passed in 1975 and designed to set regulations for all HMOs in California. But from the outset, Knox-Keene regards HMOs as businesses because they are under the purview of the Department of Corporations, not the Department of Health Services or the Department of Insurance.

"I am a long-time HMO enrollee," said Senator Herschel Rosenthal (D-Van Nuys). "Yet it wasn't until I became chairman of the Senate Insurance Committee that I realized that the DOC was responsible for regulating HMOs."

Lately, HMO regulation has been shadowed by a bigger question: What does the government do when a non-profit wants to convert to for-profit? The companies enjoyed tax benefits as non-profits, and executives in those companies stand to make a lot of money from conversion.

"I am disappointed in the non-profits," said Assemblyman Phil Isenberg (D-Sacramento) a few weeks after listening to a pre-conversion process. "The board members emphasized the lack of charity cases they took as a non-profit. Traditionally, non-profits wouldn't ever say that they didn't do charity cases. They all want to convert, so they say they didn't do much."

Many HMOs contend they have had to convert. Making ends meet without the benefit of having access to large amounts of capital — as for-profits do by selling stock — is almost impossible, they say. Competition has made health care a vicious world, and staying afloat is not easy.

"We found ourselves in the worst possible situation," said Leonard Schaeffer, CEO of the recently converted Blue Cross. Established in 1937 as non-profit insurance coverage, Blue Cross wanted to continue providing health care but was in grave danger of going bankrupt. The initial solution, said Schaeffer, was to create a for-profit subsidiary, called WellPoint Health Networks, that would be controlled by the non-profit company board.

In the past, non-profits heading down the for-profit

road were required to compensate in some way for the years of tax breaks accorded to them as non-profits. In the case of Blue Cross, all of its assets — valued at $3 billion — will be contributed to a pair of new charitable foundations. WellPoint will raise additional cash via the sale of stock. Approval of the conversion was announced in mid March.

The creation of WellPoint was well underway and almost approved in the fall of 1994 by the Department of Corporations when then-DOC Director Tom Sayles left and was replaced by Gary Mendoza, who had a different take on the conversion. Blue Cross had assumed that the money it would be required to donate to charity would be low because the conversion to for-profit was only partial, in accordance with the deal Blue Cross had struck with Sayles. But Mendoza required a much larger set-aside — a move that Blue Cross representatives say forced them to completely convert to for-profit status. "It's ironic," said Blue Cross lobbyist Bob Scarlett. "Their actions basically forced us to convert."

Blue Cross agreed to $3 billion, and the company is further required to set aside 5 percent of its assets to the foundations every year as long as Blue Cross exists. The requirement was a move away from the DOC's "hands-off" attitude. But Mendoza thinks that the foundations set up by converted HMOs can solve some of the concerns the public has with for-profit companies. "For the not-for-profits, daily operations are their societal contribution," he said. For-profits have something separate, Mendoza adds. "If the foundations are led in a meaningful way, they can make a significant contribution." Mendoza says he's gotten phone calls from insurance commissioners in other states where Blue Cross plans also are considering converting.

Hospital conversions are the next area that lawmakers such as Isenberg are watching. HMO conversion legislation that mirrors some of Mendoza's requirements for Blue Cross was passed last year. But Isenberg notes a large number of non-profit hospitals are being bought by large for-profit chains. He's working with the Department of Health and the attorney general for future regulation.

The explosion in managed care, and the concern about its growth, isn't confined to the private sector. Both MediCal and the university teaching hospitals have been affected — MediCal for the better and university hospitals for the worse. MediCal is a huge potential market for managed-care companies. "The state is somewhat belatedly recognizing the benefits of managed care," said Department of Health Services Director Kim Belshe.

California has two different HMO models for MediCal. The 12 counties with the highest number of MediCal enrollees are implementing what's called the "two-plan" model. Patients will have a choice of a county-run HMO or a private plan that has contracted with the state. The second model, a pilot project in Sacramento County called geographic managed care (GMC), allows any HMO that meets state requirements to participate. Sacramento MediCal patients now choose from seven different

> I am a long-time HMO enrollee. Yet it wasn't until I became chairman of the Senate Insurance Committee that I realized that the DOC was responsible for regulating HMOs.
> — Herschel Rosenthal

plans. While there have been some implementation problems with the program, such as confusion from school officials about students' health coverage, "geographic managed care is a very positive story," said Belshe.

The biggest advantage for patients is access, continued Belshe. Finding primary-care doctors who would see MediCal patients has never been easy. "They'd end up in the emergency room for something like a child's earache," she said. Now, MediCal patients are on an equal footing with people covered by private insurance.

Opening up MediCal to managed care is also slowly changing managed care, said Belshe. The plans approved for the two-plan models and for the GMC had to adjust for the MediCal population, especially expanding their language capabilities for the culturally diverse MediCal population. "The plans balked at first, but they're coming around," said Belshe. The more culturally diverse a plan is, the more patients it can attract. "Ultimately the plans will conclude that these type of standards make sense in a business way."

Educational institutions, on the other hand, have been hit hard by the managed-care explosion. "For-profit HMOs are not doing their part in education and research," said Dr. Gerald Lazrus, dean of the University of California, Davis, School of Medicine. Only 15 percent of the school's budget comes from the University of California. The other 85 percent is from research grants and clinical reimbursement. "We had previously been able to cross-subsidize from the money that comes from patient care."

If UC-Davis is not able to continue seeing patients in a normal setting — especially primary-care patients — "the opportunity to teach while seeing patients is really compromised," said Lazrus. Before, when teaching hospitals received the majority of MediCal patients, the federal government's medical dollars supported education. "Now the educational dollars are going into those for-profit HMOs," said Lazrus.

The universities aren't the only ones feeling out of control in this brave new health-care world. Rosenthal contends that consumers feel at a loss when it comes to evaluating their insurance. "Who protects their interest in getting reliable information to help them secure quality HMO services?" he said. HMO-initiated studies and polls lack credibility, he contends. The one national organization that monitors and accredits plans, the National Committee on Quality Assurance, has a reputation for independence. But the NCQA was recently sued by an HMO that received an unfavorable report, and Rosenthal thinks the case may taint future analyses.

Proposals for report cards and analyses are floating around the Legislature to encourage HMOs to base their companies on care not costs. But Californians are unique in their acceptance of medicine as a business, said Relman — a concept that has not caught on in the east. Part of the HMO-for-profit trend could be linked to California doctors' attitudes towards medicine. "I think California will be one of the last states to realize that a profession is not a business," said Relman. 🏛

Whither Welfare Reform

Congress' sweeping overhaul of welfare has left state and county governments arguing over who's in control and what will become of those left out of the new law

by Sigrid Bathen

Reprinted from *California Journal*, November 1996

In the baffling, statistics-laden jargon of welfare reform, numbers and categories tend to obscure the people behind them — in California, hundreds of thousands of people, many of them children, the aged and disabled. They get lost in the numbers and categories, and most especially in the stereotype of welfare recipients as being largely unwilling to work.

"I play this out in my class on Child Rights and Remedies," says University of California, San Diego law professor Robert Fellmeth, executive director of the prestigious Children's Advocacy Institute. "I ask them to guess the average age of the typical welfare recipient, and they say 19. Actually, it's 29. The picture is of a minority recipient. The reality is that AFDC [Aid to Families with Dependent Children] recipients are predominantly Caucasian...The stereotype is of a black, 18-year-old teen mother having sex with everyone she can, and I'm this white middle-class person who is supposed to finance it. That's the stereotype. Heaven forbid that reality should intrude."

Supporters of radical welfare reform dismiss advocates like Fellmeth as defenders of a broken status quo. Clearly, it was not his version of reality which was on the minds of Congress and President Bill Clinton in this election year when they approved House Resolution 3734 — The Personal Responsibility and Work Opportunity Reconciliation Act of 1996. As a result, state and county officials are gearing up for the most fundamental changes in federal welfare policies in six decades. The New Deal-era system of federal "entitlements" will end under the sweeping legislation, replaced by a system of "block grants" to states, which then, at least theoretically, will design their own programs within strict federal guidelines. Welfare recipients will be expected to work, and aid will not continue indefinitely. With some exceptions, legal immigrants would lose aid under the federal law.

While many children's ad-vocates predict sharp increases in child hunger, poverty and abuse — as well as general increases in crime, drug abuse and homelessness — under the federal law, state and county officials are scrambling to interpret the 500-page law. And California's counties, already reeling from growing budget deficits and other fiscal calamities, say they have been consulted too little and too late, when the ultimate responsibility for implementing and enforcing the changes rests squarely on their crumbling doorsteps.

"This administration typically spends a lot of time behind closed doors, shades drawn, to assess their options and develop the governor's positions," said Frank Mecca, executive director of the California Welfare Directors Association. "Time is wasted when the administration talks only to itself."

California Social Services Director Eloise Anderson, who held a long-awaited news conference the 9th of October to announce that a preliminary state plan had been submitted to the federal government, says in her typically blunt way that the "third-world" conditions predicted by advocacy groups, already exist — and that they will exist as long as the 60-year-old welfare system is allowed to continue as it has. Anderson insists counties had been consulted in the process and would be consulted further. "They say they weren't heard," she said. "But if we don't do what they tell us to do, does that mean they weren't in the process? They only have a county perspective — we have to look at it across the board, statewide."

Counties will be included in the "public input" process in a series of hearings to be chaired around the state by state Health and Welfare Agency Secretary Sandra Smoley, a former Sacramento County supervisor. The preliminary plan — submitted in part to save the state nearly $200 million in federal funds — includes a 4.9 percent decrease in AFDC (9.8 percent in regions with lower costs of living), which becomes the "Temporary Assistance for Needy Families" (TANF) program under the new federal block grant system. The grant cuts will be effective January 1st. As a result of the federal savings, Anderson said, the state will increase funding for California's GAIN (Greater Avenues to Independence) welfare-to-work program by $60 million, plus $28 million already appropriated by the Legislature.

The state plan affects only AFDC/TANF recipients — the bulk of recipients in California — and specifically does not implement the controversial cuts in aid to legal immigrants. Anderson declined to elaborate on the state response to planned cuts in federal aid for the aged and disabled who are legal citizens — an arena of considerable controversy at the local level — but said the issue is "not a factor" in AFDC/TANF at this point. "The Legislature is going to have to decide whether they pay for non-citizens," she said.

The state plan is clearly not enough for counties, who say they still lack any clear direction from the state nearly three months after the bill was signed by the president. Welfare directors, legal services and community groups remain especially troubled about the impact of the new law on legal immigrants — a provision which the state legislative analyst said will cost California millions of dollars in federal aid — and are pressing to have those aspects of the law ameliorated or repealed.

"We have many people who have been in this country 20, 40, even 50 years," said Kathy Gallagher, chief administrative officer for the Santa Clara County Social Services Agency. "They are 70 or 80 or 90 and they will lose their SSI [supplemental security income], their food stamps and Medicaid as well as in-home support services. It is very confusing to them."

"These are often people whom we have invited into our country," says Ernest Velasquez, director of social services for Fresno County. "They are legal immigrants who fought by our side in wartime, who came to this country and have worked and paid taxes. And now they find themselves ineligible for benefits."

In Fresno County, Velasquez cites the case of a 60-year-old widow who emigrated from Mexico with her husband decades ago and who lost a son in Vietnam. "She hasn't worked the required 10 years [to qualify for aid under the new law] because her husband was working, and she was raising the children," says Velasquez. "So now she finds herself being denied SSI. The fact that she lost a son in Vietnam in 1969 means nothing."

The number of legal immigrants receiving aid in California varies. DSS officials place the number of legal immigrants receiving food stamps at more than 400,000. More than 300,000 aged, blind and disabled legal immigrants receive SSI/SSP (federal Supplemental Security Income and state Supplementary Payment), and state officials estimate that many will be granted exemptions under provisions of the new law — or will have obtained citizenship by the time it takes effect. They estimate, however, that more than 170,000 will no longer qualify for SSI/SSP. Nearly 40,000 legal immigrants receive In-Home Support Services (IHSS), and nearly 400,000 receive AFDC, now TANF. The vast majority of all recipients in California — nearly 2.7 million in fiscal 1995-96 — receive AFDC, and more than 1.7 million of those AFDC recipients are children.

Although Anderson has said she would prefer to leave much of the implementation strategy to the counties, county officials are skeptical. Some sources close to the controversy say Anderson was chastised for some of her public comments by the Wilson administration. "It is my understanding that she had her wrist slapped," said one well-placed source. "The [Health and Welfare] agency has taken over primary responsibility for welfare." The governor's office, the agency and Anderson herself flatly deny those allegations.

"Nobody has told me not to give more control to the counties," she said, adding that reports of disagreements between her and the Wilson administration over strategy and public statements are exaggerated or untrue. "The governor and I are as close as two different people can get who have had different life experiences," she said.

"He's had the good fortune to have me and him and his staff in a room grappling with the issues. They're used to a director being very cautious. I'm cautious, and I'm part of the team."

Presenting further reform strategies to the Legislature will be problematic at best, although Anderson said legislators "do by and large pay attention to what we've laid on the table" — although many, especially Democrats, "wish I would drop dead." She said reforms must be based not on the original premise of AFDC that moms belong at home but on current social and economic realities.

"The larger question is about work," she said. "The old AFDC program wanted moms to stay home" — a social premise with considerable support among conservative legislators and one she said will be difficult to change. "You're talking about going into the devil's workshop," she said. "This is really harder than people admit."

The initial state planning process which so angered county governments was lengthy — and essentially closed — in order to pursue a careful, deliberative review of the complex federal law, officials contend. Although about half the states submitted plans before California, state officials say the state's diversity and size made the task more difficult. "We have many more populations with special needs, many more immigrants," said Health and Welfare Agency spokeswoman Janice Ploeger-Glaab.

Advocacy and legal services groups acknowledge the difficulty of coming up with a workable plan, but have been highly critical of the closed-door way the state they say went about it. "Determining who is exempt [from the new law] is a complex test," says Casey McKeever, directing attorney of the Western Center on Law and Poverty. "I don't see the counties getting any help from the state or federal government. A lot of people are doing work, trying to figure out what to do. The immensity of the task is overwhelming."

State officials, admittedly overwhelmed by the process, say they are being targeted unfairly. "People have to decide what they want to criticize us for," said Burt Cohen, who as the agency's assistant secretary for program and fiscal affairs is the principal point person on the California plan. "On the one hand, I'm hearing it's a closed process. Then I hear we're not doing anything. We're trying to proceed in an orderly and systematic way. We particularly want to avoid the kind of situation [that occurred] with food stamps."

When Governor Wilson attempted in September to implement a major aspect of the new law — cutting off food stamps for legal immigrants — he not only met with a firestorm of criticism, but a terse notification from the federal government that his action was precipitous and unnecessary, and he angrily rescinded it with a blast at federal officials for sending mixed signals. The incident pointed up the horrendous bureaucratic snafus which can be expected under the new law, which carries with it a series of mandates — and timelines — to remove legal immigrants from aid programs and to transition citizen recipients to jobs.

Legal services groups are watching the bureaucratic drama closely and say they will take legal action if and when aid is actually cut, particularly to legal immigrants. They say the federal law is rife with contradictions, drafting flaws, and seriously in need of clarification on many fronts — not the least of which is the glaring administrative and social services nightmare confronting California, with its huge immigrant population.

"There is no question there will be litigation," says Lucy Quacinella, staff attorney for the Western Center on Law and Poverty. "Ideally, we would like to stop implementation of the federal welfare bill. But you don't get restraining orders unless there is danger of imminent harm. At the moment benefits are cut off, we'll be there."

Nobody on any side of the welfare controversy is saying that welfare reform isn't needed, but many experts question the approach taken and contend election-year posturing permeates the legislation. They say President Clinton, harshly criticized by children's advocacy groups that formerly supported him — and by members of his own party — was pressured into signing a poorly designed and draconian measure in order to placate conservative voters.

"Clinton has moved as far as he can to the right in order to capture everything he can to his left," says Fellmeth. "They'll vote for him, and he'll moderate all the excessive provisions. But he can't rectify this. He has committed a very terrible error. He cannot bring back what he has given away, which are the entitlements, some kind of minimum floor. Mark my words, this really is going to be his Vietnam."

"We needed some changes, and I think we've been going in the right direction" says Fresno's Velasquez. "We needed some precise surgery, but Congress went out and grabbed a chain saw." 🏛

New Responsibilities, New Rules

The 500-page federal welfare bill is a complex document with many provisions. Here are a few of the major provisions, and the state's responsibility for implementing them:

Title I: Block Grants for Temporary Assistance for Needy Families (TANF)

• Eliminates Aid to Families with Dependent Children (AFDC) and consolidates federal funding for AFDC and related programs (such as job training) into a TANF block grant.

• The state must implement the block grant by July 1, 1997, but can do so sooner upon submission of a revised state plan. The date is important because it triggers the beginning of the five-year time limit for assistance.

• Prohibits use of block grant funds for teen parents under age 18 unless they are (1) attending school and (2) living in an adult-supervised setting.

• Establishes five-year lifetime limit on family use of block grant funds. States may exempt up to 20 percent for hardship.

• Requires at least one adult in a family that has been receiving aid for more than two years to participate in "work activities," including employment, on-the-job and vocational training and up to six weeks of job search.

• Requires 75 percent of two-parent families to participate in work activities in fiscal year 1997-98, increasing to 90 per cent in 1999. Single parents must work 20 hours per week in 97-98, increasing to 30 hours in the year 2,000, or 20 hours for families with a child under age six.

• Imposes penalties on states for noncompliance.

Title II: Supplemental Security Income

• Eliminates benefits to children who are "relatively less disabled." Currently, children may be eligible if an impairment exists that precludes them from "age-appropriate" activities.

• Eliminates SSI payments to prison inmates incarcerated for more than 30 days.

Title IV: Restricting Benefits for Non-citizens

• Legal immigrants already in the U.S. ineligible for SSI and food stamps. States have the option to deny benefits under TANF and Medicaid. Legal immigrants arriving after enactment ineligible for all federal benefits for five years.

• Exceptions include certain child nutrition and education programs, veterans and their dependents, refugees and asylum-seekers within the first five years of residency and persons who have worked for 40 quarters, or 10 years.

• Programs exempted include emergency medical services, noncash disaster relief, treatment for communicable diseases, immunizations and soup kitchens.

Titles III, VI, VII and VIII affect child support enforcement, child care, child nutrition programs, food stamps and commodity distribution.

Source: California Legislative Analyst

Smoking Out Tobacco

by Steve Scott

Reprinted from *California Journal*, April 1997

If, as the old saw goes, success is born of a thousand fathers, and failure is an orphan, few state programs seem more suited to multiple claims of paternity than California's eight-year advertising campaign against smoking. Financed by the quarter-a-pack cigarette tax enacted in 1988's Proposition 99, California's counterattack against tobacco advertising has been heralded as the most successful public health program in the last quarter century. Cigarette sales in the state have dropped by nearly 40 percent since the passage of Proposition 99, and the overall rate of consumption of tobacco in California is nearly a third smaller than the national average.

Yet, even as politicians shrink from any association with the tobacco industry, Proposition 99 seems to be one instance in which success, rather than failure, is the fatherless child. Neither of the program's first two political stewards — Governors George Deukmejian and Pete Wilson — has ever shown up at even one news conference to tout the unqualified success of the campaign. Both governors participated in the diversion of a total of more than $100 million away from anti-tobacco education, with the willing help of a state Legislature led by then-Assembly Speaker Willie L. Brown, Jr. (D-San Francisco), recipient of more tobacco campaign money than any elected official in the nation.

"It's just mystifying why there hasn't been more ownership of it," said Paul Knepprath of the American Lung Association. "When the governor was running for president, I fully expected to open the paper and see him take credit for this."

This past month, the state was scheduled to begin a new anti-tobacco media blitz financed by Proposition 99. By some accounts, the new campaign, which includes television, radio, and billboard advertisements, aims its lance where experts say it will do the most damage: at the industry itself. But the new campaign comes after a drought of more than 15 months, and nearly three years of on-again, off-again advertising. During that time, teen smoking has begun to climb again and the rate of decline among adults has leveled off for the first time in a decade.

"Whether on purpose or by accident, the [Health Services] department, in the early '90s came upon a successful strategy for combating tobacco use," said Dr. Stanton Glantz, the University of California, San Francisco cardiology researcher who has become something of a self-appointed truth squad on tobacco issues. "The tobacco industry has done everything they could to kill it and they've had a willing accomplice in Pete Wilson."

Such rhetorical fusillades, hotly denied as cheap shots by Wilson's allies, are nothing new in the history of Proposition 99. From the moment it was passed by voters in November 1988, the tobacco industry trained its thicket of lobbyists on the 25 percent of proceeds which go to anti-tobacco education and research. Their most important ally at the time was Speaker Brown, but with the election still fresh in memory, even Brown's muscle couldn't pull enough votes for the industry to get its way in this battle. It was one of the first major losses suffered by the industry in the Legislature until that time.

The first Proposition 99-funded ad campaign, launched in 1989, was an international sensation in public health circles. Eschewing the traditional finger-wagging approach of public-service announcements, the breakthrough ads went directly after the industry. Perhaps most memorable was a spot which depicted a group of industry executives strategizing how to replenish the supply of customers who either quit smoking or die of it. "Hey," one of the pretend executives chortles darkly, "we're not in this business for our health." The decline in the rate of cigarette smoking tripled.

When Wilson arrived in 1991, along with a crippling recession, the media campaign was canceled, and the money was shifted to direct indigent medical services. Internal e-mail messages, copies of which were received by *CJ* and other news agencies, suggested that aides to then-Health Services Director Molly Coye may have pressured researchers to downplay the importance of the ad campaign as a factor in the decline in smoking. But the administration also had some big fish to fry that year — specifically, a cavernous budget gap that eventually grew to $14 billion. Coye offered up the media campaign for temporary suspension.

"We had a direct health care problem in trying to fund essential services in a $14 billion deficit," said Kassy Perry, a former official with the state Health and Welfare Agency. "We knew it would be controversial." Eventually, the courts ordered Wilson to restore the money.

As deficits continued through the early 1990s, money continued to be diverted from the health education account into direct health services, notably for early childhood health screening. Eventually, the amount spent on anti-tobacco education dropped to 11 percent of the total tobacco-tax revenue — well below the 20 percent mandated by Proposition 99. At first, the Heart and Lung Associations and the American Cancer Society (the "voluntaries") went along with the diversions. But when the economy improved and the diversions continued, they sued again, and once again, the administration was ordered to stop sidetracking the funds.

In 1995 and 1996, Wilson fully funded the education account, but Wilson's critics are far from satisfied. The nexus of the health groups' anger at the Wilson administration can be summed up in three words: "Nicotine Sound Bites." The phrase is the title of an advertisement produced in the fall of 1994 for the Proposition 99 campaign. The spot used news footage of a 1994 congressional hearing chaired by U.S. Representative Henry Waxman (D-Los Angeles), at which tobacco industry executives claimed, one by one, their belief that nicotine is not addictive. The spot concluded with a question: "Do they think we're stupid?"

When the commercial began running, tobacco giant R.J. Reynolds threatened to sue the state, claiming it implied the executives committed perjury. State Health Services Director Kimberly Belshe strongly defended the advertisements, accusing the industry of "strong-arm tactics." Nonetheless, it was Belshe who decided to put the spot on the shelf after its one and only run.

"We had made an assessment that to [run the spot] would be an invitation to litigation," she said. "When I look at the choice between allocating our resources to defend ourselves in court against the tobacco industry or using resources to put ads on, I went with the latter."

In 1995, another controversial spot, which pointed out the paradox of insurance companies owned by tobacco companies giving breaks to non-smokers, was kept off the air. The administration did run a well-received spot, titled "Hooked," which depicts a business-suited tobacco executive hooking fish meant to symbolize the victims of smoking.

"The experience from the California campaign is clear — you have to attack the tobacco industry," said Glantz. "By attacking the industry, you open people's minds to the idea that smoking is bad."

Former Assembly Speaker Curt Pringle (R-Garden Grove) wasn't convinced. Pringle tried to insert language into the state budget which forbade the use of tobacco-tax money to attack the tobacco industry. A Pringle spokesman said the speaker was "philosophically opposed" to the use of tax money to attack an industry. Although Governor Wilson seemed sympathetic, suggesting at the time that "there is not a necessity to defame people," staffers in the Department of Health Services strongly resisted the move, and the language never made it into the budget. The former speaker still managed to have an impact on the program. As one of his last acts before turning the gavel over to Democrat Cruz Bustamante (D-Fresno), Pringle replaced two noted public health experts on the committee which oversees the education account, the Tobacco Education and Research Oversight Committee [TEROC].

The "Friday Night Massacre," as it's been called, is not the only controversy surrounding TEROC. Committee chair Jenny Cook says that over the past three years, the administration has clapped a cone of silence on the media campaign, denying access to storyboards and rough cuts. Moreover, a new condition was added to the contract renewal for ad agency Asher/Gould which forbids them from revealing anything about the campaign prior to its public release.

"Up until three years ago, there was no argument," insisted Cook, who is also the incoming national chair of the American Cancer Society. "We got all the materials, we saw all the materials, and none of it ever leaked out."

Belshe says the decision to withhold the storyboards was made to keep the state's information out of the hands of "those who are less friendly to the program." While Belshe referred largely to the tobacco industry, Perry, who is a member of the TEROC, says the secrecy is also warranted because the entire program has become politicized.

"If you could trust that the [anti-smoking] community would sit together quietly ... without everybody else going out and bashing the administration, I think there would be a little more trust in the process," said Perry. "That hasn't occurred."

A major factor in the administration's testiness is a series of increasingly-pointed newspaper ads sponsored by Americans for Non-Smokers Rights. The ANR ads highlighted Wilson's tobacco associations, including his hiring of former Phillip Morris executive Craig Fuller as the head of his abortive presidential campaign. Some of the newspaper ads reproduced an internal Phillip Morris memo which described Wilson as being "pro-tobacco." Some of the non-partisan "voluntaries", most notably the American Heart Association and the American Cancer Society, eschewed past attempts to use quiet diplomacy and signed on to the campaign.

The governor's defenders say any attacks implying Wilson is pro-tobacco are, in Belshe's words, "ill-informed and off-base." Wilson's health director ticks off a list of efforts undertaken by Wilson aimed at curtailing tobacco use. The most visible anti-smoking act taken by Wilson was his signature on the 1994 legislation banning most indoor workplace smoking — AB 13. Indeed, TEROC chair Cook, who is at loggerheads with the administration over Proposition 99, has nothing but praise for Wilson's action on AB 13. "AB 13 has done a good job," said Cook. "Very seldom do I have to look around in a restaurant to make sure there's no tobacco use going on in that restaurant." Other actions which Belshe cites in defense of her boss is the signing of the so-called STAKE act, aimed at underage smoking, and an executive order banning smoking in the state Capitol.

"No governor has signed more anti-tobacco legislation than Pete Wilson has over the last six and a half years," said Belshe. "His record is a remarkable one and his critics do him a disservice if they ignore it or minimize it."

For many in the anti-tobacco community, though, Proposition 99 is where the "rubber meets the road," and on that score, they rate Wilson openly-hostile. "That ad ["Nicotine Sound Bites] is a vaccine against smoking," said ANR's Carol.

If, as many public health groups fear, the ads pull their punches on the industry, the case for Wilson's complicity with the industry will have been made. "The tobacco industry is the vector of this disease [just as] mosquitos are the vector of malaria," said Carol. "You can't attack malaria unless you go after mosquitos, and you can't attack smoking unless you go after the tobacco industry." But Carol adds that Wilson could still be "the hero of the decade" if he would go to bat for a campaign that directly attacks the industry.

Whether Wilson will ever attain "hero" status is questionable; some Wilson aides believe they could never be radical enough to satisfy groups like ANR. But the ultimate test will be in what happens to consumption rates, particularly among the young. If, as Belshe predicts, history looks back on the latest ad campaign as "hard hitting and memorable," Wilson may yet get those laurels. But if the ads are seen as protecting the industry, Wilson could wind up on the same side of the political debate surrounding tobacco that his friend Bob Dole found himself in last year's presidential campaign.

The wrong side. 🏛

The California dream of higher education

Throughout the years, Californians have enjoyed unparalleled access to colleges and universities, but it will take a renewed commitment to maintain the dream.

By J.W. Peltason

Reprinted from *California Journal*, September 1995

The California dream has proved remarkably durable. It has survived wars, depressions, migrations, natural cataclysms, social and politi-cal unrest. That is because the California dream, like the American dream, rests on the availability of high-quality education to all who want and are prepared for it. For over 200 years, we have built a higher-education system premised on a few simple but powerful ideas: that education would serve as a path to social and economic mobility for those who lack inherited wealth; and that higher-educational opportunity thrives best in a system with a diversity of institutions — from small liberal arts colleges to large research universities — so that students have the widest possible range of educational options from which to choose. Somewhere within our system there is a college or university education suited to the talents, aspirations, income and academic preparation of just about everyone who has the motivation to seek it out.

It is still easier to get an excellent college education if you are affluent, of course. Expanding access to higher education has meant, however, that a college degree is increasingly within the aspirations of the poor, as it has long been for the rich. There's nothing surprising about the fact that it is possible to go to Harvard or Yale and end up as president of the United States. What is surprising, and what sets this country apart, is that it also is possible to go to Whittier or Elmira or Southwest Texas State College and be elected president. The American system of higher education would not score high on orderliness or organization, but it has succeeded beyond the imagination where it counts — in providing social and economic mobility, not to mention such intangibles as productive and rewarding lives for more and more people.

No state has demonstrated a clearer understanding of these realities than California. We have consistently encouraged our public universities to be as excellent as our private institutions. The celebrated

---

J.W. Peltason is president of the University of California. He is scheduled to retire in October 1995. Patricia A. Pelfrey assisted in the preparation of this essay.

1960 Master Plan for Higher Education made that aspiration possible by reorganizing California's public colleges and universities into a coherent system that emphasized quality and discouraged unproductive competition, while promising a place to any California student with the talent and motivation to benefit from higher education. The Master Plan has been, by just about any measure, an outstanding success. The University of California can carry out its special missions of providing instruction at the doctoral level and of producing the knowledge upon which our economic future depends because the California State University and the community colleges do such a splendid job of fulfilling their special roles. Our strong system of independent colleges and universities offers its own array of excellent educational options. As a result, more than any other society in the world, California has made good on the promise of educational opportunity for all of its citizens.

The system is still working, but today the doors of opportunity are beginning to close. They are closing with little public debate and less public understanding of the drastic consequences for California. Several trends threaten our system of higher education and although they are national in scope, as in so many other ways, change comes first to California.

First is the chronic underfunding of higher education. The fiscal problems facing California higher education today are more serious than those we faced during the Great Depression. Steep declines in support have occurred not because our leaders will it but because of a combination of constitutional requirements, federal mandates and expenditures for public safety that drain resources away from higher education. More than 85 percent of the state budget is protected by constitutional or statutory provisions that may only be altered by changing the law. UC, along with CSU, has the unfortunate distinction of being part of the unprotected 15 percent of the budget.

As a consequence, the share of the budget devoted to UC and CSU has declined from 13 percent in the late 1960s to 8 percent today. Unless something is done to reverse the trend, that figure will continue to decline as each year the percentage of the budget available to support higher education becomes smaller and smaller. And this is happening at a time when we are on the cusp of a reduction in federal funding for research and student aid that is so massive that it could dwarf even the radical cuts in state support we have faced over the past five years.

Solutions to the state's severe budgetary and structural dilemma have been proposed but as yet none has been adopted. The California Constitutional Revision Commission, appointed jointly by the governor and Legislature in 1993, has the formidable challenge of proposing answers to California's budgetary gridlock. The commission has released its preliminary report, and its recommendations deserve close attention by the people. The stakes are high.

Unless decisive action is taken, the long-term consequences for higher education are clear. As the California Postsecondary Education Commission put it in its report, "Challenge of the Century," public insistence that priority be given to corrections and other state activities at the expense of education means that "more criminals will be in prison, and more students will be denied college." The irony is that it is much cheaper to send someone to college than to prison; it costs over $20,000 a year to keep someone in a California state prison, while it costs little more than $12,000 annually to pay for the housing and education of a UC student.

The second trend is related to the first. A tidal wave of criticism is engulfing higher education. Even foundation heads, traditional boosters of higher education, are joining the chorus. The list of complaints is long and, if you are a college or university president, painfully familiar. There is no vision in higher education, critics say, no long-term planning, no coming to terms with the changed fiscal environment facing higher education. In particular, there are no proposals for fundamental change in the state's public universities. If professors would do less research and teach more, if fewer administrators would accomplish more, if unnecessary schools and departments and specialties were eliminated, if the various higher-education segments would cooperate more, if thousands of students were taught via distance technology and persuaded to graduate in three years rather than four, if enrollment projections were better and more consistent, then higher education's problems would be solved.

There is much to be said for a number of these proposals. Most of them already are being examined and many of them are being implemented. Some seem to miss the point, such as the assumption that research and teaching occur only at the expense of each other when every survey at UC shows that more than 70 percent of our students believe they have received a good to great education in our research-oriented environment — a record unrivaled by most human institutions, including marriage.

It should also be noted that in the contest for media attention, what we do systematically and well oftens loses out to the colorful anecdote. On an average day at UC, 160,000 students attend class unreported. One takes off his clothes, and the next day it is the "naked guy" we read about.

We will never purge our institutions of all their human and organizational imperfections, and it is not clear that it would be a good idea if we could. The worry is not the existence of criticism — which no public institution can or would expect to be exempt from — or individual criticisms themselves, some of which are true. The worry is that critics of higher education seem to have captured public attention and the public imagination. Much of their criticism is dramatically overstated and venomous in tone. But it is coming from people with tremendous influence on public perception and policy.

This criticism has not yet undermined public confidence in higher education, which still is highly sought after by parents for their children. But it has clouded and sometimes confused the public dialogue on higher education's future. That dialogue has yet to reach the level of accuracy, thoughtfulness and respect for opposing views that the subject itself deserves.

The third potentially damaging trend for higher education is what might be called the "illusion of the quick fix." There is growing support, among critics and the public, for the idea that planning will bridge the gap between what we give our colleges and universities and what it costs them to educate the young and discover new knowledge. It is a matter of vision and will, it is said, and the determination to make fundamental changes in the American university.

Universities are complex institutions that are built for the centuries. Major change tends to be incremental, not revolutionary; universities have survived as well as they have because they have not transformed themselves with every passing trend. But they must — and do — respond to the society that supports them. The very nature of what they do requires them to assess regularly changing demographic, economic, educational, public policy, and a host of other trends. This includes, of course, the likelihood of long-term resource constraints. Obviously, the transition to this new and difficult environment won't happen without will and vision and much more, but it also won't happen without minimal resources to pay the costs of educating the next generation, in addition to the other things that higher education does for California. The postsecondary education commission estimates that over the next 10 years, some 455,000 additional students will knock at higher education's doors, including an increase of 32,000 students for UC. Although UC's estimates are lower, they still are significant. The commission also anticipates that California's public institutions will need $1 billion more per year over the next 10 years to pay for new construction, repair and maintenance of existing buildings, and equipment.

Clearly, higher education in the next century will not have the resources per student that it has had in this one and will have to learn how to be more efficient and effective. But there is no way higher education can plan itself out of this budgetary straitjacket. California's public colleges and universities have made enormous efforts, in some cases with remarkable success, to increase support from private and other alternative sources. They have reluctantly raised student fees. They also have made draconian cuts in libraries, laboratories, maintenance of campus grounds and buildings and, most of all, in their people. There is no more fat to cut.

And although there is increasing discussion of privatization of professional schools within public universities or even the universities themselves, there are definite limits to that option. Increases in private gifts and research funding are helpful, but they will never bridge the funding gap. The state's share of UC's total budget, for example, has dropped in recent years until today it constitutes on 24 percent. But to say that state funding constitutes only 24 percent of our budget is like saying that your heart constitutes only 24 percent of your body. State dollars pay for the core educational activities that are at the heart of everything we do and that make every other activity possible. And no matter how small a proportion of our budget state dollars becomes, we will remain accountable to the people of California and to their elected representatives.

I also am skeptical of what may be called the "technology fix." Perhaps the most popular form of this idea is the virtual university — shorthand for the use of informational and other technologies to substitute for the traditional labor-intensive process of teaching and learning. The more enthusiastic among us even believe that the university as a physical place will wither away as information and instruction speed along the Internet to anyone who wants to take advantage of them.

Informational and similar technologies offer wonderful possibilities for expanding the scope and efficiency of teaching and research. Just as the invention of the book had a revolutionary impact on the teaching and learning process, so will the computer. We are experimenting with some of those possibilities within UC, and in cooperation with other educational institutions.

But as Stanford President Gerhard Casper has argued, in weighing the advantages of the virtual university, we also must consider "what learning and which skills can *not* be taught at a distance." Students and teachers will continue to need to get together. Despite the fact that, in the future, knowledge will be dispersed and readily available on CD-ROMs, there still will be the human and social need to meet for face-to-face confrontations, intellectual stimulation and social intercourse. Knowledge can be transmitted by a cable, but wisdom is acquired in social contexts.

Informational technologies and distance learning are not inexpensive, moreover, and the initial investment is the least expensive part of it. Nor will technology make the traditional classroom obsolete. The invention of the book and the creation of the library didn't make professors obsolete or education less expensive; they merely gave professors and students new tools for learning. The essential functions universities perform have remained intact over the centuries and will remain so into the future.

It also is worth noting that when some people talk about delivering education inexpensively through distance learning, they generally have in mind the education of other people's children; for their own, they seem to prefer traditional, residential face-to-face experience. It always is tempting to look for money saving ways for everyone else's kids to go to college. But the reality calls for something more from all of us.

The trends described here are exerting increasing pressure on our colleges and universities. Even more serious is the tremendous strain they impose on California's longstanding social consensus that public universities should be as good as private ones. The danger is that public higher education will gradually evolve into a two-track system, as has happened in many places with respect to K-12 education. If public education is allowed to drift into mediocrity, those with resources will send their children to private colleges and universities, just as they have moved their children at the lower grades into either suburban or private schools.

It must be emphasized that the governor and Legislature, despite recessions and a declining share of the state's general fund available for higher education, have buffered us from the worst consequences of California's fiscal crisis. And for the moment, at least, there are some hopeful signs. I am very much encouraged by the four-year compact Governor Pete Wilson announced in January. Through a combination of a modest increase in tax dollars and reasonable fee increases, coupled with additional aid to needy students, the compact will stabilize higher education during the next four years and give us the chance to make the changes we will need to move into the next century.

Important as it is, however, stability isn't enough. As earlier generations of Californians have done, we must invest in our future. And for the first time in a long while, California is not getting ready for the next generation.

The Master Plan hasn't failed. Our colleges and universities, despite their imperfections, haven't failed either. What has failed is public understanding of the unyielding fact that we can't go on simultaneously insisting on more prisons and refusing to pay for them through increased taxes. As a result, we are depriving ourselves of the chance to build California's infrastructure, including the educational infrastructure that has helped make this state into the sixth-largest economy in the world. We are asking our colleges and universities to run on empty. If we don't begin questioning our willingness to live with this situation, it will not be long before California and the California dream both will be going nowhere. 🏛

back to basics

When the subject is education and schools, the debate is a Babel of conflicting expertise, statistics, prejudices and preconceived notions. Lost in the debate are the most elemental questions: Why do we send our children to school, and what do we expect them to learn?

By A.G. Block

Reprinted from *California Journal*, June 1996

"Why should my son be a scholar when it is not intended that he should live by his learning?" asked satirist Jonathan Swift in an 18th Century essay on education. "By this rule, if what is commonly said be true, that money answers all things, why should my son be honest, temperate, just, or charitable, since he hath no intention to depend upon any of these qualities for a maintenance?"

Swift's taunting question was designed to mock the families of wealth, whose offspring often ended up squandering the ancestral fortune in a lifetime of sloth and idleness. But his barb serves to illustrate, in terse relief, those elements of an education that exist beyond the three "r's."

Controversies gripping the education community today would amuse Swift, for they seem to have little to do with the results of schooling and scholarship. These arguments have seethed for years over issues such as vouchers, assessment tests, funding, block schedules, charter schools, state and federal control, school bonds, integration, busing versus neighborhood schools, Eurocentric versus ethnocentric curricula, new math versus old math, whole language arts versus phonics,

class size versus teacher salaries, *ad nauseum*. However important these issues, the noise they create overshadows some real basics: why we send our children to school in the first place and what we expect our schools to teach them.

To this end, Neil Postman, chairman of the Department of Culture and Communication at New York University, painted a broad stroke in his new book "The End of Education" when he wrote: "At its best, schooling can be about how to make a life, which is quite different from how to make a living." To Postman and others, we educate children for a variety of reasons, all important but all in competition for the limited time and resources allocated to schools.

Basically, schools prepare children for jobs and careers, to be involved citizens and for a lifetime of learning. Finally, and perhaps most important for California, schools provide children with a common meeting place in which to learn common values. As such, schools are the crucible where Americans are made and where children discover a heritage grown from a myriad of diverse cultures. How this is accomplished, however, is the grist for controversy.

Thomas De Quincey, a 19th Century English philosopher, suggested that there are but two kinds of literature: that of knowledge and that of power. By "literature," he meant everything, including poetry, sermons, speeches, writings, novels, textbooks, scientific tracts, encyclopedias and almanacs of data. The literature of knowledge is meant to impart information or ideas but often is ephemeral, changing as new information comes to light. The literature of power, on the other hand, is designed to move and is more likely to be eternal.

To illustrate, a 1930s history textbook taught students about, among other things, the Reconstruction era that followed the Civil War. This "literature of knowledge" faded from view, however, as new facts were unearthed and different ideas emerged. But the "literature of power," as embodied in W.E.B. DuBois' robust 1935 essay "The Propaganda of History," remains as inspirational today as when first written to discredit accepted views of Reconstruction and to celebrate what he termed the "magnificent drama" of slavery and the resurrection of an entire race.

To De Quincey, therefore, an education system was effective when knowledge and power were woven together to form a tapestry of learning.

Clearly, however, schools must give students the knowledge necessary to earn a living and to enter society. "Kids need to have the skills and abilities that allow them to compete, to earn a wage, and support a family," says Maureen DiMarco, secretary of Child Development and Education in the Wilson administration. Those skills include the ability to read and write, to calculate and perform higher math, and to have some understanding of the sciences.

Historically, the country moved away from the notion of church schools during the mid-19th Century precisely because of the demand for a more skilled workforce. "In 1865, we were coming off a civil war, and half the country was bankrupt and the other half was in ruins," says Superintendent of Public Instruction Delaine Eastin. "Yet by the turn of the century, we were the number-one manufacturing nation on earth, and many economists believe this happened because we had compulsory public education. ...In the information age, education has an even more important role because workers have to use complicated skills." If we don't impart those skills to our children, Eastin warns, jobs and wealth will go elsewhere.

But in a world where it is estimated that students will have as many as nine different jobs over the course of a lifetime, career preparation means something different than it did 50 or 100 years ago. Consider, for instance, this passage from Mark Twain's "Life on the Mississippi," one of the great literary studies of education.

"If you take the longest street in New York," Twain wrote, and commit to memory every cobblestone, lamppost, building, sign and street crossings, and then add to that the knowledge of the depth of mud at every spot along that street "so accurately that you can instantly [identify where you are] when you are set down at random in that street on an inky black night, you will then have a tolerable notion" of what a Mississippi River pilot must learn. But, Twain added, your education will not be complete, not until you can take half the street signs and *change their places* once a month and still know their new positions on a dark night.

Twain attributed this accumulation of knowledge to an acute ability to memorize. But rote learning was meaningless to a pilot cruising a river that changed daily. More important were the tools of learning which allowed that pilot to understand the significance of snags, floating logs, eroding banks and sand bars. "Life on the Mississippi" is a paean to the art of learning, which serves a student in any endeavor.

"We can't just teach things," says DiMarco. "We must also teach ... attack skills. The ability to learn how to learn is far more important than preparing a student for a specific career."

But if schools only taught job skills, this would be a nation of drones. Nor would it long be a democracy. Therefore, schools also must prepare students to be informed citizens — a role that Thomas Jefferson considered paramount.

"In every government on earth," Jefferson wrote in his "Notes on the State of Virginia" in 1781, "is some trace of human weakness, some germ of corruption and degeneracy. ...Every government degenerates when trusted to the rulers of the people alone. The people themselves therefore are its only safe depositories. And to render even them safe, their minds must be improved to a certain degree."

Jefferson wanted people educated as a guard against tyranny, but others also see citizenship as a combination of responsibility and pride in a uniquely American heritage. "We must [inculcate] our students to the great principles of our nation and our founding documents," says Assemblyman Steve Baldwin (R-El Cajon), chairman of the Assembly Education Committee. "We must teach students what made America what it is." Baldwin emphasizes teaching about our basic system of government and justice, but he also stresses teaching aspects of the American character such as independence and self-reliance.

Good citizenship also evolves from a sense of duty, something Benjamin Franklin understood when he urged the study of why governments are formed, and that youth be steeped in "the advantages of liberty, the mischiefs of licentiousness, benefits arising out of good laws and a due execution of justice..."

Yet in a place as diverse as California, preparation for jobs and citizenship must be supplemented with an understanding of what is common to all Americans, regardless of background or heritage. According to Postman, "Schools are the affirmative answer to the question: Can a coherent, stable, unified culture be created out of people of diverse traditions, languages and religions?" Schools, Postman insists, "must fashion Americans out of the wretched refuse of teeming shores." To do this, he says, they must teach, among other things, common values: restraint, social responsibility, humility, empathy, tolerance. They also teach the value of sharing, respect, fair play, collaboration, patience and the need to follow rules.

The task is daunting for a state fractured along so many ethnic fault lines. Other places at other times have been faced with educating large numbers of immigrants, but California is unique. It is not, for example, New York at the turn of the 20th Century. True, New York schools once coped with Polish, French, German, Swedish, Russian, Italian, Spanish, Hungarian and a variety of other European tongues. But most of those languages shared a common alphabet and common roots. In addition, most of the children were white. Today, one Orange County school district alone, reports DiMarco, must deal with 89 different languages and dialects — from Russian to Laotian to Mandarin to Spanish to Hindi and points in between. And not all the faces look alike.

Yet mixing that diversity into a single, multinational culture may be the most critical task facing schools. School is the place where the children of those cultures come together, providing an opportunity to foster tolerance and understanding. School also is the place where children first feel as though they are invested in a system common to all.

"It is really important that people think of themselves as Americans and have a stake in society," explains Dr. Diane Ravitch, former U.S. assistant secretary of education in the Bush administration and now a professor at NYU. "And one of the purposes of education up to the 1960s was to engage in assimilation — to make us all Americans."

But the 1990s are not the 1960s. Assimilation is more complicated today, says Ravitch, and schools may be part of the problem. "Schools ... have fallen in love with diversity," she warns, "and this ... probably heightens racism and the alienation of peoples toward each other. It takes us away from the notion that everyone is part of a common endeavor." Ravitch believes that society — and, therefore, schools — must get back to a time when there were no "hyphenated Americans, just Americans."

That's fine, agrees Eastin, but much of the urge to hyphenate is coming from those who feel that the education system doesn't provide for them. "In the history of this country, there were always people who were excluded, to our regret," she says. "But in the old days, the excluded wanted a world of inclusion. In the future, the excluded will be the least educated, and many of them ... seem to yearn for a world of exclusion." Eastin argues that exclusion — separatism — is the result of anger and frustration on the part of have-nots from all cultures who "have rightfully understood that they cannot participate in the ... information age" without education. "There are the seeds of real trouble."

Children from diverse cultures and backgrounds "often are trying to negotiate two different worlds," explains Morgan Appel, a senior research associate for education at the Claremont Graduate School's Tomas Rivera Center. "The classroom world often does not reflect the home world."

"All children learn, but they learn in different ways," says Senator Diane Watson (D-Los Angeles), who has a doctorate in education. Referring to black children, Watson says that many come from "environments that are highly stimulating. Our children live in areas that are highly depressed ... and violent." Those conditions must be taken into consideration when preparing programs to educate black children, she insists. Otherwise, the risk of alienation spreads.

Appel and Watson especially worry that schools suffer from a lack of teachers from diverse ethnic backgrounds. "If Latino kids, for example, do not see that Latinos are represented among respected adults with authority," Appel says, "it sends a powerful message that not only the school doesn't value the contribution of Latinos, but that the system doesn't value it." He says that message translates to any culture. "Kids need to see their faces represented in that larger face of America."

The task is further complicated by the very idea of teaching common values. "The devil is in the details," says Rick Simpson, principal consultant to the Senate Education Committee. "What exactly are those common values? That's where you begin to see conflicts."

Baldwin, for one, is uncomfortable with the notion that some schools may teach that all cultures are morally equal. "I don't believe they are," he says. "I don't believe that the way women are treated in an Arab culture, where they have to cover themselves, is on the same plane, morally, with the way we treat women in the west."

"It is a challenge to balance respect for other cultures against the real need to have a buy-in to being an American," argues Eastin. "You can teach what values are held by various peoples, and teach kids to respect them, but you better bring it back to what binds us together: equality of opportunity, fairness, liberty and justice."

Can the schools inculcate children with common values and blend cultures in a balanced way — in addition to all of their other duties and mandates?

Most observers insist that schools have no choice. If American society is to move along in harmony, schools must be a salad bowl where all the diverse cultures can be mixed into a cohesive public. "It has long been the public school that has been the institution that has created a sense of a 'public' — that is the principal value of a system of public education," says Julia Koppich, a director at the Policy Analysis for Public Education (PACE) at the University of California, Berkeley. And if that "public" is not created, she warns, "we might as well give up on being a country."

For her part, DiMarco sees great strength in diversity. "This state is sitting on the richest raw diamond find ever put on this planet," she says. "Yet, when we look out, do we see the raw diamond mine? No. We see a field of pointy sharp rocks that make it hard for us to go down our path — we think. But if we only would recognize those diamonds for what they are — something that needs to be polished and placed in the proper setting. As such, they will provide this state with a multicultural work force that will give us the chance ... to dominate the global economy."

But the only way to get to that point, DiMarco says, "is to educate people in the American culture and to circle back to that common ethic and values system. To do that, they must be educated — together." 🏛

Education Politics

California's hydra-headed education governance system features an elected state superintendent, a board appointed by the governor — and major confusion over who is accountable.

By Sigrid Bathen

Reprinted from *California Journal*, June 1997

The present state school administrative organization in California is double-headed, and contains elements that could easily produce discord and destroy its efficiency.

—Report of the Special Legislative
Committee on Education, 1920

Even though I almost ran for it, I've come to the conclusion that the office of the superintendent ought to be abolished.

—Former State Senator Gary Hart, 1997

In 1978, Nancy Reeves, who was appointed to the state Board of Education by then-Governor Jerry Brown, resigned after some 18 months on the board. A lawyer, Reeves said she was resigning because the board was "paralyzed by ambiguities" in state law regulating the massive task of governing California's schools.

"With a budget of almost $8 billion," she said, "this knowledge industry is one of the largest enterprises in the state — and yet the board that oversees it is paralyzed by ambiguities in the California Education Code that prevent it from even governing itself, let alone the state educational system."

Unlike most other states, she noted, California's state board is "subordinate to its executive officer, the superintendent of public instruction, instead of the other way around."

Although a landmark 1993 state appellate court decision in State Board of Education v. Honig gave the board considerably more clout, California's system of educational governance remains a hydra-headed creature of questionable efficiency and frequent bouts of pique. Reeves' characterization of the process as one of virtual paralysis is as apt today as it was when she quit the board nearly 20 years ago — although

the education budget has mushroomed to some $30 billion.

Despite decades of studies and hearings, a raft of assorted legal opinions, and years of legislative and administrative end runs around the system — as well as several unsuccessful ballot measures to abolish the elected, ostensibly nonpartisan state superintendent — it remains much the same: an unwieldy, gerry-built vehicle lurching along a pothole-ravaged road toward vague visions of "educational excellence" in a state where students score near the bottom of school performance in the nation. It is a circuitous, tortured passage, fraught with the constant likelihood of collision, breakdown and wrong turns.

In any detailed review of education governance in California, one is struck by how little it all seems to do with children, how much with elemental, down-and-dirty politics. Not that the players don't care about kids; although ego is certainly not an unknown quantity among the state's top educators, most care deeply. At the same time, they find themselves trapped in a maze of conflicting regulations, duplicative and overlapping jurisdictions, the crazy-quilt Rube Goldberg instrument that is the California Education Code, and a fragmented gover-

nance system embedded in the state constitution and unlikely to be changed any time soon. It's not a pretty picture.

"The way we have structured our state education leadership politicizes education," says Assembly Education Chair Kerry Mazzoni (D-San Rafael), a former school board president in Marin County. "It's a setup for dysfunction. And if there is one area that should not be politicized, it is education."

"I'm not optimistic," says former state Senator Gary Hart, longtime chair of the Senate Education Committee who now heads the Institute for Education Reform at California State University, Sacramento. "The Constitutional Revision Commission suggested eliminating [the elected superintendent], but it didn't go anywhere. Whoever holds the office opposes it, and almost considers it a personal insult. Any change would require a constitutional change, and the electorate jealously holds on to its elected officials."

Hart and others suggest a system already in place in many other states: a Cabinet-level position overseeing education, appointed by and reporting to the governor, and perhaps an advisory state board. But under the current system, he said, "Everybody is bumping into everyone else. I would really like to make it clean, streamline it."

Since any immediate changes are unlikely, the players in the process say the next best thing is to work cooperatively. "If you were to design a system that would be efficient and practical, it would not be the system we have, "says former state Senator Marian Bergeson, a former teacher who is Governor Pete Wilson's secretary of education and child development, an influential but largely ceremonial post that Wilson has unsuccessfully pressed the Legislature to raise to Cabinet-level status. "But the goals are too important to break down in bickering."

In the day-to-day flow of running the 1,200-employee state Department of Education as well as overseeing California's 1,000 school districts — not to mention advising elected county superintendents and boards of educations, yet another layer of bureaucracy that many critics say could be abolished or consolidated — California's state superintendent generally does "get along" with the board, the governor and the various sub-strata of the state's educational system. Textbooks get adopted (still one of the board's principal tasks), money gets disbursed, standards debated if not adopted, local disputes mediated if not dispatched.

"Given that the Constitutional Revision Commission efforts were not successful, we don't spend a huge amount of time trying to make it different," says Mary Kirlin, chief of staff to Superintendent Delaine Eastin, about the state system. "We try to make it work. . .There are many, many things going on around here that are extremely important to children and parents. The bulk of the state budget goes to education. There are 5.5 million kids. It ought to be important to people. Given how huge and how complicated it is, we do very well in a less than perfect governance situation. I think we work together very well 95 percent of the time."

Robert Trigg, the highly regarded former superintendent of the Elk Grove Unified School District near Sacramento who was appointed to the state board last year, says, "It's one thing to read about the issues, and it's another to be a participant. Obviously, it's different at the state level because the superintendent doesn't serve at the pleasure of the board, and that is by design. I certainly am very aware that the superintendent is elected by the people, and that packs a lot of weight. ...One should expect

disagreement, and I think that is healthy as long as we don't personalize it."

The complex relationship between board and superintendent took a nasty turn in April 1997 when board president Yvonne Larsen fired off a sharply worded letter to Eastin — and another, slightly less acerbic letter to U.S. Education Secretary Richard Riley — castigating the superintendent for meeting with President Bill Clinton to support his push for national testing standards, at a time when California officials are attempting to reach agreement on state testing. Eastin insisted she was not speaking for the state, but the widespread publicity about the trip, which the board apparently didn't know about in advance, helped fan the fires of discord.

Larsen and Eastin both say they quickly buried the hatchet after the testy public flap and now are getting along just fine, thank you. "It's come and gone and is over as far as I'm concerned," says Larsen. "Delaine and I have had a conference and shaken hands and are working together. ...I will try to maintain civility and respect."

Eastin had a somewhat more colloquial response: "I have real interest in mending those fences as quickly as possible. All that happens when you don't mend the fences is the cattle get out."

In addition to serving as the executive secretary to the board — which recently was allocated its own staff and its first executive director — the superintendent is a member of the University of California Board of Regents, the California State University Board of Trustees, and a plethora of local, state and national boards, commissions and advisory bodies. As education has hit the front burner as a political issue in recent years, the superintendent is also, increasingly, a politician — much in demand for speeches, utilizing that most powerful of the office's limited powers, the bully pulpit, to effect change. Board members and representatives of state-wide education groups have sometimes privately criticized Eastin as "too political" and not sufficiently attentive to the day-to-day operation of the department and the school system. Some criticize her for not attending the entire two-plus-day monthly board meetings, although she generally sits in for part of every board meeting and always sends a high-level representative.

Interviewed by cellular phone while she was visiting schools in a four-

county area, Eastin says she has missed only one board meeting since she took office in 1995 — "when I was in Hawaii on my first vacation with my husband in years. I also missed the Democratic convention. I could be gone 24 hours a day on events. I work pretty much seven days a week." Scheduling her time, she says, "is a very close call. ...I've tried to have a big tent philosophy and to that extent, I've been criticized for being too inclusive."

"The original constitution said the superintendent should buy a horse and visit the schools," she adds. "When you go to the schools, as I do, you get a very different picture."

When she first became superintendent, Eastin — a fiery orator who was known for aggressively pursuing her goals in the Legislature, a liberal Democrat who chaired the Assembly Education Committee — was criticized by liberals for working with the governor and conservatives on education issues. When she travels to schools or particularly out of state, she is criticized for not being in Sacramento. When she doesn't go to schools or participate in national policy-setting agendas, she is criticized for being too parochial. Although she holds bachelor's and master's degrees in political science from the University of California, and taught political science and women's studies in community colleges for seven years, she is criticized by others in the huge and contentious education community as lacking an "education background," because she doesn't come from the traditional — some would say hidebound — ranks of full-time professional educators. In the end, says Eastin philosophically, "You're damned if you do and damned if you don't."

And, when the clash of divergent viewpoints about what is best for kids in school becomes a clash of egos — with no programmatic agreement or results — Eastin observes: "The kids lose, big time."

While 14 other states have elected superintendents, some are partisan and others, like California's, nonpartisan. According to the Council of Chief State School Officers in Washington, D.C., the majority (25) are appointed by a state board that itself is generally appointed by the governor, although 12 of the state boards are elected. A few states have boards which are a combination of elected and appointed members. Only one state — Wisconsin, with a nonpartisan elected superintendent — has no board. In states with elected superintendents, the superintendent is very often a member of a different party than the governor, as well that of his appointed board of education and, in California, the secretary of education and child development. To say that arrangement creates a certain tension is an understatement, and the tension sometimes takes a partisan bent, especially during budget deliberations over which the governor and the Legislature wield far more power than the superintendent.

When the relationship between the superintendent and the board becomes strained — as it has on countless occasions through several contemporary administrations — it is often over a policy issue of major statewide consequence, such as academic standards, testing or teaching methods. In the late 1970s and early '80s, with a contentious board comprised of members appointed by former Governor Ronald Reagan and then-Governor Jerry Brown, huge battles were fought over bilingual education. The superintendent during much of that time, Wilson Riles, who served three four-year terms from 1971-1982, spent as much time at board meetings being a mediator as he did a policy adviser.

"The superintendent must have the understanding and the knowledge of how to pull the members together," says Riles. "If the superintendent follows what should be followed, he or she helps the board set policy and provides them with the information they need. Their job under the law is to set policy, but not to run the department — they have an executive [the superintendent] to do that." The 1993 appellate court decision clarifying the board's policy-setting role came out of years of conflict between the board and former Superintendent Bill Honig, who succeeded Riles, eventually prompting the board to take the issue to court. Honig argued, according to the court opinion, that he was "under no clear, present, and ministerial duty to implement" board policies. The court flatly disagreed, directing the superintendent to implement specific policies, including the board's request for additional staff.

In a fascinating history of education governance in California (the first board, established in 1852, was established by the Legislature and consisted of the governor, the surveyor-general and the superintendent), the court noted that subsequent constitutional and statutory embellishments to the role of the board and the superintendent created a system designed for confusion. After a 1921 legislative reorganization that created a "unified Department of Education," the court noted, "Predictions of open conflict were realized in 1926, when a newly appointed Board refused to confirm the candidates the Superintendent appointed as presidents for the state colleges at San Francisco and San Jose." Responsibility for the state colleges and universities has long since passed to separate bureaucracies and boards appointed by the governor.

Bill Whiteneck, who was a deputy superintendent in the Department of Education from 1973-1983 and chief consultant to the Senate Education Committee from 1983-1994, served as an adviser to the Constitutional Revision Commission, which recommended abolishing the position of elected superintendent in California. Like many other top state educators, Whiteneck supports the commission recommendation, and says the "laser beam of accountability for education should be with the governor," since he controls the budget. "Most of the time, the governor gets a free ride on education," he says. "If things are going well, whether financially or programmatically, it's very easy to take credit or leverage credit. If things are going badly, they can blame it on the state superintendent. The public has a terrible time sorting out whose cage to rattle."

Whiteneck says the 1993 court decision "just cries out for the Legislature to do something to clean up the governance structure." As for the role of the current elected superintendent, Whiteneck says, "You can do what Honig did, and what I see Delaine doing, running up and down the state. ...You're not an equal in the legislative process. You have no veto authority. ...Right now we have stereophonic noise coming out from multiple offices."

For her part, an embattled but tenacious Eastin, never one to back down from a fight, faces a recalcitrant Legislature reluctant to embrace her push for tougher high school graduation standards and a policy-setting board whose members are all appointed by a Republican governor who wants to be known as California's "education gov-

I am building a house. I am a carpenter. This is the door. This is my tool box. The light switch is on. I put the doorbell in. — Andrew Parker

ernor" — and, with his popular class-size reduction initative, has scored major points in the increasingly political race to shore up the state's troubled schools. "Everybody has an opinion about a school experience," says Eastin. "Not everybody has an opinion about surgery because they haven't had surgery, and they may not know anything about auto insurance because they haven't had an automobile accident. But everybody has had a school experience."

"It is true that my job is really to get the job done for kids," Eastin adds, "and that is what I'm trying to do with a limited amount of authority." While Eastin believes an elected superintendent offers an independent voice and should be retained, board president Larsen, a former school board president in San Diego, says the board provides "empowerment" to local school groups who otherwise would have a limited voice. "We are the only entity where a distraught citizen can come if they don't get comfort from the local district, the one entity which will hear testimony," she says. "We do give them that forum, which they don't have with the Legislature or the governor."

Riles says elected superintendents and appointed boards stumble when they lose sight of their constitutional roles. "Even though the superintendent is a constitutional officer, you just can't dictate to the Legislature, to the board, but you do have a bully pulpit and can provide leadership by advocacy," he says. "Although the board is not elected, but appointed by the governor, they set policy for the Department of Education. Some superintendents forget that, and, of course, that creates all sorts of problems." 🏛

Doing more with less: class-size reduction

By Steve Scott

Reprinted from *California Journal*, June 1997

The muffled scratch of pencil lead on coarse lined paper is the response which greets teacher Jacquie Cranston as she recites the week's study words to her second grade class at Hillside School near Sacramento. The 19 children squirm with the invisible tension possessed of all young children, but they are also quiet and listening to their teacher. As she recites each spelling word, Cranston makes a slow circular sweep through the middle of the horseshoe-shaped desk arrangement, glancing at every paper as she strolls by. When the time comes to reveal the correct spelling, she is able to note that many missed a particular sequence of letters.

As the spelling test ends, and a new round of words is assigned, Cranston directs her attention to a new student, bundled in her coat as if plotting an escape route. Instructing her on the format for writing out spelling words, the teacher kneels down next to the child and quietly administers an on-the-spot assessment of her reading skills. While she whispers softly to the child, the other 18 children in the room — essentially on their own for the moment — keep their seats, hold their tongues, and await the teacher's return to the front of the room.

Two years ago, the prospect of teaching students 20 at a time in any California classroom seemed the stuff of fantasy. The average class size in the state's schools approached 29 students per teacher, a ratio that ranked California near the bottom among the 50 states. With a student population of more than 5 million, any attempt to reduce the average class size by even one student was prohibitively expensive, even as the revenue crunch of the early 1990s eased.

Well, times have changed for California classrooms. By spring of 1997, more than half of all eligible primary grade school children — kindergarten through third grade — were being taught in classes of 20 or fewer children. Class-size reduction is being hailed as the education reform of the last two decades in California. And for the first time in recent memory, parents and teachers are being drawn toward, rather than away from, the public school system.

"It's the best thing that's happened in my 15 years as a teacher," said Marjorie Sahs, a first-grade teacher at John Erhardt Elementary School near Sacramento.

Reviews of the new program are so uniformly glowing that Governor Pete Wilson has proposed expanding funding for the program to insure that as many K-3 children as possible are able to take advantage of it. But the rapid implementation of class-size reduction has also created an instant teacher shortage, and again called attention to a facilities crunch that, by some estimates, will require a long-term investment of as much $40 billion.

In at least one respect, class-size reduction is truly the "accidental reform." Although education leaders of just about every stripe paid lip service to the notion that smaller classes equaled better learning, neither the Legislature nor any governor in recent memory had made class-size reduction a budget priority. The first hint that things would be different came in the governor's May budget revision last year. Wilson proposed a modest $500-per-child incentive for schools to lower classes to 20 children in grades one and two.

Given that the actual cost to some districts would likely run twice that amount, few took the plan seriously until Wilson later proposed expanding it to three grades. While he mockingly suggested an ad campaign by the powerful California Teachers Association had convinced him, Wilson's primary motivation appeared to be to take a shot at the CTA by keeping a large chunk of roughly $1.8 billion in new education revenue out of any program which would have allowed it to go to teacher salaries. While Democrats suggested Wilson was trying to "partisanize" the issue, they were ultimately caught in their own education rhetoric, and the plan for three grades was approved, at a rate of $650 per student.

Notwithstanding its origins as a political maneuver, the program is predicated on the simplest of notions — the fewer children a teacher has to deal with, the more time she can give to each child. That extra attention is, by nearly all accounts, most crucial in the early grades, when a child's work habits and even the brain itself, are still developing. "The younger you can get to children with enriched stimulation learning experiences, the better will be their foundation," said Dr. James A. Fleming, superintendent of Capistrano Unified School District in San Juan Capistrano.

"You learn to read in the first three grades, you read to learn from then on," said Marian Bergeson, Governor Wilson's secretary of child development and education.

In its first year of implementation, teachers from all over the state report they are anywhere from one to three months ahead of where they were last year at this time. Some have had to push into the next grade's curriculum to find new challenges for children who finished up the current year's program in February or March. "I can give more thorough and more frequent assessment, and can give immediate feedback," said first-grade teacher Sahs. "You can even do some teaching while you're assessing."

Most teachers also report they have fewer discipline problems in the classroom. In part, this is a product of broader parental participation on a day-to-day basis. The prospect of teaching in smaller classes drew many teachers from the higher grades into the primary level, and attracted many private school teachers. Kim Book spent 15 years in Catholic schools, teaching to classes of 38, before moving over to Hillside School this past year.

"It took a month to get used to teaching to half the children," said Book. "I kept saying, 'Where are the rest of them?'"

From the educational standpoint, the closest thing to a problem at the school site level has come from upper grade teachers whose main question is, will our turn come? "You could see the resentment," noted one primary teacher. "It would get noticeably quiet in the lounge during that first month." Some superintendents report difficulty convincing upper grade teachers and parents that the issue is larger than simply a question of equity. Even here, though, there seems to be general agreement

that teachers in higher grades will ultimately reap the benefits of a better prepared, more controlled student pool. An internal membership survey conducted by the CTA shows overwhelming support for the program even among those who likely will never see their own classes get any smaller.

"Every sixth grade teacher in California knows that if we could do a better job of teaching basic skills in third grade, it wouldn't be so big a problem that classes are bigger in sixth grade," said state Superintendent of Public Instruction Delaine Eastin.

The popularity and educational appeal of class-size reduction has made many in the education community reluctant to be too critical of the particulars for fear the Legislature might change its mind and take the program away. Nonetheless, there have been a few hiccups on the road to implementation which many educators say must be addressed if the program is to be truly successful. The three most visible issues are facilities, teacher supply, and long-term funding.

Facilities. While school districts showed a surprising amount of creativity in managing their space, dozens found themselves forced to put 40 children and two teachers together in the same room. While Hillside School teachers Ona Lee Camp and Teri Thomas were able to develop a good working groove together, others have not. "I know of situations in our district where the teachers don't even speak to each other," said Camp. "You can't just teach with anybody." The "40-2" scenario was only one of the ways districts were forced to improvise in order to get the classes down. Music rooms, computer labs, special education labs, teacher lounges, libraries, and even cafeteria space was given over to classroom activities. The music program at Hillside, for example, was shifted out of a music room and on to the stage in the cafeteria, and Cranston's second-grade class has to learn about music amid the decidedly atonal clatter of unfolding lunch tables.

The problem is especially acute in large urban districts, tiny rural districts, and rapidly growing suburban districts. In the giant Los Angeles Unified School District, said LAUSD lobbyist John Mockler, "they have 100 schools that are so overutilitized, it's just impossible to bring in any more classroom space." The suburban Elk Grove Unified Dis-

trict near Sacramento was forced to hold off on implementing the program for any grade other than first because there just wasn't enough space.

"In many cases what we've done is renovate classrooms, dividing two classrooms into three spaces," said Elk Grove superintendent Dave Gordon.

Teacher Supply. More than 18,000 additional teachers were hired this past year to accommodate class size reduction. According to a report by the Legislative Analyst's Office, these teachers were less experienced than those hired in past years. Many districts plundered their substitute pools to find teachers for the program, while others raided internship programs they'd set up to bring new teachers along slowly. In some cases, such as the San Juan Unified District near Sacramento, the administration took a chance by hiring teachers before the Legislature and the governor had even approved the class-size reduction plan.

Both Eastin and Bergeson suggest the teacher supply problem may have been somewhat overstated. Eastin maintains the number of emergency teaching credentials issued this past year is no greater than usual, and Bergeson says the supply problem "isn't nearly as significant as was touted." But the same may not be true if, as expected, the program is expanded to four full grades this coming year. The analyst says that will require the hiring of an additional 16,500 teachers, forcing many districts to recruit out of state.

"We're in Minnesota, we're in Texas, we're in Florida," said Capistrano Unified's Fleming. "The pool is drying up quickly."

Funding. Administrators complain of two problems related to funding — local flexibility and the encroachment on other locally-funded programs. Officially, class-size reduction is an "incentive program," something that districts are being encouraged, but not required to do. Since it was not a formal mandate, legislators had the political cover for not paying districts for the entire cost of the program. But the overwhelming popularity and common sense of the program have made it something of a de facto mandate, and school officials worry that, as newly hired teachers move up the pay scale, the program will consume more and more of the resources available for other grade levels. Elk Grove's Gordon says his district was forced to eat 14 percent of the cost, and the encroachment could swell to as much as 31 percent if nothing changes.

"The program doesn't pay for itself, and as a consequence, we have to encroach on other district programs," said Gordon. "If that continues, there's no way we can maintain the program over time."

In addition to the general funding issue, many district superintendents complain about the rigidity of the 20-to-1 prescription. The implementing legislation imposes a severe penalty for any class that rises above a maximum of 20 students. For some small districts, this makes it almost impossible to take advantage of the program, as one new mid-year transfer could wipe out all the funding. "You can't get a new facility, and you cannot be creating a lot of combination classes at that point," notes David Walrath with the Small School Districts Association. "In those situations, the districts are at tremendous fiscal risk." District superintendents have proposed allowing the 20-to-1 ratio to be averaged throughout a school district, with a cap of 22 per class. This change is unlikely, though, as neither the Wilson administration nor Superintendent Eastin support it.

On the overall funding question, however, there appears to be some encouraging news. Revenue estimates as of early May indicate the state will have about $2 billion more than expected for the coming budget year, thanks to an improving state economy. Governor Wilson has proposed funding all four grades at $800 per student, the figure which has become the accepted definition of "full" funding. Although even at this rate, many districts will have to swallow a portion of the cost, Mockler says at $800 per student "you solve everybody's problem of messing around with higher grades' funding."

Solving the per-student funding issue still leaves the larger question of where to put all these new classes. While schools won't be allowed to double up at 40-to-2 the way they were last year, music rooms, libraries, and cafeteria stages will still be taken away for classroom space. Partisan squabbling in the Legislature last year killed a school bond for last November's ballot, and Eastin now says the next election should include a $4 billion bond, including $1 billion for class-size reduc-

I am a police officer. I am directing the traffic. The cars are stopping. I like being a police officer. I am wearing my police uniform. I am happy because I am a police officer.
— Osagie Omoruyi

tion. Eastin is also proposing a longer-term funding plan which includes a relaxation of the two-thirds vote requirement for local school bonds, a proposal also backed by Wilson.

As for the issue of finding teachers, the solutions most offered involve expansion of local apprenticeship and mentoring programs. As a senator, Bergeson authored legislation creating the Beginning Teacher Support Program, which helps mentor new teachers by pairing them with more experienced teachers. Bergeson says the promise of a less stressful environment may also help ease any teacher crunch by attracting new people to the profession. "There's a good deal of interest in education," she said. "People are regaining trust in their schools."

That trust, however, doesn't extend to the Legislature or the governor. In doing their own soundings on the issue, the California State PTA found that the biggest concern among parents is that the program might disappear if the economy goes south, or the political winds shift. "They're concerned about the resolve of the Legislature and who the next governor will be," said Betty DeFea, the PTA's legislative director. Eastin says these fears are eased by the constitutional protections afforded

education spending under 1988's Proposition 98.

The facilities, funding, and recruitment concerns all led the legislative analyst to suggest delaying further implementation of class-size reduction for a year, to give districts time to catch up. But that scenario seems highly unlikely, particularly in light of the new revenue figures. It isn't often that the Legislature hits on something that is so universally acclaimed, and when it does, the temptation to do more is great.

One thing is certain: Just about everybody involved in the program has noticed the difference, including the children themselves. Back in Jacquie Cranston's second-grade class, the students tell a visitor how much calmer things are this year. "Last year, the teacher had to, like yell out words and stuff," said one child. "It was hard to hear the teacher." "I get a lot more treats this year," volunteered another. Later, Cranston marveled at how much more relaxed she was this year. Although her union has always emphasized teacher salaries, this is one area where Cranston is more than willing to pay the price.

"Speaking for myself, I'd rather have a reduction in class size than a raise in my salary," she said. "The stress is just much less intense." 🏛